THE
SOVEREIGN
GHOST

THE
SOVEREIGN
GHOST

STUDIES
IN
IMAGINATION

DENIS DONOGHUE

THE ECCO PRESS
New York

First published in 1990 by The Ecco Press
26 West 17th Street, New York, NY 10011
Printed in the United States of America

This edition by arrangement with University of California Press

Library of Congress Cataloging-in-Publication Data

Donoghue, Denis.
  The sovereign ghost: studies in imagination
Denis Donoghue.—1st ed.
    p.   cm.
  Reprint. Originally published: Berkeley:
University of California Press, c1976.
    1. Imagination.   2. Literature—Philosophy.
3. Creation (Literary, artistic, etc.)   I. Title.
PN56.I45D6   1989   809—dc20   89-16874   CIP

ISBN 0-88001-239-0

10 9 8 7 6 5 4 3 2 1

For Frances

Contents

Preface

In this book, as in my *Thieves of Fire* (1973) and *The Ordinary Universe* (1968), I am concerned with the poetic imagination. In *The Ordinary Universe* I looked at certain works which, running against the modern grain, acknowledge the validity of common experience as a force with which the imagination deals on terms pretty nearly equal. The imagination does not insist upon its rights at the expense of nature, the world, or reality. Or at least the insistence is not gross. In *Thieves of Fire* I looked somewhat nervously at certain writers whose imaginations are intransigent, peremptory, strident in the presence of common experience and the received poetic forms. In the present book I try to deal with some of the questions raised by imagination itself, its character and relations, the claims regularly made on its behalf, the problems it proposes. I take largely for granted a current interest in literary fictions and the theories which sustain them. I also take for granted the historical meanings of the word "imagination," especially its association with divine frenzy or the madness which Leontes invokes when he is on the point of thinking the statue of Hermione a live thing:

> O sweet Paulina,
> Make me to think so twenty years together.
> No settled senses of the world can match
> The pleasure of that madness. . . .

Chapter 2 was given in a much shorter form as the W. P. Ker Memorial Lecture for 1974 at the University of Glasgow and published as *Imagination* (Glasgow: University of Glasgow Press, 1974). Chapter 5 is a revised version of the Ewing Lectures given at the University of California, Los Angeles, in 1971. Chapter 4 was published, in a shorter form, in *Sewanee Review,* and an earlier version of Chapter 6 in *The Waste Land in Different Voices*, edited by A. D. Moody (London: Edward Arnold, 1974). I am grateful to the editors for the hospitality extended to me in their pages.

                                                                    D. D.

This love more intellectual cannot be
Without Imagination, which in truth
Is but another name for absolute strength
And clearest insight, amplitude of mind,
And reason in her most exalted mood.
                    William Wordsworth, *The Prelude* (1805), XIII, 166-170

Nota: man is the intelligence of his soil,
The sovereign ghost. As such, the Socrates
Of snails, musician of pears, principium
And lex. Sed quaeritur: is this same wig
Of things, this nincompated pedagogue,
Preceptor to the sea?
                    Wallace Stevens, "The Comedian as the Letter C"

The Essential Power

In the *Essay Supplementary to the Preface* (1815) Wordsworth turns aside from his argument at one point to say that "the word, imagination, has been overstrained, from impulses honourable to mankind, to meet the demands of the faculty which is perhaps the noblest of our nature." On the whole, this is no longer true, imagination is not one of our key terms. Very little energy is spent upon its use, or upon any other effort to distinguish among the faculties of our nature. Our nature is no longer an object of sustained reflection; we are not certain that we possess such a thing, and are in any case far more strenuously exercised by the conditions in which we live than by the "nature" we maintain or abuse. There is no need to degrade the case by asserting that nobility is a moribund value; its presence has never been measurable. It is enough to say that Wordsworth's concern for imagination was a token of his concern for human nature and the nobility it embodied. He studied the nature of man by brooding upon man's highest and noblest attribute, a sublime power. It is still possible to find poets brooding upon the imagination, but they rarely construe it as the essential power, the attribute in which man is most gloriously expressed. Power is still a crucial question, but glory is no longer deemed interesting.

The modern way of using the word "imagination" is shown clearly enough in I. A. Richards's *Coleridge on Imagination* (1934) and *Principles of Literary Criticism* (1924), where it is a word like any other and is put to work without special privileges beside such words as communication, value, pleasure, mind, memory, emotion, form, experience, permanence, truth, and belief. If the situation has changed in the past fifty years, it has resulted in a further suppression of the word in favour of such words as style, genre, and structure; it does not figure prominently in current linguistics. The best that can be reported is

1

that imagination has survived as a critical term, without flourish-
ing, while other terms of equal grandeur in Romantic criticism
have disappeared. Only a wilful or nostalgic critic would now use
Blake's terms "genius" or "vision." The tone of modern criticism
is cool, disinterested, and suspicious of any words which would
drive the study of art beyond the reach of discussion. We are
patient with problems, but not with mysteries.

Most people would therefore accept the six meanings which
Richards distinguished in Chapter 32 of *Principles of Literary
Criticism* as applied to the word "imagination," and would think
it unnecessary to add a seventh. The six are (i) the production of
vivid images, (ii) the use of figurative language, (iii) the
sympathetic sense in which we share and reproduce the feelings
of others, (iv) the inventive faculty by which a man brings
together elements not ordinarily connected, (v) the scientific flair
for choosing productive elements from a given field of phenomena, and (vi) imagination in the poetic sense which Coleridge
defined in *Biographia Literaria*. This last, the only meaning to
which Richards gives close attention, is implied by Coleridge's
celebrated phrases: "that synthetic and magical power," "the
balance or reconciliation of opposite or discordant qualities . . .
the sense of novelty and freshness, with old and familiar objects;
a more than usual state of emotion, with more than usual order;
judgment ever awake and steady self-possession with enthusiasm
and feeling profound or vehement; the sense of musical delight
. . . with the power of reducing multitude into unity of effect,
and modifying a series of thoughts by some one predominant
thought or feeling." Richards's gloss upon (vi) would also be
generally accepted. He emphasizes "the heightened power of
combining all the several effects of formal elements into a single
response," "the resolution of a welter of disconnected impulses
into a single ordered response." The imagination holds simultaneously and without suppression many impulses which are intrin-
sically and in ordinary experience opposed; not merely heterogeneous but specifically at war. "The equilibrium of opposed
impulses" is for Richards the central value of imagination: when

the imagination animates our experience, we find more forces in our personality actively engaged, we cease being one-sided or partisan, we become genuinely disinterested. We do not vacillate, we find ourselves composed. A neurologist would proclaim us healthy.

Richards's account of imagination has been severely questioned, mainly by those who disapprove of its practical or positivist character, the presentation of imagination as good medicine for the nerves, art as therapy. I am not concerned to pursue the quarrel, but to show in Richards's account the modern determination to use the word without mystery or privilege. Richards takes the Romantic harm out of the word, and the only question is whether or not he has also taken some of the good.

As a general statement about imagination, Richards's version accords with its time, it has pleased more people than it has irritated. But it has moved away from Coleridge in at least one respect. Coleridge was engrossed in the imagination because, like Wordsworth, he was committed to a fundamental concern for the definition of man. The imagination is man in the role of maker. Coleridge studies a poet's works so that the feeling aroused by the experience may then suffuse his sense of the poet in particular and man in general. The works are evidence of the man, they certify his creative nature. Objects are valued because they disclose the subject, the creative source. Coleridge's entire work in criticism is therefore biographical, he is writing a biography of man to elucidate the nobility of his nature. Everything returns to the subject, poet, maker. Richards does not share this exhilaration: when he writes with enthusiasm, the object of praise is the language, not the poet. Richards is avid to discover the resources of language rather than the attributes of man. What he thinks of man is quickly said: he thinks he needs to be treated for nervous instability. What he thinks of language can only be given by responding to Richards's entire work in criticism, rhetoric, and poetry. He is engaged with a poet only for his poetry, and for the poetry only as the embodiment of the language, revealing some of its resources. His chief interest is turned upon the linguistic system as a field of possibility, not upon the individual poet as maker or even as instrument. The animating motive of his life is to help to discover all the resources contained in language. It is significant, for instance, that when Richards placed a passage from Donne beside a passage from Dryden it was to illustrate "the interaction of words," not to distinguish between the merits of two poets. The Donne was preferred to the Dryden because the first more than the second exhibited "a prodigious activity among the words." Donne's lines were more challenging than Dryden's because they took the risk of setting up, among the words, mighty oppositions and contradictions; the poem became a minefield, intrepidly negotiated not only by Donne but by an English language wonderfully capable of such feats. Richards is a patriot in criticism, he treats the English language like a splendid army, its foot-soldiers Basic English, its officers the major poets, but it is the army as a whole that wins battles.

It is easy enough to account for the shift of attention which Richards has represented and in large measure enforced. Many people have tired of the sublime, and of admonitions which drive us toward it: they feel themselves intimidated by the rhetoric of Romanticism. Images of ultimacy and perfection are tedious, we want to be left alone, we do not want to be raised from our mundane selves. More often than not we feel as William Gass's protagonist feels in "In the Heart of the Heart of the Country" when he addresses the cat Mr. Tick: "You are a cat so easily, your nature is not something you must rise to."[1] If we have a nature, we want it to be something to fall upon, for ease and justification: preferring to identify it with our bodies rather than our souls. We aspire to our best selves only as a Sabbath exercise, finding the effort exhilarating because occasional. When the imagination, like a Russian Formalist, proposes to intensify our perceptions by making things appear strange, sponsoring estrangement as a way of life, we are edified, but the effort is unnatural, we crave to sink down into the fleshpots of routine.

There are other causes. When imagination comes under

question, it is often because of its association with the licence of
self-consciousness, which can easily be given a bad name as
curiosity or self-regard. Despite the philosophical objections to
Idealism, devotees of imagination insist upon living in a
Ptolemaic universe with the self as centre. They inevitably incur
the disapproval of poets moralistically inclined. Donald Davie
has praised Pushkin for turning away from this temptation:

> The poet exhibits here
> How to be conscious in every direction
> But that of the self, where deception starts.[2]

It starts with self-deception, and goes on to larger sins, functions
of its own morbidity, unless it is fortunate enough to be
disciplined by a better tradition, a sounder code of manners.
A. R. Ammons has a more rueful version of the same rebuke:

> we never talk about anything but ourselves,
> objectivity the objective way of talking about ourselves.[3]

Yes, but Narcissism is not inevitable, even in an extreme
aesthetic of imagination. There are moods in which the imagination suppresses its exorbitance in favour of the natural forms:

> I could not think but
> vanished into the beauty
> of any thing I saw
> and loved,
> pod-stem, cone branch, rocking
> bay grass.[4]

There are also imaginative enterprises which, incorrigibly subjective as imagination is, can be construed as acts returning upon
the subject rather than acts beginning and ending with the
subject. It is possible to brood upon matter, as Gaston Bachelard
did, in such a way that matter seems to speak or dream or
breathe through the perceiving subject, and in those moods the
only meaning of subjectivity is the point at which matter, under
this brooding pressure or provocation, becomes spirit. Images
become not pictures of something or even actions of a subject
but phases in a process of transformation. Bachelard's *The*

Psychoanalysis of Fire is classic proof that an act of the mind, at once inward and elemental, may be utterly innocent of self-regard. Musing the obscure, Bachelard engages his subjectivity to release from matter a spirit which it is not fanciful to regard as creative. Nature becomes what the perceiver already is, a spiritual being. The process is alchemical but not hermetic. Yeats's conflicts of self and anti-self are corresponding attempts to give subjectivity grounds other than itself. The validity of Yeats's procedure is not at all undermined by the fact that both self and anti-self are in equal measure imaginative constructions: the poet is setting his imagination to do for its own sake what Richards, following Coleridge in this respect, has named as the special work of imagination; taking the risk of oppositions, tensions, contradictions, so that the unity at last achieved will be correspondingly and richly earned. Imagination is not obliged to wait for Nature to provide the ideal conjunction of appearances, it may provoke them for its own sake. As a general strategy the imagination is wise to resort to the method of conflict, encouraging every instance of recalcitrance in the available forms, because its characteristic temptation is to subdue every force to itself, defeating every object by turning it into subjective terms. It is important that unity come only when it has been earned. "Pure" poetry is inferior to "impure" poetry for precisely this reason, that it secures its purity too soon and too easily by suppressing potentially difficult elements, its rhymes are facile. Bachelard's brooding is astonishingly daring because it seems to establish conditions which repel every impurity, but the appearance is deceptive: the mind finds impurities in the elements which incite its meditation.

But we need a systematic argument. In April 1972 Lionel Trilling gave the Thomas Jefferson Lecture in the Humanities under the title "Mind in the Modern World." The lecture was a work of true nobility, exhibiting those qualities of care and urbanity for which Trilling is widely if inadequately praised. On that occasion, as often before, he addressed himself to fundamental questions in the life of our society, reflecting upon the sense of insecurity with which the values of mind are now sponsored. He maintained that our contemporary ideology exhibits a disaffection from history; "an uneasiness has come into our relation to mind," indeed the mind itself is increasingly discredited on the grounds that its typical activity is indirect, "it cannot be in an immediate relation to experience, but must always stand merely proximate to it." Toward the end of his lecture Trilling spoke of the modern "ideology of irrationalism" which celebrates "the attainment of an immediacy of experience and perception which is beyond the power of rational mind." "In our day," he argued, "it has become possible to claim just such credence for the idea that madness is a beneficent condition, to be understood as the paradigm of authentic existence and cognition."[5] I shall not comment upon the argument beyond saying that I share Trilling's sense of a crisis in modern culture as a perturbation in the relation between mind and experience. But I am concerned at the moment with one aspect of the matter, the reasons which led Trilling to speak of mind rather than imagination when he came to represent the values he would defend. I shall have to risk impertinence at this point.

Perhaps the first reason is that Trilling associates mind with "the idea of order," even the idea of hierarchy, "the subordination of some elements of thought to others." He puts the force of his moral authority in favour of the ideal of objectivity, which he describes as "the respect we give to the object as object, as it exists apart from us," the fullest possible recognition of "the integral and entire existence of the object." These are his congenial terms, and we know that his advocacy of order, hierarchy, and a culture devoted to these values is magnanimous. But it is my impression that he is deeply suspicious of imagination or genius not in themselves but in their capacity to serve as the authority of a valid culture. He speaks of genius as "a unique originating power of mind," and he has shown himself profoundly responsive to its manifestations in literature, but he does not invoke its qualities when he describes the ideal of a true society. Partly the reason is that he would like to think of a

nation's intellectual resources as invested not in a few but held in
common. On the whole, the Romantic theory of imagination
does not align itself unequivocally with order, reason, and
hierarchy. The order it proposes comes late rather than soon,
and is often opaque to common forms of sense. It may be that
Trilling thinks imagination, viewed as a possible organizing
principle in society, gravely compromised by its history and by
the experience of two hundred years in which it dominated
European thought as a rhetoric of feeling and will. It is even
possible that he blames the Romantic and post-Romantic
rhetoric of imagination for the very predicament he describes in
"Mind and the Modern World." According to that judgment,
the rhetoric of imagination favours subjectivity, undermines
knowledge of "the object as in itself it really is," offers intuition
as a profounder sense than knowledge, and proposes as its ideal
the direct, unmediated access to experience in preference to the
distance imposed by rational categories. To put the matter much
too crudely, the imagination proposes that we come to know
experience by touch, not by sight: distance is abolished. I am not
ascribing to Trilling sentiments to which he has never committed
himself. I am trying to divine from his books certain values and
preferences which make the idiom of mind more congenial to
him than the idiom of imagination. Mind can be translated into
practical terms and put to work in society: imagination cannot
be translated, because a fiction put into practice becomes a
myth, an extremely dangerous force at large in the world.
Perhaps Trilling's vocabulary is to be explained along these lines.

It must be conceded that much Romantic theory can be
received as a licence to self-indulgence, sponsoring bizarre
conjunctions of imagery, exorbitance of will, and claims upon a
secular version of divine power. But there is no inevitable
quarrel between imagination and mind. There are indeed
differences between them, each is a mood of the other and is
moody in its own favour. The mind complains of imagination
that it is wayward, irresponsible, self-engrossed. Imagination
complains of mind that it is totalitarian, it demands immediate

obedience, imposes its categories upon experience with little thought for the nature of the experience, it is premature in its orders and conclusions. Imagination regards mind as a civil servant, a bureaucrat, illiberal in administrative zeal, too Roman for its own good. If it comes to a choice between mind and that mindlessness which Trilling indicts, the fashionable subversion of knowledge and truth, then the choice is clear: I choose mind with all its limitations. But I think imagination can be preserved as the grander term. There are occasions on which we feel that nothing less than the full resource, the essential power of imagination is adequate. I think this is what Wallace Stevens had in view when he observed that Santayana's life was "a life in which the function of the imagination has had a function similar to its function in any deliberate work of art or letters." The sentence is not happily phrased, but it is clear: there are lives "in which the value of the imagination is the same as its value in arts and letters."[6] It is implicit in such praise that the lives in question are freely chosen rather than constrained; they are sensed and lived as a continuous act of imagination, with such freedom as is consistent with the nature of things, the limitations imposed by time, place, and body. There are also occasions and objects of perception which demand something more intimate than the response of a mind bent upon orders and conclusions. Theophil Spoerri has spoken of the dialectic of nearness and distance in Hölderlin's poems, the great counterpoint of life and intellect. Bacchus, he says, is the god of nearness, in whose presence all barriers fall, everything fixed becomes fluid, and all sober rationality dissolves in a rapt yielding to nature. Hercules on the other hand is the god of distance and light, skilled in the art of discrimination, clear consciousness, laws, language, in "all that tears us from the lap of the mother," as Emil Staiger phrases it. These rival principles are then united in Hölderlin's Christ, the Only One, "Der Einzige":

> Wie Fürsten ist Herkules. Gemeingeist Bacchus. Christus aber ist
> Das Ende.[7]

Is not this a theme for imagination, a motif that requires not a
particular response, an answer to its question, but the condition
of intense responsiveness, a sustained act of consciousness in
which the end is indefinitely postponed and the mind is content
to lavish its resources upon a grand cause? Before such a theme
the mind is patient, willing to live forever in the midst of its
means without a thought for its end, entirely free of conclusions
and purposes. If this is so, imagination seems a more accurate
name than mind on such an occasion.

I think of another such occasion. There is a moment in
Fellini's *Amarcord* in which the boys of the town are throwing
snowballs: the scene is high-spirited, the boys in good humour.
Gradisca, the town beauty, comes along and the boys throw snow
at her. The hero denounces them, Gradisca escapes into the
café. When the boys pitch their snowballs against the café
window, the proprietor rushes out shouting and waving his
hands. Suddenly there is a strange noise in the sky, everyone
looks up to see what it is. After a few moments the Count's
peacock glides down, lands in the square, opens its gorgeous
feathers. The screen is filled with the peacock's spreading tail,
like an Impressionist painting. Everyone stops to gaze upon the
peacock, the whole town seems to stand breathless. Then the
scene changes, the story continues toward Miranda's death. The
peacock has come from the Count's garden, or from nowhere, it
does not matter. What matters is that its coming stills the
commotion, the snow-fighting scene, and that it fulfils at that
moment our desire for ease, calm, beauty, the unpredictably
gorgeous. Nothing in the story requires that the peacock come,
it comes and goes, is never seen again, but remains as a presence
for the rest of the film. Its coming is as palpable as the
fluffballs, the bonfire, Gradisca's glamour, the Grand Hotel,
the great ship looming up in the fog, the boys dancing in the
storm.

It is difficult to say precisely why the peacock is so powerful in
its coming. The best explanation may be entirely formal, in

keeping with Kenneth Burke's understanding of form, in *Coun-
terstatement,* as that which arouses and satisfies a desire in the
audience, the fulfilment coming as a surprise. We are responding to the finesse of form when, our desires having been aroused,
we find them gratified and appeased when we least expect such
felicity. I am not sure that I can explain why it is especially
satisfying that the entire screen is occupied, for a moment, by
the great peacock's tail; unless it is to ensure that every desire,
need, fear, and frustration in the hero and in us is resolved, for
the moment, and there is nothing more. The explanation does
not matter, because it offers itself as an answer to what it deems
to be a question. The incident in *Amarcord* is not a question or
a problem in that sense, it is a poetic image, and we respond to
it as we acknowledge a gratifying presence, when absence is
feared. The situation is imaginative in fact, and we respond to it
with a corresponding attitude, we lean and hearken after it.

It may be useful at this stage to look at a passage which has
received sustained attention from critics with an interest in
defining the Romantic concept of imagination. In Chapter 15 of
Biographia Literaria Coleridge quotes these lines from Shakespeare's "Venus and Adonis," the scene in which hero abandons
heroine:

> With this, he breaketh from the sweet embrace
> Of those fair arms, that held him to her heart,
> And homeward through the dark lawns runs apace:
> Look! how a bright star shooteth from the sky,
> So glides he in the night from Venus' eye.

Coleridge has remarked of the poem as a whole "the perfect
sweetness of the versification," Shakespeare's use on this occasion
of a subject remote from his own "private interests and circumstances," and lastly the poetic use of images. Images become
poetic, Coleridge says, "only as far as they are modified by a
predominant passion; or by associated thoughts or images
awakened by that passion; or when they have the effect of
reducing multitude to unity, or succession to an instant; or

lastly, when a human and intellectual life is transferred to them from the poet's own spirit." The lines quoted, he says, give us "the liveliest image of succession with the feeling of simultaneousness."[8] Quoting the same lines in a lecture, Coleridge commented:

> How many images and feelings are here brought together without effort and without discord—the beauty of Adonis—the rapidity of his flight—the yearning yet hopelessness of the enamoured gazer—and a shadowy ideal character thrown over the whole.[9]

In *Coleridge on Imagination* Richards concentrates on the same lines from "Venus and Adonis," emphasizing that all the separable meanings of the words are brought into one:

> *Look!* (our surprise at the meteor, Venus's surprise at Adonis's flight)
> *star* (a light-giver, an influence, a remote and uncontrollable thing)
> *shooteth* (the sudden, irremediable, portentous fall or death of what had been a guide, a destiny)
> *the sky* (the source of light, and now of ruin)
> *glides* (not rapidity merely, but fatal ease)
> *in the night* (the darkness of the scene, and of Venus's world now)[10]

Perhaps we may add a few footnotes to these perceptions, before commenting on the main consideration between Coleridge and Richards.

Look! gives both situations as pictures to be compared, the scene in the sky, and Venus lying on the ground, distressed, while Adonis races away.

bright: Adonis running "through the dark laund" (line 813); capable of giving light to the Sun (line 864) rather than receiving it from that source.

star: force of nature, more inhuman than human, but almost human in one respect, its caprice.

shooteth: in Shakespeare generally, shooting stars are seen as by Salisbury in *Richard II* (II.iv.18-20):

> Ah, Richard! with the eyes of heavy mind
> I see thy glory like a shooting star
> Fall to the base earth from the firmament.

So the comparison is probably not neutral, but tipped in Venus's favour, Adonis has at least partly ruined himself.

from the sky: so heavily parallel to "from Venus' eye" that it has something of the feeling of Oberon in *A Midsummer Night's Dream* (III, ii, 107f.):

> When his love he doth espy
> Let her shine as gloriously
> As the Venus of the sky.

glides: faster than its modern meaning, but it has the "fatal ease" that Richards mentioned. Probably as in *Romeo and Juliet* (II, v, 4-6):

> O, she is lame! Love's heralds should be thoughts,
> Which ten times faster glides than the sun's beams,
> Driving back shadows over low'ring hills.

in the night: Venus "having lost the fair discovery of her way" (line 828). On Coleridge's "shadowy ideal character thrown over the whole," he does not say how this is done. Clearly there are several factors, but the important one is probably the juxtaposition of a figure of distance (star/sky) and a figure of nearness (Venus and Adonis, "the sweet embrace / Of those fair arms which bound him to her breast"). The stellar situation is "brought home" by the phrase "from Venus' eye." Spoerri's terms are well in tune with the passage. On Coleridge's point about "the liveliest image of succession (combined) with the feeling of simultaneousness," the clue is in the syntax, the "As . . . So" form. Successiveness corresponds to the movement of one line into the next, each complete in itself. The impression of simultaneousness is given by the grammatical and metrical unity of the couplet. Incidentally, the "As . . . So" form reverses the temporal order, gives the event second and the comparison first; this has the effect of keeping temporal considerations in suspense, they are not allowed to make themselves felt until the sentence and the couplet are complete. The coinciding of grammar and metre is important, each "half" of the sentence coincides with a line of verse, there are no run-on syllables. This emphasizes not only the similitude, each part and each line being in that respect like its partner, but also the consonance of each component. "So" is coupled with "look how" in grammar, and receives from it some imperative force. Further couplings link "shooteth" with "glides," "from the sky" with "from Venus' eye," and "bright star" with "he." The music is made more intricate, and the risk of flatness avoided, by the fact that the first line of the couplet gives subject and then predicate: in the second, the verb comes first, then the subject, the pronoun. It is also important for the "shadowy ideal character thrown over the whole" that the particularity in the first line is of species, not event (a bright star shooteth; any shooting star, not a particular one) and in the second it is unique ("So glides he"). The rhyme of "sky" and "eye" is unfortunate, incidentally. Even Shakespeare cannot avoid flatness if he insists on rhyming two monosyllables which are the same parts of speech.

A further point about the "shadowy ideal character." The structure of the couplet is metaphoric rather than metonymic, to recall Jakobson's distinction, the source of the statement is similarity rather than contiguity.[11] Adonis rushing away from Venus is like a shooting star in the sky. As with metaphor generally, we hold in our minds simultaneously the sense in which the relation between tenor and vehicle is valid, and the resistance of common sense which has to be overcome before its validity can be received. All the other attributes of Adonis have to be kept away so that one of them (he is like a shooting star) may be enforced. Resistance is overcome mainly by the vicinity of *shooteth* and *glides;* these, the only verbs in the couplet, bring tenor and vehicle close together before they part again on the way to "Venus' eye." Presumably the shadowy ideal character of the whole is caused by every element in the lines which works against the sheer successiveness of the report, since successiveness tends to keep things separate, marching in single file, but these resistances seem especially hard-working.

It is sometimes maintained that in the best figures of comparison there is no need to block off any attributes; if the comparison is really valid it can take all the risks implicit in the figure. Every reader takes, as the weight of the comparison, whatever relations the figure gives him, he senses the comparison in various aspects. If a reader does not take the full weight, it is because he is not sufficiently interested to go to the trouble of doing so, not because the figure is such that it has only one point of comparison to make. This is probably too much to maintain: the chemistry of a shooting star has no bearing upon Adonis or his situation, so it would be fruitless to look there for yet another point of comparison. In any reading we have to draw the line somewhere. This touches upon Coleridge's distinction between Imagination and Fancy, since Fancy is "the faculty of bringing together images dissimilar in the main by some one point or more of likeness distinguished."[12] The images of Fancy are "fixities and definites," they resist the tendency of words in imaginative use to fuse or yield themselves in favour of some higher unity; they are brought together as an act of will, according to a relation already sponsored by the association of ideas or by "accidental coincidence." Fancy is satisfied by bringing into conjunction images which are normally comparable at one point only: when that one point is registered, only a fool would think of persisting. The fact that nearly any images can be compared in some one respect accounts for the inferiority of Fancy to Imagination; though Coleridge clearly means that a poet ought to be gifted in both respects. The lines he quotes to illustrate Fancy in "Venus and Adonis" are these:

> Fully gently now she takes him by the hand,
> A lily prison'd in a gaol of snow,
> Or ivory in an alabaster band,
> So white a friend engirts so white a foe.   (lines 361-364)

Obviously, the first line could not be used to distinguish Fancy from Imagination. It could lend itself to either. Richards's comment takes the second and third lines as the work of Fancy on the grounds that the comparison between Adonis's hand and a lily ends when you have sensed that both are fair, both white, both, perhaps, pure; and in the comparison of Venus's hand

with a gaol of snow you have to put up with the fact that while
gaol and hand are both enclosures and both white, a lily has no
desire to escape and Venus's hand does not resemble a gaol of
snow. "There is no relevant interaction, no interanimation,
between these units of meaning," Richards argues. The links are
merely accidental, pondering them does not enrich the poem.
This does not apply, he maintains, to the last line, which is the
work of Imagination rather than of Fancy. Venus is Adonis's
friend in two senses, he says; she is his lover and, if he had
yielded to her, she would have been his preserver. "With the
second sense," he continues, "there comes a reach and a
repercussion to the meaning, a live connexion between the two
senses and between them and other parts of the poem, con-
siliences and reverberations between the feelings thus aroused,
which were missing in the other lines." But to go back to the
second and third lines: William Empson has argued against
Richards that the pun on "fair" is at the back of it: "all
beautiful women were white like Elizabeth, and this made their
beauty display their virtue (sensuous idealism); 'fair' is light-
coloured, beautiful, and calmly good without the effort of
imposed standards (cf. 'fair play')." Furthermore, Empson
argues, "the suggestion that the rowdy and lustful Venus keeps
all these qualities makes her a goddess because she resolves the
contradictions of normal life; it puts her into a fairy-tale world
as cool as the metaphors."[13] It is certainly one of the aims of
the entire passage to subdue the force of prison, gaol, and band
to an impression of statuesque relations, as in a severe ballet.
Richards says that "the commonest characteristic effect of Fancy
is the coolness and disengagement with which we are invited to
attend to what is taking place," but there are occasions, and the
lines from "Venus and Adonis" make such an occasion, when we
are invited to remain disinterested precisely for as long as the
events seem utterly in command of themselves. For the moment,
Venus seems to be leading Adonis by the hand as if the beautiful
combat were over and she the winner; an effect mimed by the
grammar and prosody of the last line. In such a scene every

factor must keep its place, the words must keep their distance
from one another. Richards is soon bored by these scenes, he
responds only to language in which "interaction" and violence
are the substance and the composure comes hard. Empson is
ready to give the lines from "Venus and Adonis" the best chance
they can have, but he agrees eventually that they are Fancy
rather than Imagination and that the distinction is real: "the
implications of whiteness are taken conventionally, as a matter of
course, as an accepted myth, and do their work under cover of
this solid 'form'." I think the second and third lines of the
passage are indeed the work of Fancy, for the reason given, that
the first effect of the lines is the only effect they will ever have,
no amount of pondering will make them glow. They provide
Shakespeare with an opportunity, and he is an opportunist on
this occasion. But Empson's reason is not convincing. In a style
of Fancy, according to his view, the poet is content to have most
of his work done by others; particularly by genre, conventions,
well-established figures, rhetorical cliches. He takes whatever he
can find as a matter of course. In the style of Imagination,
presumably, the poet does all the work by himself.

I find it strange that Empson will not allow a poet to use
whatever there is to use, or to resort to an accepted myth.
This seems to relegate nearly everything achieved by way of
tradition, form, and figure, as if these were merely second-hand
instruments rather than earned perceptions. To make any
genuine use of a convention, however, is to earn the perceptions
it contains; this is presumably what Eliot had in mind in
sponsoring a relation between tradition and the poet's individual
talent. I have no quarrel with Empson and Richards when
they regard Imagination as superior to Fancy, since Fancy
corresponds to the mind's grasping at straws, settling for a
relation between two things merely because it is possible. But
more is involved. Coleridge thought Imagination a superior
faculty to Fancy because it draws upon the full activity of
man's mind and is noble for that reason: it is man's highest
attribute, a token of his gravity and freedom. Richards and

Empson arrive at the same preference, but for a different reason; because the poet is the exemplary modern man and he must exemplify the lonely struggle to make sense of things without aid from church, doctrine, or belief. In the exercise of Fancy, according to this idiom, a poet does not take risks, he accepts myths as a matter of course, deploys forces already defined and fixed. He is like an unthinking believer, living by rote and convention. But in the exercise of Imagination the poet runs the whole enterprise as a matter of risk; like the speaker in Empson's poems, an adept of despair. A similar assumption of risk underlies Richards's poems, in which the mind resorting to its speculative instruments is like a mountaineer trusting to his individual skill. When Richards writes about Coleridge and imagination, it is in the determination to force the condideration of imagination into an area of risk, disavowing the aids which Coleridge and Wordsworth, however differently, thought the imagination could call upon.

What is common to Coleridge and Richards is emphasis upon unity as the imaginative ideal, but each has a different kind of unity in mind. For Richards, poetry is the risk and the shock value of language, and words are evidence of the strain the linguistic organism can bear; proof that the strain has been borne is the composure of the form. In Coleridge it is unity of effect, a qualitative resolution expressed in atmosphere and feeling: the otherwise hard edges of things are softened; the imagination is therefore a modifying or "coadunating" faculty because it draws intimations of an ultimate unity from imme-diate severances and divisions not by excluding the difficult forces but by accommodating them; it deals with quarrelling children not by separating them and dispatching each to his room but by emphasizing kinship, a family likeness, in the disputants. In Richards the unity is sought as composure, by analogy with nervous composure in the human body: he is interested in difficulty rather than ease, and values tension as a constituent of composure. Hence his devotion to poetry and mountaineering, systems complex but manageable: even when you have climbed a mountain, you have the problem of getting down again; there is more in a great poem than meets the eye, so it is wise to train the eye, hence *Practical Criticism*. Richards approaches events as if they were nerves cut adrift from their nervous system: he then tries to discover the system, the relation between one nerve and another, and to help the system to realise itself in action. Structuralists find him companionable for that reason, though he is not in other respects of their fellowship.

Emphasizing unity as the central aspiration in Coleridge and Richards, we have to ask what unity means and why it has achieved unquestioned status as a moral and aesthetic criterion. So it may be useful to rehearse some few of the paradigms of unity exemplified in literature and thought. I start with instances in which unity is achieved by taking two terms, subject and object, and moving toward a situation in which one lives in the light or the shadow of the other. Or perhaps a dynamic balance of the two terms is achieved, and this balance is unity. Later I shall make some rudimentary comments on the possibility of circumventing the dualism of subject and object.

Since our theme is the imagination, we may begin with the Romantic relation of subject and object: in extreme cases the unity consists in the continuity of impressions, the increasingly complete process by which objects are dissolved to become impressions or flavours in the subject's inner life. In more genial forms of Romanticism, including most particularly Wordsworth, there is an attempt to give object its full measure of identity, and subject is deemed to be ideally first among equal forces. In Eliot, subject is still the dominant term. The animating power is consciousness, which in Eliot corresponds to virtue except that it is not its own reward, and to conscience because of its scruple, the anxiety with which it proceeds. Consciousness responds to whatever resistance it meets in objects, and at length it meets its own conscientiousness, a sense of its inadequacy as a moral principle: this is the last resistance it meets. At that point it hands itself over to a higher authority which then certifies the only unity that counts. Self gives itself to a higher principle, in

the later poems God. In the early poems, as in *The Waste Land,*
higher principle is represented by higher perspective, that for
which Tiresias stands as intermediary. In Yeats, a deliberate conflict is set up between subject and object for the sake of the energy
engendered and released. The poet seeks a resolution, but provisionally rather than definitively. It is vital that whatever resolution
or harmony is achieved contain enough misgiving to propel the
next phase of conflict: and so a poet's life is lived without recourse
to transcendence. Unity is at every moment provisional, however
imperial its tone. When it comes to a choice between subject and
object, Yeats chooses subject, but he postpones choice in the
interest of conflict: postponement is itself subject, of course.
Opportunism becomes aesthetic. In Hegel, unity is sought by
having Reason receive the irrational, accommodate it, thereby
transforming itself into a higher principle of Reason. Meanwhile
man is in the place of unrest *(Unruhe)* because he negates the
partial convictions available to him, hence the continual movement of dispersals and re-gatherings. Unity in Hegel is therefore
the condition in which subject and object at last, but only then,
become identical, in an identity received by consciousness in the
form of Absolute Knowledge, which accommodates everything
except death. In all these cases, subject is the predominant
value, always problematic but always decisive in its relations.
When object is the prior or determining term, we find a
different set of possibilities. It is possible for subject to discover
itself so deeply expressed in the natural forms that it flies to that
Abraham's bosom and demands nothing more. Hofmannsthal
speaks of that condition in his Chandos letter. He does not
confuse himself with things, or lose the distinction between his
nature and the nature of things, but he finds in nature a spirit
so akin to his own that he feels no need to declare the
independence of his spirit as a separate presence. It may be said
that this experience is still a function of the subject: more
accurately, it is a stroke of luck, or a gift received by subject
from object's hands. Generally, however, there is no such luck,

those who start with object face the problem of somehow
insinuating a subjective term, since they can only find their
freedom by breaking their logic. They have no difficulty finding
unity, except that the unity they find is premature and mechanical. Structuralists start with structure, a theory of relations, and
never quite get over the problem that in studying items and
objects they merely seek evidence in their own favour. The verve
with which they run to ideology is understandable, since they
start from a term which is already an ideology, "an interest
disguised as an idea," and are pointed in a political direction. In
Marx, unity is sought as a form of collective harmony achieved
in a victory of the true proletariat and the withering of the state:
conflict disappears with its cause. Marx ascribes to the true
proletariat a creative spirit capable of transforming the world,
and he refuses to give credence to any notion of historical fate
defined in advance: there is still time to alter the conditions of
economic exchange and therefore to erase every fateful mark
presumptively inscribed in things. Unity is the millenium, on
these terms. Lucien Goldmann also takes object as his primary
term, identifying it with "the ensemble of the historical process":
the individual subject is invited to make his sensibility coincide
with that ensemble, sinking all differences. (I choose to represent
this "objectivity" in ideologies of the Left, but the imagination is
just as sceptical of ideologies of the Right, it cannot endorse the
congealed interests in either cause. "When in Rome, do as the
Greeks." That is why Richard Blackmur said that "the politics of
existing states is always too simple for literature; it is good only
to *aggravate* literature," and again that "the true business of
literature, as of all intellect, critical or creative, is to remind
the powers that be, simple and corrupt as they are, of the
turbulence they have to control."[14] It is also why the imagination
reacts to ideology pretty much as Lambert Strether reacts to
Mrs. Newsome in *The Ambassadors* when he remarks of her to
Maria Gostrey, "There's nothing so magnificent—for making
others feel you—as to have no imagination." Finally it is what

caused Goethe to say to Eckermann—July 5, 1827—that "if imagination did not originate things which must ever be problems to the understanding, there would be little work for the imagination to do." An ideology has become what it is by sacrificing imagination to mechanical force.

These examples depend upon the dualism of subject and object, upon dialectic as such. "The revolt against dualism" is a long story, well told in A. O. Lovejoy's book of that title, but it has not yet reached a conclusion. There are many people who reject the dualism by preventing conflict, vetoing its constituents before they have started upon their dualistic way. Many of them are devotees of Zen and the style of "flower power," which I interpret as an attempt to maintain the subjective mode without its stridency and aggression. Their unity is unity of feeling, in principle an attempt to replace competition by community. The "negative capability" which Keats ascribed to Shakespeare is another way of fending off the logic of subject and object: instead of raging for certitude, one chooses to live with doubts, question marks, divisions. Unity then means the equanimity with which the choice is made and pursued. There are many other versions, but it is unnecessary to list them, their motive is clear. If the argument is pressed, they do not in fact evade dualism, since their efforts are made in their own favour as persons and artists, they seek themselves first and then the world. Even negative capability is a power devoted primarily to the ease of an organism.

The question arises: does the imagination favour any particular form of unity? Since it is a subjective term, it is bound to approve any form that recognises the subject and guarantees its validity: assertiveness in that cause is not required. Imagination is that "uncommitted energy" which Yeats in *A Vision* ascribed to the Greek rather than the Roman mind, with an implication that such energy scorns the bureaucratic mentality. Freedom is its cardinal value, and the richest freedom is that which finds its limits within itself, a sense of decorum not imposed but acknowledged. Certainly the imagination does not welcome totalitarian orders, premature categories, or the censoring of possibilities, it would prefer to be aberrant rather than prim. Idealism is imagination's favourite philosophy, partly because it is extreme in its claims; it claims that the world is mine, is indeed "I." But the truth is that the imagination is at once exorbitant and modest. In some terminologies the imagination is a colonial enterprise which judges its merit according to the number of its possessions and captives. The object of its activity is power rather than wisdom, and the artist becomes hero of his own exploits, master in a world he has made. It is possible that this emphasis has been pressed too far, and that the analogy of divine creativity has been outrageously deployed in man's favour. Theories based upon imagination as the primary term are often pretentious, disproportionate to any produced evidence: their sponsors need to be reminded that consciousness does not account for everything in anyone's experience. On the other hand the imagination is modest in one respect, its claims are merely virtual, it does not propose to put its fictions into practice or to remove the formal parentheses within which it works. Auden was right: poetry makes nothing happen. Indeed, that is why it resents every attempt to translate its fictions out of themselves and into practice. The order it seeks is figurative, its unity is virtual, its energy uncommitted, so it is patient of any form of unity except those, if they are any such, which have no time or place for the perceiving, creative subject. Within its parentheses, the imagination is appropriately liberal, it can afford to be; its modifying power is exercised by having words attract to their orbit meanings over and beyond those required by the plot of the occasion. This is what Coleridge and Richards value in poetry, the vital tensions aroused by a liberal rather than a restrictive bearing of words, and the correspondingly vital experience embodied in their resolution.

As for unity itself, why we seek it, and why we posit a close relation between unity as end and the imagination as means: presumably we think of unity when we ascribe to our beginnings a marvellous plenitude of experience—no severances or dichotomies. We want either to regain a lost Paradise or to create a new Paradise from our own resources and the resources we have

captured. This is Coleridge's theme in one respect; self-consciousness as the very proof of division and alienation, the loss of
Adam's unity with his language; and yet at the same time
self-consciousness as the only act by which being and consciousness may yet become one. Coleridge was traditional rather than
bold in his analogies. Much of his thought on the question of
consciousness assumes for mind a divine origin. What Henry
Adams wrote of the thirteenth century would have been entirely
congenial to Coleridge. That century supposed, according to
Adams, that mind was "a mode of force directly derived from
the intelligent prime motor, and the cause of all form and
sequence in the universe—therefore the only proof of unity:
without thought in the unit, there could be no unity; without
unity no orderly sequence or ordered society. Thought alone was
Form. Mind and Unity flourished or perished together."[15]
Coleridge would not have used "motor" and "unit" in this way,
but otherwise the assumptions are accurate. He thought of the
imagination not only in relation to psychology but in relation to
theology; its highest manifestations at once solicit and defeat
explanation, like the Word of God. If you posit in man a
creative faculty, it is easier to suppose for it a religious rather
than a secular origin since the most plausible analogue for
creativity is its "original" form, the divine act of creation.
Chapter 14 of the *Biographia Literaria* is a haunted meditation
on this analogue, the original act of creation and unity, the
infinite I AM. When Coleridge elsewhere speaks of a man
becoming a distinct consciousness and of bringing "the whole
soul of man" into action, he has in view the divine act of creation
as the type of such action. When he meditates on the nature of
Form, he notes that "the contemplation of Form is astonishing
to Man and has a kind of trouble or Impulse accompanying it,
which exalts his Soul to God."[16]

The trouble is a baffled sense of one's origin in unity, and
one's fall into division. Indeed, the Romantic theory of imagination, as M. L. Abrams has argued in his *Natural Supernatural-
ism*, is a late theology of the creative Word, animated by

religious belief or by nostalgic brooding upon the effigies of belief and the ideal of a transparently true language. The difference between Coleridge and Adams in this respect is that Adams's idiom is now entirely secular: he is so much a product, though not a creature, of his time that his brooding upon the unity of the thirteenth century is picturesque rather than nostalgic, it is too late for nostalgia. When he says that energy is the inherent effort of every multiplicity to become unity, he brings his several commitments together. Energy is the word we need when we propose to translate imagination into modern terms; we understand it, as we do not understand imagination, in its relation to force. The question it proposes is D. H. Lawrence's major concern in *Women in Love, The Rainbow,* and *St. Mawr:* if energy is the inherent effort of every multiplicity to become unity, does this mean that man is always hopelessly out of tune with life's "natural" intimations and rhythms, like Gerald Crich in *Women in Love?* Or is this energy the very power by which man is moving in archetypal rhythms — while those rhythms are themselves a paradigm of seeming violations and acceptances, a winding path, a turning wheel, a cadence of lapses and renewals? If we speak of unity and multiplicity, and then of energy, the missing term is that which energy circumvents or forestalls; it cannot be anything but death, the definitive form of inertia.

We should not evade these questions, even if we have little hope of answering them. Answers may not be necessary, if we think of answers as strategies and solutions; responsiveness may be enough. Equally, we should not evade the full responsibility of imagination, even in the good cause of sponsoring mind, order, hierarchy, and subordination: there is an even better cause. We should not hand over the unconscious and the aboriginal to the Surrealists, or the irrational to R. D. Laing. But if we propose to establish our values in the light of imagination, we must try to understand what we are doing, and why, and the character of that light. I propose therefore to use the word "imagination" in the following sense: imagination, as

distinct from mind, is that mental power which finds unnecessary the strict separation of conscious and unconscious life, of
primary and secondary processes, in Freud's terminology; which
deals with contradictions not by subordinating one to another
but by accommodating all within a larger perspective; and which
entertains feelings and motives before they have been assigned
to categories or organized into thoughts, attitudes, statements,
values, or commitments. It is not necessary to suppose that the
literary imagination differs in kind from the imagination which
exerts itself in other forms: that it is generous in providing
evidence of its action is of course convenient as well as gratifying.

It is widely agreed that nearly everything can be discussed
with reference to three cardinal points of perspective: God, Man,
and Nature. It is clear that the concept of imagination became
problematic when the first two of these terms suffered confusion,
notably when the idea of God lapsed into the idea of Man. The
God-term was not deleted: instead, it was assimilated to the idea
of Man, which in turn was enormously aggrandized. Man, no
longer content to see himself as servant or vicar of a divine
power, the ability to create something from nothing, procreator
if not Creator, was exalted to receive by his own desire the
creative power traditionally ascribed to God. The "supreme
fiction" of Man as God became portentous in the later years of
the eighteenth century: the idea of Man as creative vicar of God
goes back of course much further, Ernst Kantorowicz finds
versions of it in medieval jurisprudence.[17] The elevation of Man
was not achieved without cost, and we sense the cost when we
say that the spirit of the elevation may be heroic or rueful or
desperate: nearly any mood is possible. It is heroic if we mark
the sheer scale of the role and repudiate the nostalgic note which
obtrudes. It is rueful if the elevation is observed as merely
virtual, theoretic, an act in principle rather than in effect. It is
desperate if we feel that the cost is exorbitant or the pretention
gross. The subjective aura which imagination casts upon experience may be deemed valuable or miserable, a major enhance-
ment of life or a mere delusion. It is my impression that

imaginative acts are now performed and received in a spirit more
rueful than either heroic or desperate; mainly because the heroic
note is virtually impossible or at best naive, and a truly desperate
note is hard to sustain. But it is impertinent to be positive upon
a question so large and so loose.

The essential power: why essential? Not merely (though this
would be cause enough) because it is all we have, but because it
is the only force that has the slightest chance of coping with the
vast miscellany of arbitrary and ordained events which constitute
the occasions of our experience. No force on earth can cope with
everything; certainly no force of mind. The artist does the best
he can, trusting to the imagination's favourite trope, the synec-
doche which takes the part for the whole. Richard Blackmur has
observed that "the artist is concerned with all the world of actual
experience to which human response is possible, and he has
therefore the impossible double task both of finding means
adequate to represent what experience he has had, and of
finding, through the means he has, the experience he has not
had."[18] The only means he has is the imagination, which at
least in principle confronts whatever experience the artist has
had and goes on to create in a spirit of need, risk, possibility, or
fulfilment, the experience he has not had. It is not his business
to assert that the experience, real and imagined, is at any
moment complete: that is a question for others and answerable
only in retrospect. But it is his business to put into relation to
"the world's body" the body of his own imagination, since that is
what he has and all he has. I refer to his own possessions and
needs, and take for granted that he will have recourse to
whatever he can use from the possessions and needs of others,
made available in forms, traditions, structures, morals: he does
not choose to be a barbarian. Otherwise put, imagination as the
complete act of the mind is the only power an artist can bring to
bear, from his own resources, upon the world he is bound to
confront, "a doomed world, nevertheless surviving, throwing up
value after value with inexhaustible energy but without a
principle in sight."[19] Blackmur's phrases are good enough to

remind us that the modern artist takes himself on trust by
believing that his craft is the only morality worth his time, and
that what he seeks is an ethic of achieved form. If what he
achieves turns out to be a value entirely personal and as
arbitrary as driftwood, that is not his fault alone but the fault of
anyone who tries to get along without a principle. I mention
these matters not to deal with them at all adequately but to
suggest something of the context in which the modern artist's
imagination is likely to act. As the artist is merely a special case
of the ordinary man, his circumstances are bound to be exemplary and of general significance.

But while we say, with whatever qualification, that the
imagination is all an artist has, we have also to say that in a
sense he has it at one remove from himself; this is why T. S.
Eliot has insisted upon a distinction between the man who
suffers and the writer who creates. Imagination is like love, not
in general but in the particular instance, it is like love to the
lover, a force in which he feels himself implicated and expressed
rather than a force of his own. The narrator in *The Sacred
Fount,* thinking of Gilbert Long and Lady John as lovers, muses
on "the way other people could feel about each other, the power
not one's self, in the given instance, that made for passion."
Imagination is another such power: it is one's very self in the
sense that he, the artist, cannot feel himself embodied except in
its terms; and yet it is outside one's self, like a force of nature,
which is why till recently aesthetics posited for art a source in
divine frenzy, madness, or the gods. We think of imagination as
a man's "secret ministry," corresponding to the intentionality of
the mind in its desire to range beyond the limit of what is merely
given. The only restriction an artist accepts is marked by the
nature of artistic form: he has come upon his limit and must stop
or turn aside when he finds himself unable to bring his feeling
to the condition of form. Imagination is the power by which that
which is considered natural, conventional, or axiomatic is transfigured to become truly known, possessed in the form of
knowledge and action. When the transfiguration is sudden and is

achieved in a form that could not have been anticipated, since it was not in the cards or the script, we are in the presence of the Sublime, and the only question is its source: either the gods or the human imagination.

Let us say, then, that imagination is the secular name we apply to the soul when we wish to live peacefully with our neighbors. I cannot believe that the imagination is other than divine in its origin; but even if we leave that belief aside, or disagree upon it, we may agree that the imagination is a form of energy, demonstrable in its consequences if not in its nature, and that it strives to realise itself by living in the world. Like the soul, the imagination seeks to inhabit not only a human body but a human world. Even if the given world is regarded as a mere transit camp in a journey toward the abiding City of God, it is the only world available to us in the meantime. So a question of the imagination ranges beyond itself to raise further questions: the nature of the body, and of "the world's body"; the character of imagination itself, if such a question is answerable; the bearing of imagination as living energy or soul upon the world it inhabits; and the bearing, gentle or aggressive, of that world upon its spiritual inhabitant.

This is to say that the question of imagination bears upon fundamental issues in metaphysics and politics. In metaphysics, the question touches upon definitions of consciousness, being, action, fiction, and so forth. Even if we start by saying, with Kenneth Burke, that man is the symbol-making animal, we have to go further and ask questions about the nature and status of the symbol. Is the symbol-making faculty enough to confer identity upon the one who uses it? Could we base a definition of man upon imagination as his essential quality? There is a famous passage in Proust's novel in which Marcel describes a scene in his room when the afternoon sun sends its beams through the almost closed shutters: the light, he says, contrived to slip in upon its golden wings, staying motionless in a corner between glass and woodwork like a butterfly: ". . . où un reflet de jour avait pourtant trouvé moyen de faire passer ses ailes jaunes, et restait immobile entre le bois et le vitrage, dans un coin, comme un papillon posé."[20] Would it be reasonable to base a definition of man upon the faculty by which the movement of sunlight is seen and felt as the wings of a hovering butterfly? It would be reasonable, provided one could show that the act was genuinely imaginative, not merely a tic of subjectivity, and that the symbolic nature of the act characterised Marcel's way of living in the world and making sense of that life. I make this point not to end the matter or even seriously to start it, but to show the kind of question raised by a metaphysics of imagination. In politics, the most pressing question would turn upon the conditions in which an act of imagination is possible, the scene which corresponds to the act. A politics of imagination would object to any account of imagination which made it utterly self-centred, a category of one's private life cut adrift from questions of natural history, society, and culture. I have in mind here the objections brought by Adorno against Heidegger's concept of *Dasein* as the self's possession of itself. The main objection is that such a concept allows philosophy to give up concerning itself with the conditions of any particular life, the conditions which make it possible for a man to become himself, to be himself, or to change.[21] The way to avoid such charges, in a theory of imagination, is to emphasize the intimate relation between imagination and its enabling correlates: nature, the world, other people, society, history, the language, forms, genres. I emphasize this point because there is a real temptation in discussing imagination to make it a property of subjectivity and to isolate it for that reason. A politics of imagination would resist that temptation by describing its results. Adorno is again a case in point, partly on the strength of a passage in *Minima Moralia* in which he points to "aesthetic subjectivism" as one of the causes of modern mass-culture. Parodying Heine's lines about making small songs from great sorrows ("Aus meinem grossen Schmerzen / mach' ich die kleinen Lieder"), Adorno pictures the artist making his journey into the interior and coming back with psychic treasures which, far from being ineffable, are saleable on the open market:

> The progress in technique that brought artists ever greater freedom and independence of anything heterogeneous has resulted in a kind of reification, technification of the inward as such. The more masterfully the artist expresses himself, the less he has to 'be' what he expresses, and the more what he expresses, indeed the content of subjectivity itself, becomes a mere function of the production process. . . . The transformation of expressive content from an undirected impulse into material for manipulation makes it palpable, exhibitable, saleable. The lyrical subjectivism of Heine, for example, does not stand in simple contradiction to his commercial traits; the saleable is itself subjectivity administered by subjectivity.[22]

The merit, but not the sole merit, of Adorno's passage is that it warns us against considering the imagination as if its ideal character were entirely reflexive, self-defined, self-engrossed; or as if it always acted in conditions of spiritual purity. Proust is instructive again on this point. The "reification of the inward as such" is recognised in that passage in which he reports that when he looked at something, his consciousness that he was seeing it would remain between the object and himself, so that he could never come into direct contact with the object: "Quand je voyais un objet extérieur, la conscience que je le voyais restait entre moi et lui, le bordait d'un mince liséré spirituel qui m'empêchait de jamais toucher directemente sa matière; elle se volatilisait en quelque sorte avant que je prisse contact avec elle, comme un corps incandescent qu'on approche d'un objet mouillé ne touche pas son humidité parce qu'il se fait toujours précéder d'une zone d'évaporation."[23] The "mince liséré spirituel" may be taken as standing for the necessarily mediated character of consciousness; or for the presence of consciousness to itself, reified in Adorno's terms as the object of its own attention. Proust breaks out of the circle of solipsism by opening his experience to the force of chance. It is not a mark of naivete that he allows chance to initiate his consciousness: it is absurd to say that he takes seriously anything he happens to remember merely because he has remembered it. He deems authentic any experience initiated by chance and developed or tested by consciousness: this is his way of ensuring that his art is sustained by a just relation between inward and outer experience. It is as if he ascribed to certain external events the destiny of being chosen by his imagination as suitable objects of transformation. Only a peculiarly humble politics of imagination, it may be said, would be content with such an acknowledgement. Most critics who devote themselves to the politics of literature have a sharper axe to grind. But I am merely describing the smallest acknowledgement which makes a political aspect visible: a more demanding politics would have to come later.

I think it only reasonable to admit that a theory of literature which takes imagination as its ground or point of departure lays claim to certain axioms: that art is the inspired work of a few rare souls, adepts of a sacred mystery; that while common minds slide upon the surface of things, artists search the depths. The imagination cannot believe that what it comes upon or aspires toward can be merely contingent, the poet believes that the direction of his work is a kind of destiny. Much of this is implicit in the terminology of imagination, because it features man in his creative role. It is of course entirely possible to reject the rhetoric of imagination and to scorn the psychological, social, and political ambitions which imagination sponsors, the claims upon depth, reverberation, soul, community, and mystery. Robbe-Grillet's fiction arises from that scorn, as his essays insist. The fiction of Wyndham Lewis deploys the same logic, as Fredric Jameson has shown in a remarkable study.[24] Lewis's sinister comedy presents reality as obedient to its stereotypes, the public world becomes a gestalt drilling its mechanical atoms. The main feeling behind such comedies is that the forms of imagination have now been captured and put to ignoble work by the forces of commodity culture: the most convincing way to show what has happened is to devise an art in which those degraded forms move like robots marching upon the surface of our lives. The closest comparisons point to *A Tale of a Tub* and *The Dunciad,* works which use the methods of Fancy, deploying "fixities and definites" and refusing to let them aspire to a condition higher than their own.

Yet another programme is outlined in a famous phrase of Beckett's, which I set down here without gloss: Imagination Dead Imagine.

Notes

1. William H. Gass, *In the Heart of the Heart of Country, and Other Stories* (New York: Harper and Row, 1968), p. 184.
2. Donald Davie, "Pushkin: A Didactic Poem" in *Collected Poems* (London: Routledge and Kegan Paul, 1972), p. 18.
3. A. R. Ammons, *Collected Poems 1951-1971* (New York: Norton, 1972), p. 334.
4. Ibid., p. 92.
5. Lionel Trilling, "Mind in the Modern World": *Times Literary Supplement,* November 17, 1972, p. 1385.
6. Wallace Stevens, *The Necessary Angel* (New York: Knopf, 1951), pp. 147-148.
7. "Like princes is Hercules. Common to all is Bacchus's spirit. But Christ is the Ultimate." Quoted in Theophil Spoerri, "Style of Distance, Style of Nearness" in Howard S. Babb (editor), *Essays in Stylistic Analysis* (New York: Harcourt Brace Jovanovich, 1972), p. 77.
8. Coleridge, *Biographia Literaria,* edited by J. Shawcross (London: Oxford University Press, 1962), reprint, Vol. II, pp. 14-18.
9. Coleridge, *Shakespeare Criticism,* edited by T. M. Raysor. (London: Dent, 1967), reprint, Vol. I, p. 189.
10. I. A. Richards, *Coleridge on Imagination* (London: Routledge and Kegan Paul, second edition, 1950), pp. 82-84.
11. Roman Jakobson and Morris Hale, *Fundamentals of Language* ('S-Gravenhage: Mouton, 1956), pp. 77f.
12. Coleridge, *Shakespeare Criticism,* Vol. I, p. 188.
13. William Empson, review of *Coleridge on Imagination* in *The Criterion,* April 1935, Vol. XIV, pp. 484-485.
14. R. P. Blackmur, *The Lion and the Honeycomb* (London: Methuen, 1956), p. 41.
15. Henry Adams, *The Education of Henry Adams* (Boston: Houghton Mifflin, 1961), reprint, p. 429.
16. Coleridge, *Notebooks,* edited by Kathleen Coburn (London: Routledge and Kegan Paul, 1962), Vol. II (1804-1808), Entry No. 2223, October 1804.
17. Ernst Kantorowicz, "The Sovereignty of the Artist: A Note on Legal

Maxims and Renaissance Theories of Art" in *Selected Studies* (New York: Augustin, 1965), pp. 352f.

18. R. P. Blackmur, *The Lion and the Honeycomb*, p. 219.

19. Ibid., p. 205.

20. Proust, *A la recherche du temps perdu*, edited by Pierre Clarac and André Ferré, Pléiade edition (Paris: Gallimard, 1954), Vol. I, p. 83.

21. T. W. Adorno, *The Jargon of Authenticity*, translated by Knut Tarnowski and Frederic Will (London: Routledge and Kegan Paul, 1973), pp. 114-116.

22. T. W. Adorno, *Minima Moralia*, translated by E. F. N. Jephcott (London: NLB, 1974), pp. 214-215.

23. Proust, *A la recherche du temps perdu*, Vol. I, p. 84.

24. Fredric Jameson, "Wyndham Lewis as Futurist" in *Hudson Review*, July 1973, pp. 295f.

The Sovereign Ghost

On February 18, 1900, W. P. Ker delivered a lecture to the London School of Ethics under the title "Imagination and Judgment." He told his audience that "the mind attains its proper freedom through imagination" and that the imagination, far from being opposed to judgment, is indeed "the ground and source of right judgment, being the habit of mind which is both comprehensive and definite, both long-sighted and minute."[1] Ker found it an easy matter to defend the imagination. He assured his students of ethics that the imagination is neither wild nor capricious but sound, and that it participates in every act of moral choice. Judgment is a critical act of the mind so far as its conditions are specific and local, it is an immediate possibility guaranteed by the greater possibility which we call the imagination. Judgment and imagination are concentric circles, and imagination is the larger one. The terms are in partnership, not in opposition.

I have chosen Ker's lecture as a point of reference because it was given with the confidence of a scholar in full possession of his theme, and upon a subject thoroughly established. The imagination was praised as a faculty well authenticated and in good standing, a personal attribute which one was not obliged to curb. I do not find that these happy conditions still obtain. Before we praise the imagination we are now challenged to establish it; the concept of imagination is under attack. It is too soon to assess the damage already done to a concept which, making common cause with Romanticism in certain respects, has until recently negotiated with some nonchalance the challenges it has met: it may shrug off the present challenge even yet. Like any other paradigm, it will stay in office until a new spirit of the time produces a new terminology; such occasions arise from a

35

slow process of doubt rather than from one spectacular challenge. It would be premature to report that the concept of imagination has been dislodged and that we must give it up for lost, but it would be ingenuous to deny that it is under attack. Perhaps it will survive by resorting to the strategy adopted by Christian apologists after the publication of Darwin's *Origin of Species*, allowing nearly everything to be explained in terms of evolution and natural selection while insisting that a divine intention must be posited as intervening at some point. The lines of defence were pulled back and concentrated. Critics of a Romantic persuasion may offer the imagination as the divine intervention which thereafter makes secular history possible.

We need a text, otherwise the theme may extort a consideration too abstract to be useful.

II

On January 31, 1931, John Stanislaus Joyce wrote to his famous son to wish him a happy birthday and a bright New Year. "I wonder," he wrote, "do you recollect the old days in Brighton Square, when you were Babie Tuckoo, and I used to take you out in the Square and tell you all about the moo-cow that used to come down from the mountain and take little boys across?" I propose to place that question beside one of Joyce's "epiphanies" where the novelist transcribes an incident that happened in 1891 when a neighbour, Mr. Vance, came into the house in Martello Terrace, Bray, waving a stick:

> Mr. Vance: . . . O, you know, he'll have to apologise, Mrs. Joyce.
> Mrs. Joyce: O yes . . . Do you hear that, Jim?
> Mr. Vance: Or else—if he doesn't—the eagles'll come and pull out his eyes.
> Mrs. Joyce: O, but I'm sure he will apologise.
> Joyce *(under the table, to himself):*
> Pull out his eyes,
> Apologise,
> Apologise,
> Pull out his eyes.

Apologise,
Pull out his eyes,
Pull out his eyes,
Apologise.[3]

These two episodes participate in the beginning and the end of
my text, the first page of Joyce's *A Portrait of the Artist as a
Young Man*. I bring them together because they remind us, with
a certain force at a time when we are infatuated with fiction and
theories of fiction, that in the relation between reality, imagination, and form as represented by that page reality has a good
deal to show for itself, it does not merely wait upon the attention
of a novelist. Mr. Vance was a fact before the *Portrait* was a
fiction. We should not assume that facts are always soluble in
the displacements of memory and fiction.

The question proposed concerns the existence and the nature
of the imagination. For some years I had supposed the question
easily answered, the imagination was understood to mean the
mind in its fictive or creative capacity, a personal faculty for
every purpose as free as its occasions required. John Smith's
imagination differed from Picasso's only in force and direction.
Unashamedly subjective, the imagination claimed the privilege
of consciousness, including most particularly self-consciousness,
it constituted its experience and organized it in its own terms, it
was the centre of every circle it drew. Now we are aware that
within the past ten or fifteen years these assumptions have been
challenged. If it were merely a question of the attributes of the
imagination, or of its practical influence upon the world at
large, the challenge would not matter, no one has claimed that
the imagination will save the world, even if we think that it is
unlikely to be saved without its ministry. Many years ago
Hannah Arendt expressed a doubt, a fear that the imagination
could not in any way deal with such facts as Belsen and Dachau;
she thought it must resign, baffled and humiliated by such
evidence. Perhaps we have claimed too much for the imagination: when you have a toothache you need a dentist, not a poet.
But this is not the present dispute: the challenge turns rather

upon the character, form, and place of the imagination in relation to other powers. The privilege of subjectivity is now questioned along with the philosophy of consciousness, the status of the perceiving or speaking subject. It is common again to hear the assertion that consciousness is determined by social existence, and individual speech by social and linguistic codes. We are often warned that what we take to be the freedom of the imagination is a delusion, it is not free. The warnings come in one idiom or another from structuralists, anthropologists, critics, especially from those who take their bearings from Marx and Freud. It will be convenient to refer to them as structuralists without distinguishing one from another or establishing the attribution in any individual case. I am referring to an intellectual spirit at large, nothing more than that. It may be true that the spirit is merely reacting against the exorbitance of Romantic assertion, and especially against the mystification it sponsors, the insistence that the imagination is holy ground and must not be examined. Such an assertion makes research impossible. Scholars do not like to be told at the beginning of their studies that certain areas are beyond their range and must be reserved as the ground of mystery; to conclude, late in their studies, that there are indeed mysteries and impenetrable questions is a much more tolerable experience. To be specific: it is sufficient if the reader agrees that there are intellectual forces at work which, faced with the terms I have given in the first group, would emphasize rather those I give in the second:

Genius	System
Poem	Text
Poet	Language
Genetics	Linguistics
History	Structure
Origin	Relation
Creativity	Displacement
Subject	Function
Hero	Chorus

The lists are meant to indicate a tendency; there is no need to quarrel over individual items. If the second is called Structuralism, the first may with equal if no greater accuracy be called Romanticism. The idea of imagination is secure in the first, not in the second. So the question may be refined: is it necessary to revise the standard account of the imagination under pressure from those forces which would displace man from the creative centre of experience and make him rather a function of certain governing systems or codes?

I refer to the standard account of the imagination as though there were some such agreed thing, and I suppress the differences between one man's version and another's. I do so for ease and because the differences are comparatively slight and they nearly disappear when ranged against those forces which threaten the concept of imagination in any version. From Kant, Hegel, Coleridge, and Hazlitt to Stevens and Valéry there is substantial agreement on the nature and scope of the imagination; the differences are matters of shading or emphasis. It is understood in this tradition that the imagination is a free power; as Aristotle says in *De Anima,* "imagining lies within our own power whenever we wish." The imagination is distinct from the will, but it is propelled by man's desire to create, to transcend himself, to surpass in his real experience that portion of it which is merely given, like Mr. Vance to Joyce. As such, imagination is a form of man's spirituality. We refer to the transcendental subject when we want a more precise terminology, but the difference need not delay us, both phrases run happily together. The subject constitutes its experience; when the experience is under full control, it is featured as a circle; when it is not, it is featured as a void or a vortex. As a classic instance of the imagination in control of its material and superbly confident of its powers, we may cite the narrative of Cellini's mastery in his *Perseus,* on the evidence of the sculpture itself and a famous chapter in Cellini's *Vita,* the confidence is exhilarating to us because it seemed miraculous to him.

III

According to this tradition there are three enterprises especially congenial to the imagination as an act of consciousness: in principle, it is possible for an artist to practice all three, but he is likely to give most of his allegiance to one. In the first, the imagination lavishes attention upon the natural forms and proposes to "contemplate them as they are in their rich and contingent materiality."⁵ We think of this as the secular equivalent of religious devotion in which a certain mode of consciousness corresponds to love. The object of attention is the particularity of nature, and the imagination is disposed to reveal it in its plenitude with the result that the objects contemplated take to themselves a certain radiance which marks the feeling they inspire. According to this intention the imagination does not interrogate the objects or question their validity, it approaches them only for appreciation. The merits of the objects are deemed to be either intrinsic and therefore valid by definition, or representative, as tokens of a higher power embodied in them. The mode of this imagination is, let us say, Franciscan rather than Augustinian. The motive is acknowledgement, celebration, lest anything of value in the world be lost. Beyond this, there is no philosophical commitment, such an imagination is not required to bring in an optimistic account of the universe, though it may be difficult to reconcile a thoroughgoing scepticism with celebration or acknowledgement. "Snow in the Suburbs" begins:

> Every branch big with it,
>   Bent every twig with it;
> Every fork like a white web-foot;
> Every tree and pavement mute:
> Some flakes have lost their way, and grope back upward, when
> Meeting those meandering down they turn and descend again.
> The palings are glued together like a wall,
> And there is no waft of wind with the fleecy fall.⁶

You cannot write like that unless you pay attention and take care. The care is in the attention, lavish because the snow makes the speaker see everything as if he were just now struck by the great net of analogies in which each object, held, reaches out to another object according to laws entirely natural. The branch is big, like a pregnant woman. The forks in the trees are like ducks' feet. The pavements' noise is suppressed, the flying snowflakes are meeting, turning, meandering. An ostensibly lifeless scene is full of life. What we call description is an act of imagination, a fiction animated by goodwill toward its object. The object excites and fulfils the attention it receives. In painting, think of Matisse and his "Red Interior, Still Life on a Blue Table."

In the second enterprise, the imagination proposes to set against the natural world a rival fiction which owes as little as possible to nature and nearly everything to itself. The motives at work are sometimes opportunist, sceptical of nature or aggressive toward it; in any case the imagination regards natural forms not as moral emblems or aesthetic criteria but as mere occasions, obstacles to be overcome or grist to the mill. But the motives are not always ruthless. Sometimes the act of imagination is felt as a desperate necessity, like an act of faith in the absence of evidence in its favour. Natural forms are not felt as sustenance, and the leap of faith is made in the needy hope of aspiring beyond nature to more complete satisfactions. If nature is not enough, the imagination must act upon its own authority. Such an imagination is often "angelic," to use Allen Tate's description, and it results in a hypertrophy of feeling, will, and intellect; of feeling, since it exhibits "the incapacity to represent the human condition in the central tradition of natural feeling"; of will, since it features "the thrust of the will beyond the human scale of action"; and of intellect, since it shows "the intellect moving in isolation from both love and the moral will, whereby it declares itself independent of the human situation in the quest of essential knowledge."[7] In other words, the imagination is never satisfied. Elsewhere I have described some of its motives as Promethean, marking its restlessness and defiance.[8] On a show of hands I suppose most imaginations would declare themselves dissatisfied with the available forms: else why does our vocabulary entrust so much feeling to words like *make, assume,*

construct, create, conceive, imagine, and (most of all, as making
a leap of faith) *act?* Why is it natural for poets from Plato to
Hart Crane to call the imagination "the fury" and to set it
against "the broken world"? In "Voyages II" the lover speaks to
his beloved of the sea:

> Mark how her turning shoulders wind the hours,
> And hasten while her penniless rich palms
> Pass superscription of bent foam and wave, —
> Hasten, while they are true, —sleep, death, desire,
> Close round one instant in one floating flower.[9]

In these lines the relation between imagination and reality is so
favourable to the imagination that reality, the sea, may hardly
be said to provide more than an occasion. In such a sublime
cause, the sea is amenable. It is perhaps vulgar to say that the
sea must curb itself, keep itself impoverished, if the style is to
become richly agglutinative. It is improper to invoke another
sea, different from the one the speaker sees, and complain that
the true sea has not been adequately described. Poetry which
trades in agglutinative textures charges high prices, as much as
the market will bear. The feeling rides upon the style, not upon
the waves. It is impossible to prescribe the amount of plot which
is capable of carrying so much diction, so much metaphorical
freight: shoulders, clocks, palms of hands and palm trees,
coinage, signatures. But it is natural to such a style to cause
tension and, if necessary, embarrassment between its subject
matter and the feeling it is required to sustain. We often feel of
the extreme images in a poetry such as Crashaw's that the figures
are daring us to be embarrassed and disgusted, since the
speaker's love of God can take anything in its stride. The figures
are not fully explained by reference to Bernini and Baroque
styles generally, they are what they are so that a certain rush of
feeling may be expressed by surmounting them. In any event, a
sense of rivalry is necessary if this kind of imagination is to
thrive, the poet must refuse to be satisfied with nature's offering.

In the third enterprise the characteristic act of the imagination is negation. Hegel is its sponsor, notably in the Preface to

The Phenomenology of Mind, where he speaks of the mind engaged with distinctions and difference: "difference itself continues to be an immediate element within truth as such, in the form of the principle of negation, in the form of the activity of Self."[10] Critics as diverse as Freud, Bergson, and Kenneth Burke have proposed negation as the essentially human act: there are no negatives in nature, there are only positives. Human language alone contains the principle of negation. Negation is therefore a linguistic marvel by which the mind repudiates its dependence upon objects. The objects exist, they are there, but the mind exerts itself by rejecting them. I assume a direct relation between the principle of negation and Pater's account of those moments in which the mind replaces the object in nature by a wealth of sensations and impressions: these are the only remaining traces of the object, and thereafter their intensity is independent of the object. The demand of the mind on these occasions, as Pater says in *The Renaissance,* is to feel itself alive, presumably by feeling its power in dissolving the natural object. This form of imagination differs from the second version in dissolving the object: in the second version the imagination counts upon the recalcitrance of the object so that the relation between object and style may be tense and difficult, the sea is not meant to yield to Hart Crane's imagination too easily. The third form is like solipsism in Tate's account, "a philosophical doctrine which says that we create the world in the act of perceiving it."[11] There is no question of recalcitrance, objects do not exist even to the point at which an effort is made to dissolve them, they come into existence only upon the mind's *fiat.* In practice, I concede, negatives often give their positive opposites more existence than their formal grammar would permit; if you banish something with vehemence you make the reader aware of the vehemence necessary to banish it at all. So there is a gray area between my second and third types of imagination, depending on the degree of presence we feel clinging to the dissolved or vetoed object. Empson discusses this in a later chapter of *Seven Types of Ambiguity* when he points out that in Keats's

"Ode to Melancholy" "No, no, go not to Lethe, neither twist /
Wolf's-bane . . ." tells you "that somebody, or some force in the
poet's mind, must have wanted to go to Lethe very much, if it
took four negatives in the first line to stop them."[12] Even in
Marlowe's "Ugly Hell gape not: come not, Lucifer" there is also,
Empson argues, "a demand for the final intellectual curiosity, at
whatever cost, to be satisfied: *'Let* ugly Hell gape, *show* me
Lucifer." This case is not as convincing as the Keats, but there is
enough in it to show how words can work perversely against
their official purposes. Anyway, I only wanted to say that the
second and third offices of the imagination are akin, though
still, I think, distinguishable.

Of the three offices, the only one to which the structuralists
would object is the second. The first would be acceptable to
them because it is philosophically realist, quite straightforward,
it does not fuss about the status of objects. The second would be
thought objectionable because it posits the imagination as
creative source, and this would be spurned as romantic mystification. The third would be endorsed because it does not claim
the power of creating from nothing; or, more precisely, negation
could be regarded as a formal operation applied to a series of
elements already given. Structuralists would say that negation
acknowledges objects by negating them, and they would interest
themselves in the formal operation as something capable of
being studied without mystification. They would not trouble
themselves about the origin and status of the objects. In fact,
structuralists will take pretty nearly anything they are given, so
long as it does not involve an occult source or a ruling
principle deemed to be beyond the reach of analysis.

This standard account of the imagination distinguishes it, in
degree but not necessarily in kind, from perception. Perception
is normally considered a sad fellow, pursuing the bourgeois
virtues. Imagination is then construed as vision, with an implication that it sees what it insists on seeing. In a milder version a
distinction is made between perception, in which the mind
accepts the object of its attention as a vigorous partner in its

fiction, and imagination, in which the mind regards the object of its attention as variously suggestible, responsive, malleable, ready to be enhanced, suffused, and perhaps even dissolved by the feeling it occasions. Perception and imagination are both events in the history of individual feeling, and the distinction between them is a matter of degree. In perception, as in imagination, I am not a camera. A percept and an image are both fictions. The main distinction is that imagination proposes to be present throughout the process of the mind's engagement and to concentrate upon the quality of that presence: nothing is more important than the presence of the imagination to itself. Perception is also the mind's engagement with objects, but it is casual about its presence, and much more concerned with things to be done, decisions to be taken. In perception, the mind creates from the given appearance of a chair the satisfying impression which extends to a body an invitation to sit down: it is not concerned with the quality of its own presence. Perception, then, expects to meet the resistance of objects, it does not press the case too far, its fictions are not violent, it has no design upon objects except to sense their presence, their relation to other objects and to the mind, it acknowledges that objects have another life in which they are not perceived, though they may be deemed to await perception. But the imagination exercises its freedom by determining to what extent if at all it will yield to the weight or force of objects, and it is ready to surpass them if its freedom calls for such a show of violence. Hegel points to this attribute of imagination when he says that there is no merit in speaking of the unity of subject and object if they are taken to mean "what they are outside their unity."[13] The imagination is the name we give to the mind when it is prepared, if feeling requires it, to see everything change except itself. Such a faculty has naturally been regarded as omnipotent. Wordsworth thought it, as he writes in *The Prelude* (XIII, 168) "but another name for absolute strength / And clearest insight." Coleridge thought it, in one of its capacities, the finite counterpart of the creative word of God. The chief trouble with these associations is that they incite the human imagination to scorn its humanity and make direct, unmediated designs upon essence, thereby separating itself from perception and its sustenance.

IV

This is, I think, a reasonably accurate account of the imagination in its standard Romantic version. Clearly, the faculty I have been describing depends upon the notion of a privileged consciousness, an act of the mind which could hardly be conceived if subjectivity were to be suppressed or dislodged. A man who begins by rejecting subjectivity is in the worst position to say where he will end; he would abolish the imagination in all its offices, thereby denying himself the habitual skill by which we relate ourselves to a world in many of its moods opaque and hostile. It is improbable that we would be persuaded to go far in that direction; we would retain the skill under any name. It should also be remarked that many people who no longer take the integrity of the transcendental subject for granted still maintain the force and status of subjectivity, under whatever degree of pressure. "I want at all costs to save the subjectivity of literature," Georges Poulet has declared, a reasonable desire in a critic whose entire work depends upon his sense of the poet's constituting consciousness and the reader's ability in some measure to participate in it.[14] According to that emphasis, the source of value is to be found not in an object or even in a subject, separately construed, but in the energy of feeling for which an object provides the occasion and a subject provides the desire. The object may be real or imaginary, nothing is said of its objective status, the subject is deemed to manifest unity of presence. The reflective subject is challenged in many respects but not in its unity; unity is embodied feeling, nervous, vibrating, and free. Romanticism is the name of that unity so far as it has revealed itself in historical terms: the real problem of Romanticism is to determine what its proclaimed fusion of subject and object really means, a problem which Coleridge did much to clarify but not so much to resolve. To be a critic in Poulet's terms is to enhance one's subjectivity by projecting it into the more achieved subjectivity of the poet in his poems. But I cannot find that Poulet has established subjectivity with any theoretical precision, unless he has in mind that a convincing theory is bound to emerge from a commitment so forcibly expressed. Merleau-Ponty is on stronger ground than Poulet because he proposes to save man's subjectivity not for its own sweet sake but to establish man's being in the world, his engagement with everything else. Hence the proposal "to restore to subjectivity its inherence in history." History is not merely the past, or the sense of a past in anyone who has that sense, it is not an antique drum, it is whatever evades the exorbitance of consciousness and refuses to be intimidated by the *élan* of fictions. Merleau-Ponty has attacked as a fallacy the notion that "the thinking subject can absorb into its thinking or appropriate without remainder the object of its thought, that our being can be brought down to our knowledge."[16] To make sure that being is always the larger term, Merleau-Ponty has emphasized not only the subject's inherence in history but its inherence in the human body. The subject is not in itself or in its isolation a primary source, meaning is a communal possibility, utterly dependent upon the relation between person and person. The subject is not transparent to itself. The body is neither subject nor object, it is a "subject-object" of capacities and solicitations, hence its central role in a philosophy which "puts essences back into existence."[17]

V

If the concept of imagination is under interrogation, there is no reason to think the concept of the image secure. Those who have an interest in retaining the term see their best hope in translating it from the terminology of knowledge into that of action. Sartre has argued that images are not what we see or know but what we do, an image is an act, "a certain kind of consciousness"[18] defined by its direction rather than by any content ascribed to it. It is not a thing or even a mental picture of a thing. Since it is an act, it is subjectivity itself, it cannot be anything else, an act requires an agent. Sartre's concept of imagination is essential to his understanding of freedom and his sense of man as one who acts in a given world. Freedom is illusory if we are constrained to wait for the delivery of impressions by the senses and then to arrange them in various patterns, retaining self-consciousness as an exotic diversion. In his first essay on imagination Sartre overwhelms the terminology of subject and object by representing every ostensibly visual element of imagery in terms of action and gesture. But in his later treatment of the theme he is not quite so extreme, he is still ready to drive the idiom of action as far as it will go and to make it supersede the notion of imagery as a gallery of little pictures in the mind—as scholars speak of Shakespeare's imagery —but he admits difficulties more liberally than before, even to the extent of allowing the idiom of subject and object to assert itself, though in a dispirited form. The image is described now as a relation, it denotes the way in which consciousness presents an object to itself. The image does not "stand" for an object, it is an act of consciousness occasioned by an object. This enables Sartre to propose his own definitions of perception, conception, and imagination, in that order, because he treats perception as the lowest act on the creative or fictive scale. "In perception I *observe* objects." I look at a cube, see only three of its sides, and remain content with that restriction; my interest in the cube is likely to be utilitarian or prudential. Conception is defined as "knowledge which is conscious of itself and which places itself at once at the centre of the object." In conception the limitations of the "point of view" are surpassed; acting upon earlier knowledge in similar situations we choose to "see" all sides of the cube because our experience assures us that they are there. Conception is therefore an act which enhances what we see by

taking the advantage of what we remember and what experience
has taught us. Imagination, finally, is "a synthetic act which
unites a concrete, non-imagined knowledge to elements which
are more actually representative." It is therefore an act which
produces the object as an image, but since the image is complete
at the very moment of the act it cannot avoid a certain
impoverishment, it presents the object not as being but precisely
as not being. "No matter how long I look at an image,"
Sartre writes, "I shall never find anything in it but what I put
there." But Sartre is veering here between an old terminology of
consciousness and content, on the one hand, and a new terminology of acts and gestures, on the other. He professes to have
rejected the old notion of imagery, but he has allowed it to creep
back into the book. I do not understand why I am allowed to
"look" at an image now if I have been scorned for doing so
before. If Sartre's sentence is taken loosely I suppose it means
that whatever the image is at that moment it can never become
anything more, it has no resources in itself, it is only what the
subject has made it, giving it some of his life. Reading Sartre's
account of the image, I find it difficult to decide how much
credence to give to his rhetoric of impoverishment in imagery,
because it is in his interest to reduce the "content" of the image
to zero before giving it a new character in terms of action. The
image has character but no content. Sartre is therefore bound to
deprive images of the plenitude we ascribe to objects, he cannot
even allow them to live as shadows of objects, if he is to give
them roles in a drama of freedom. Sartre's imagination deals
with every object by cancelling it in the mind, reducing its
hypothetical content to the zero of absence; it may then be
translated into the terminology of action, where it is deemed rich
according to its intensity and force. The process is the reverse of
Stevens's in "The Snow Man," where the listener is invoked:

> . . . the listener, who listens in the snow,
> And, nothing himself, beholds
> Nothing that is not there and the nothing that is.[19]

The listener acknowledges what he sees, such as it is, and adds to it his own nothingness. "The nothing that is" means, I assume, the listener's imagination which relates itself to reality as a flick of feeling, a nuance, a light added to reality; the result is "the real made more acute by an unreal," as in "The Bouquet." Stevens's imagination in these poems is the zero which, added to plain reality, makes all the difference. But Sartre does not allow images to compete with objects according to rules prescribed by objects and therefore grossly in favour of contents and density. To Sartre the image is that marginal act which holds the given world at a distance and therefore certifies the world and itself. Images and objects are different in kind. The image is not overwhelmed by reality, this is the sign of its freedom, that it does not compete. It is like a free improvisation on the world's theme. In relation to reality the image is spontaneous, it acts as an incantation, it is "constitutive, isolating, and annihilating" because the action it proposes is bound to exhibit "a certain trait of nothingness in relation to the whole or reality."[20] If the world is deemed to be present, the image causes absence, not merely nullity or void but a deliberately ensured absence which is a condition of existing beyond the world and outside its reach. The image is necessarily poor by comparison with objects since poverty refers to content, but the poverty of the image, according to Sartre, is the sign of its freedom; as an act on the margin of the world, it is free to do anything. If consciousness were limited to perception and conception — I am using Sartre's definitions still — it could not escape from reality, it would be overwhelmed by cubes; this is the condition so often described by Blake, Wordsworth, and Coleridge, in which the mind is enslaved to the objects of its attention. Imagination is the act of free creation, and it receives objects in the world as occasions, dealing with them as diversely as we have seen, with gratitude, truculence, or disdain. It is the pleasure principle inscribing itself on the margin of the reality principle.

Much of this account is commonplace, so it is possible to quote in its favour writers otherwise different in their inclinations.

Stevens says of the imagination that it is "the liberty of the
mind," in other words "the power of the mind over the
possibilities of things," and he gives as an example of the
imagination in one of its enterprises the ease with which a man
looking at the Jesuit Church in Lucerne might "pass from the
real to the visionary without consciousness of change."[21] Sartre
and Stevens agree upon the clairvoyant power of the imagination, its sublime addiction to freedom and pleasure; they agree
on nothing else. I shall press the matter further by quoting
Merleau-Ponty again because he has the further merit of including Sartre and Husserl in his critique. He remarks that the word
"image" has fallen into bad repute because "we have thought-
lessly believed that a design was a tracing, a copy, a second
thing, and that the mental image was such a design." (I might
say, incidentally, that the same error often arises in theories of
art based upon "imitation," *mimesis,* or representation, and the
problem in that case is to decide where to stop, along the
fictive line, short of thoroughgoing solipsism.) The image is not,
Merleau-Ponty continues, "a content in my consciousness but
rather an operation of my whole consciousness." That consciousness acts by exerting "a claim to the presence of the imagined
object, which is unfounded: it is an absence of the object which
tries to pass as its presence." Up to this point Merleau-Ponty is
merely reciting his agreement with Sartre that we must not
understand the image in any reified sense, it is rather an act of
absence, "a nothing which tries to present itself as a something."
Presumably he and Sartre are also in agreement that imagination is the name given to one's whole consciousness: perhaps the
best reason for exercising ourselves about it is to discover, in
principle as well as in practice, what that phrase, "one's whole
consciousness," means. But at this point Merleau-Ponty accuses
Sartre of an error in logic; he maintains that in *L'Imaginaire*
Sartre puts his account of the image in serious question when he
analyses "certain states where a clear distinction between the
perceived and the imaginary cannot be made." If the image were
nothing but empty and absent, he says, we would not confuse it

with a perception, and illusions would be hard to understand. "Thus in so far as Sartre raises the question of illusions, he necessarily suggests the possibility of a situation anterior to the clear distinction between perception and imagination which was made at the start. But this means that it is impossible to understand the image by an examination of the pure possibility of an image in general and by a definition which we would then merely apply to the analogous empirical examples."[22] This is not the end of the dispute, nor am I competent to end it. But it seems reasonable to say that while illusions are failures of perception they do not embarrass the imagination. Perception, according to Sartre's definition, addresses itself to a given object in the hope of studying it in its practical relations. Illusions would leave the hope intact while humiliating knowledge and observation: it may be difficult to prove them wrong, since we already allow for the fictive nature of perception, and it seems clear that they can only be disproved in practice by acting upon the illusion and finding it wrong. The illusion of a chair cannot be sat on. But if the imaginative act is free, it is not constrained by practical criteria, it is not required to submit to verification. Magritte is safe. Bachelard has declared that the imagination is never wrong, because it does not ground its actions upon any general sense of what it would mean to be right or wrong. It cannot be shown to be wrong, though anyone is free to regard its products as wilful or extravagant. Excess, judged by strict criteria of knowledge or action, is not a sin of the imagination, it is one of its characteristic signs. There are no illusions in imagination, only caprices arising from the freedom of its behavior.

VI

Everything I have said has arisen directly or indirectly from the general Romantic and post-Romantic accounts of the imagination. I see no great difficulty in regarding Sartre and even Merleau-Ponty—though he has affiliations with Structuralism, too, and it has been argued that Structuralism is an event in the history of Phenomenology—as included in that tradition. Admittedly, their concern is mainly for the imagination in its second enterprise, that of securing for itself, in relation to the given world, sufficient freedom and space, a fictive range free of traffic. (One of the purposes of fiction is to clear a space for the imagination, making a playground for the mind.) I propose to consider now the relation between imagination, according to that tradition, and language; starting with the assumption that in reading literature we engage the words not to translate them out of themselves into something else—such as a meaning—but to register their presence. We are interested in words and the relation they bear to their history and the even more dramatic relation they bear to their present moment, which is largely a question of the magnetic field in which they participate with other words. There is always a temptation to withdraw words from their field, or otherwise break their circuit. In reading merely practical language, we do this with impunity, it makes no difference, such language asks to be used once and thrown away. In literature, it makes all the difference. Merleau-Ponty has quoted Husserl as saying that "to speak is not at all to translate a thought into words. . . . the intention of signifying is not found outside the words or at their side. It is rather the case that in speaking I constantly achieve an internal fusion of the intention with the words. This intention animates the words, and as a result all the words, and indeed each word, incarnate an intention; once incarnated, they bear this in themselves as their meaning."[23] I assume that this means we are not to think of translating words into thoughts, ideas, or even feelings, extracting their juice and throwing the fruit away. We are to respond to the intention of the words as to their presence and vitality. These terms seem to call for a personal analogy; we respond to the words as we respond to a person's voice. Given the words, find the speaker. Much of the criticism of fiction since Henry James has been preoccupoed with this pursuit, especially where the words are ascribed to a narrator. Hence considerations of "the implied author," and so forth. But these pursuits are not enough. It is true that some uses of language call attention to the nature of their speaker rather than to the delivery of words in comprehensible sequences, but it is just as reductive to translate words into an impression of their speaker as it is to translate them into a sequence of ideas, thoughts, or feelings. In the first case we go through the motions of character-building, and we regard the work as concluded when the character seems to be built; in the second we think of the sentence as delivering more and more of an otherwise secret meaning, the disclosure of which will end the book. Either way, much is lost, the juice must be kept in the fruit. We read badly if we replace the words by their presumed speaker, or by noises in the head which have ceased to be verbal. The defect of these methods is that they make us helpless in dealing with forms of language which do not dissolve themselves in our impression of their speaker. The defect of the Telex method of reading is that it encourages us to treat literature as a secret file, interesting only for the secrets it eventually reveals. We should ask not what the words mean, as though they contained secrets, but what are they doing, as though they embodied actions.

VII

Here is the passage from the *Portrait.* I propose to read it first in Romantic or subjective terms; later I will try to read it in more structuralist terms. For the present I confine myself to an interest in the imagination as a form of freedom, and I take for granted the integrity of a transcendental subject:

Once upon a time and a very good time it was there was a moocow coming down along the road and this moocow that was coming down along the road met a nicens little boy named baby tuckoo . . . His father told him that story: his father looked at him through a glass: he had a hairy face.
He was baby tuckoo. The moocow came down the road where Betty Byrne lived: she sold lemon platt.
    O, the wild rose blossoms
    On the little green place.

He sang that song. That was his song.

    O, the green wothe botheth.

When you wet the bed first it is warm then it gets cold. His mother put on the oilsheet. That had the queer smell.

His mother had a nicer smell than his father. She played on the piano the sailor's hornpipe for him to dance. He danced:

    Tralala lala,
    Tralala tralaladdy,
    Tralala lala
    Tralala lala.

Uncle Charles and Dante clapped. They were older than his father and mother but uncle Charles was older than Dante.

Dante had two brushes in her press. The brush with the maroon velvet back was for Michael Davitt and the brush with the green velvet was for Parnell. Dante gave him a cachou every time he brought her a piece of tissue paper.

The Vances lived in number seven. They had a different father and mother. They were Eileen's father and mother. When they were grown up he was going to marry Eileen. He hid under the table. His mother said: O, Stephen will apologise.

Dante said:

— O, if not, the eagles will come and pull out his eyes. —

    Pull out his eyes,
    Apologise,
    Apologise,
    Pull out his eyes.

    Apologise,
    Pull out his eyes,
    Pull out his eyes,
    Apologise.[24]

The passage depends upon its establishing an ostensibly third-person narrative voice, to begin with, and then allowing the voice to modulate into other voices, notably Stephen's and his father's. "Once upon a time": here an event breaks in upon time in such a way that the father's voice takes as its own form for the time being the ancestral voice of the storyteller. This is the first of several moments in which the feeling does not demand a special form for itself but accepts a linguistic convention as satisfactory for its purpose. In these first lines the father's voice reconciles the otherwise diverse worlds of storytelling, Brighton

Square, baby talk, and the simple identification by which
Stephen becomes baby tuckoo who may be taken across the
mountain by the moocow. According to this basic rhythm there
are many worlds of experience but there is no reason why they
should not make harmony together: this is what storytelling does.
It may appear that Joyce's words on the page are merely
transcribing reality, taking dictation from the facts, but they are
also establishing what the mere facts did not or could not
establish, cadences of feeling flowing between them. "His father
told him that story": the sensory events reach Stephen's mind one
by one as though each were given the duration as well as the
syntax of a short sentence and were suppressed by the full stop
of vacancy. Stephen's mind receives the events like atoms, it has
not yet begun to complicate their relationships or to give each a
relation to its neighbours more elaborate than contiguity. But
the sentences embody a movement of feeling from the intimacy
of "His father told him that story" to the objectivity of "he had
a hairy face." "The moocow came down the road where Betty
Byrne lived": the child's mind is beginning to deal with experience in such a way as to make fact and fiction cohere to form a
lived event. It is no distance from the imaginary moocow to the
real Betty Byrne and her real lemon platt because everything is
active in the same mind and the movement of feeling is the
syntax we are to trace. We can take this as the moment in which
Stephen "accepts language as (his) sole mode of existence,"[25]
since only in language do Betty and the fictive moocow live on
the same road. It is pointless to ask which comes first, Stephen
or a linguistic form; self and language dissolve into each other
because this is a novel and not a life. Mr. Vance came into
Joyce's life, and a trace of his existence went into Joyce's novel,
but the novel takes from Mr. Vance only the little it needs, a
note or two from which, with other notes, a cadence may be
made. The same applies to the father telling stories to his son in
Brighton Square. "He sang that song. That was his song." But
Stephen changes the song to make it his own, making it responsive to his feeling for the bright halos of freedom and possibility.

The wild rose becomes a green rose and its blossoms are drawn
out by Stephen's feeling, not his father's. The fact that you can't
have a green rose is conceded ten pages later and resolved by
the reflection that "perhaps somewhere in the world you could."
But Stephen's feeling does not allow itself to be curbed by
botany, green roses grow in language when you want them to
grow there. "O, the green wothe botheth": I read this as a pure
act of the imagination, effected by recourse to possibilities
secreted in language and not in nature. Such blossoms grow
profusely in the field of nonsense, the wildest field of language.
Alice in Wonderland is full of them, and therefore an example
of passing with ease from the real to the visionary with or
without consciousness of change; with, if we think the transitions
bold or histrionic; without, if we think them natural. In any
event, Stephen's sensibility is now turning facts into cadences as
the Promethean child under the table diverts eagles by turning
them into rhyming verse. In this passage the imagination is
engaged upon its three major enterprises. It is receiving things
and delighting "in their rich and contingent materiality," as if
they were lemon platt: taking things as they come, making what
it can of each without giving it more than a simple relation to
other things. But in literature things come as they are called.
Stephen's mind is beginning to shape the possible, singing a
private song in response to old Dedalus's song, sensing possibilities of fiction where otherwise there are only necessities of fact.
Finally, I do not think it fanciful to suggest that Stephen's mind
is also engaging in the third enterprise, negation, taking the
harm out of fact by dissolving it in his feeling. William Gass
said of Valéry that he regarded the arbitrary as a gift to form,
and of Henry James that words were those servants who did his
living for him.[26] The first statement is also true of Joyce, and the
second of Stephen Dedalus in this passage. The arbitrary is
received as a gift to form because it is there, it is given, and the
novelist finds it easy to assume that it is a gift from the gods,
like the first line of a poem. Look what Mr. Vance started.
Words were the servants who did Stephen's living for him, and

especially his escaping, they provided the boat from Kingstown
to Holyhead. Turn eagles into rhymes, and save your eyes. Mr.
Vance's stick becomes a metronome, and Stephen is free.

I am approaching the words in a deliberately old-fashioned
spirit and entertaining assumptions which are now vigorously
challenged. I am assuming, for instance, that what we want to
know is the story of Stephen's life, his feeling, and we therefore
interest ourselves in other things, other people. The words on the
page are turned into a psychological graph, they at once conceal
and disclose a speaker who is deemed to be as complete in his
implied nature as the words are complete in their linguistic
nature. Since the words are distinctive, we divine for them a
speaker who corresponds to them according to laws which are
easy to obey because they appear natural, we have drafted them
for ourselves. Thus we make characters in a play, and speakers
for printed words. I am also assuming in an old-fashioned way
that a speaker uses language as his instrument, and that he is at
every moment in command of the situation. These assumptions
are regularly challenged. It is argued that we should be interested in the life of the words, not merely in Stephen's life, that
both lives may be distinguished one from the other. It is also
argued that in any event we should not dignify as interpretation
what is merely the translation of words into psychology. What
about the linguistic medium as such, which retains its opacity
even when we have abstracted from it whatever we choose to
designate as feeling and character? Then there is the question of
the instrumental nature of language. Structuralists maintain that
in speaking we are more the slaves than the masters of our
language, we are used by language at the very moment in which
we think ourselves most independent in the use of it. It is true
that language would remain silent, speechless, and would die if
no one spoke it. But structuralists insist that as soon as we speak
we put ourselves in the hands not only of language in general
but of the particular language, its structure and bias; we are
permitted to say only what the structure authenticates. When we
write, we are written, the particular language inscribes itself on

our thought and, in that measure, controls it. While old-fashioned critics refer to the omniscient author, structuralists ascribe to Language superior knowledge short of omniscience, and to any individual language only such knowledge as its structure contains. Barthes's *S/Z* is the classic text for the structuralist position on this point and on subjectivity, his position being that subjectivity is not the ship but its wake *(sillage)*, not the plough but its furrow. It is not the plenitude of an autonomous self. Correspondingly, objectivity is not generically opposed to subjectivity, not the opposition between an autonomous self and "others," but only an imaginary systematization of the codes which arise as one works through them, trying to derive a self by distinguishing self and others. Barthes's text reads, at this point:

> Ce 'moi' qui s'approche du texte est déjà lui-même une pluralité d'autres textes, de codes infinis, ou plus exactement: perdus (dont l'origine se perd). *Objectivité* et *subjectivité* sont certes des forces qui peuvent s'emparer du texte, mais ce sont des forces qui n'ont pas d'affinité avec lui. La subjectivité est une image pleine, dont on suppose que j'encombre le texte, mais dont la plénitude, truquée, n'est que le sillage de tous les codes qui me font, en sorte que ma subjectivité a finalement la généralité même des stéréotypes. L'objectivité est un remplissage du même ordre: c'est un système imaginaire comme les autres, . . .[27]

We are required to question, therefore, the notion of the self as creative source, autonomous and therefore mysterious. If experience is a circle, the self is not the central point. Structuralists who proceed upon the diverse auspices of Marx, Freud, and Mallarmé point to structures which "put in place an experience for the subject they include."[28] The subject is not free: nevertheless, he is indispensable precisely as a function of the codes or systems in which he is placed, the point at which these codes and systems disclose themselves and put themselves on trial. We associate this general argument with Derrida, who speaks of the characteristic act of displacement or de-centering, dislodging the "presence" of the speaker, and forcing him into the general traffic of things. The figures in this mode of thought are spatial rather than temporal, structuralists are more interested in what has become than in how it became: if consciousness is determined by the codes of social and political existence, then the proper study of mankind is the law of that existence. Structure is understood as the constraint in the elements of a system, and the main object of research is this constraint as a set of formative marks in horizontal or simultaneous relations. Structuralists reading Joyce's *Portrait,* for instance, would be more interested in Stephen's linguistic competence than in his feeling; and generally more interested in linguistic possibility and its limits than in anything to be discovered in a child's response to arbitrary or contingent events. The reason is that they want to examine the conditions of social and political existence by taking a cross-section of it in a given society, they look across rather than before and after. They assume that history has already expressed itself in structure. But they never get over the problem of stationing themselves outside the very structure they study as though they were uniquely immune to its force and to their own mobility.

To come back to the question of a speaking subject. We have tended to think that the symbolic codes deployed in Western languages have the force of natural law. In recent years this axiom has been challenged. The resurgence in the appreciation of the ancient civilizations of India and China has raised a certain scruple, we are no longer disposed to claim that the situation of a transcendental self confronting a given world is necessarily the universal paradigm of knowledge. Julia Kristeva has argued that we must make a new definition of the transcendental subject so as to allow for its freedom within a social code which the subject at once "rends and renews."[29] If this sounds like the old song of free will and determinism transposed into semiology, I do not object to the sound, because it leaves us the consoling possibility that we may be permitted to speak, subject only to the constraint of whatever linguistic and social codes we are ostensibly using. We are warned not to take the speaking subject for granted, as for instance by positing him as sole origin and source; we are not to assume that in speech we have a subject heroic in his self-possession set off against an objective world complete in its character. If we were to maintain this assumption, we should set up conditions so favourable to the subject that he would be supposed to command every structure he encountered. It would be an unruly project, on the other hand, if not absurd, to represent the speaking subject as dissolved beyond redemption, merely the noise of a ship's wake or a ventriloquist's dummy. Nothing so extreme is intended, so far as I can find in Barthes's practice. It is intended only to show the speaking subject as vulnerable to social and political forces. *Tel Quel's* apparent cult of China has this in mind, along with the stimulating fact that Peking is not Paris. Structuralism certainly includes a number of moral terrorists, but Julia Kristeva is not among them. According to her programme, the speaking subject is to be constructed, not taken for granted. We are not allowed to produce the subject as the magisterial speaker, but rather to enact the construction of the subject in language; we are to go through the signifying process by which the subject may be established, not once for all but for the moment, and constantly re-established. This points to a reasonably peaceful conclusion. Just as the speaking subject "rends and renews" the code, so the code rends and renews him. If we want a figure to represent the process, we may think of the processes involved in writing a poem, or even in reading one, the "intolerable wrestle with words" which Eliot invokes in *Four Quartets*. The linguistic code does not remain unmoved as though it were a telephone directory, it registers the force of the poet's mind just as that mind registers the strain involved in wrestling with the language. I. A. Richards has argued that understanding is not a preparation for reading a poem, it is itself the poem, "a constructive, hazardous, free creative process, a process of conception through which a new being is growing in the mind."[30] This is useful because it gives the relation between speaker and code, like that between poet and language,

as a dynamic relation in which each member exerts pressure
upon the other. There is no difficulty in accommodating, under
such terms as "poet" or "reader," the plurality which Barthes
describes. It is not a matter of pure instrumentality or pure
creativity. The situation is comparable to Engels's famous assertion that men make their history but that they make it on the
basis of real anterior conditions; nevertheless it is they who make
their history, and not the conditions.[31] If you say the conditions
are irrelevant, you claim for men the attribute of angels, direct
access to essence; there is no merit in the claim. Men act upon
a scene which imposes constraint upon their actions, but they
cannot be reduced to the scene, they remain agents and
therefore human. I interpret R. D. Laing as establishing the
same ground for subjectivity when he says that "subjectivity is
neither all nor nothing: it is a moment of the objective process
(that of the interiorization of exteriority) and this moment
pertetually eliminates itself and is perpetually re-born."[32] Note,
incidentally, that critics as different in other respects as Sartre,
Merleau-Ponty, Kristeva, and Laing agree upon one consideration, the rejection of any reified model of consciousness or self,
the insistence upon representing both as actions, processes,
lapses, and renewals. According to this emphasis, the words
"Stephen Dedalus" are a summary of an action which takes place
in a certain book, a continuous story of fracture and becoming.
There is no such thing as "the reader," there are only readers,
each in Barthes's sense a plurality of the texts he has read and
been read by.

VIII

It may appear that in yielding even as much as this to
modern interrogation we have lost the right to invoke the
speaking subject or the imagination, that by throwing the subject
into the idiom of processes and codes we have allowed him to
drown in his *sillage*. It is well to look at the *Portrait* again. My
first account of the passage underlined the freedom with which

Stephen places himself in the scene of his experience, not only
the world of contingency but the inner world certified by the
continuity of his feeling. He appears to live in an arbitrary or
historical world but also, when he chooses, in his mind and in
the concessions of language. He does not merely use or exemplify
the code in which he speaks, he astonishes it and thereby
refreshes it. His speech cannot be adequately described by a
theory of meaning or a theory of communication because any
account of it must allow for the heuristic aspects of his language,
his recourse to play, pleasure, and possibility as creative impulses
active on his own responsibility. Well, that was a way of reading
it, making everything minister to the "character" of Stephen,
and making our account of that character as full as possible.
Presumably a structuralist would still insist that the tokens of
creative freedom are illusory, that instead of free acts we are
witnessing formal operations of language, that language pens the
penman, and that the first paragraph represents not only the
elder Dedalus's story but Stephen's reception of it as the gentle
dominion of society, other people. Thereafter, Stephen releases
himself from his father's narrative and converts every event to
his own purposes, mostly freedom and pleasure. A structuralist
would make a good deal of the grammar of Stephen's feeling,
though he would interest himself more in the grammar than
the feeling. The feeling is not absolutely free to find its form, it
is partly coded before it is registered. So a structuralist would
emphasize the priority of codes, linguistic systems, cultural
norms, genres of narrative, the ancestral procedures of storytelling, and the fact that Stephen's inner life is mediated for him by
the five cardinal senses and is not at all autonomous: he hears
his father's voice, sees the hairy face, feels the wet bed and the
oilsheet, registers his mother's smell, tastes the cachou. Then
there is the fact that much of the energy of the passage arises
from comparisons and juxtapositions: father, son; moocow, baby
tuckoo; moocow, Betty Byrne; warm, cold; father, mother;
Uncle Charles, Dante; Davitt, Parnell; the maroon brush, the
green brush; Eileen's father, Eileen's mother; the wild rose

blossoms, the little green place; cachou, tissue; eyes, apologise. Some of these pairs are provided by the sounds of the words, others by discrimination among opposites, still others by association, as in Uncle Charles, Dante, and Davitt, Parnell. Presumably a structuralist would think it worthwhile to mention these pairings, whether or not he thought them worth underlining as binary oppositions. I assume he would interest himself in them as featuring a property of the language rather than as marking one of Stephen's personal attributes; a linguistic pattern rather than a psychological bias. If an old-fashioned reader were to say that the prose carries a stream of consciousness, on Stephen's part, and that everything begins and ends in Stephen's alert sensibility, the structuralist would argue that the movement of revery from one moment to the next gives an impression of words issuing not from Stephen's ordaining mind but from Language itself. But Kristeva's point is useful again. The speaking subject must be constantly renewed. Stephen is not given to us once for all, he is not what we take him to be as though he had an existence apart from the language, but what we make him become, moment by moment, under the gentle but absolute sway of the language. The novelist's function is to make other things appear to exist in the way in which real things appear to exist; irrefutably, when the novel succeeds. Joyce's language "utters" Stephen as one word presses the next into existence. This child is delivered by words. Lévi-Strauss has quoted from Rousseau the feeling that "there exists an 'it' which thinks in me, and which makes me doubt whether it is I that think."[33] There is no need to repudiate the assertion unless we repudiate every other version of constraint, or rather everything that testifies to our sense of living by constraint: language, time, place, work, society, history, duty, morality, and most particularly our bodies. Even inspiration can be felt as constraint, since it is an "it" that thinks in me. That the source of inspiration is now called Language rather than God or the Muse does not affect the issue. Following this idiom, one would speak not of a stream of consciousness but of a reservoir of language. The mind in question would not be thought to command its experience but rather to make itself available as a vehicle or function of experience to a large extent social and cultural, in a form indistinguishable from the form of language. If we are reluctant to put the case in these terms it is because we still hanker after the old correspondence of word and voice, voice and person, one who stands out boldly from his setting. This touches again upon the question of language and character, whether we meet it in considerations of Shakespearean drama or modern fiction: words or people? How many children has Lady Macbeth now? It is a good question, but there is no need to take it up again. Every reader of *Between the Acts* knows that Mrs. Manresa does not exist, but he also knows that one of the achievements of that novel is to create and enforce an impression that she does. If this makes difficulty for the theorist of fiction, he must put up with it. At the same time it must be conceded that there are many styles, especially in modern literature, which discourage any direct correlation of words and implied speaker. In Mallarmé's later poems, Joyce's *Finnegans Wake,* and much of Proust it is harder to receive the words as issuing from a person, fictive or real, than from Language:

> Choit
>   la plume
>   rythmique suspens du sinistre
>   s'ensevelir
>   aux écumes originelles
>   naguères d'où sursauta son délire jusqu'à une cime
>   flétrie
>   par la neutralité identique du gouffre[34]

This is 'pure' in the sense described by Mallarmé in "Crise de vers":

L'oeuvre pure implique la disparition élocutoire du poëte, qui cède l'initiative aux mots, par le heurt de leur inégalité mobilisés; ils s'allument de reflets réciproques comme une virtuelle traînée de feux sur des pierreries, remplacant la respiration perceptible en l'ancien souffle lyrique ou la direction personelle enthousiaste de la phrase.[35]

The disappearance of the poet, his voice suppressed, the ceding of initiative to the words; these gestures represent the movement of style toward a level of abstraction at which, ideally, no trace of a merely personal sensibility would remain. The self would be relegated to the void or the past. Mallarmé refers to the spiritual universe seeing itself and developing through a self now superseded, "à travers ce qui fut moi." His later style is secretive not because it is obscure but because it refuses to allow its disclosures to be translated directly into personal terms; it has transcended the marks of a personal expression, the audible breath, the old lyrical puff of inspiration. Appropriately, Mallarmé refers to this in visual rather than in oral terms, reflections and glancing lights flashing from word to word, now that oral affiliations have been suppressed and we are directed toward "concrete poetry." Language disposes itself through the words without reference to distinctions between one voice and another, the words appear to come from a source beyond anyone's personal experience as if to identify themselves with pure spirit. This style is congenial to structuralists because it presents itself as a network of simultaneous relations and does not imply a source more mysterious than language itself.

A similar impression, though much less scandalous to devotees of sensibility, arises from a style in which the claims of individual feeling seem to yield themselves to a genre, a formula, or a form which testifies to communal experience. The words present themselves not as individual expression or pure spirit but as the vehicles of an anonymous or racial style, as in the formulaic passages of an epic. The singer of tales does not draw attention to himself, his voice, or personality. We feel that age-old forms of life are enacting themselves through the words rather than that an individual is saying something and bidding us to listen. "Once upon a time and a very good time it was." Dedalus is not speaking on his own behalf but assimilating his feeling, for the time being and while the story lasts, to that of all the storytellers there have ever been, it is as impersonal as "tralala lala," the traditional syllables of a hornpipe. Formulaic expressions are persuasive, whatever their origin and function otherwise, because they give us the sense of an anterior life, free from the abrasions and frictions of personality, they join our lives to other lives and give us a sense of the continuity of life itself. No one has ever regretted the invention of personality, whatever its cost in lacerations of feeling, but it is an immense relief to escape from the high-pitched insistence of personality into ancestral forms which imply that people are the same rather than different. For the same reason we respond to a solo violinist and to a full orchestra quite differently. And for this reason, too, we value in literature the things that stay the same while everything else changes: conventions, five-act tragedies, forms, motifs, metres, figures of speech, "Once upon a time. . . ."

If we go on to say that Stephen's consciousness is one with his experience, the reason is that the experience is to some extent monitored for him by sensory categories, the nervous system, and the ordinances of language. The short sentences testify to the adequacy of the linguistic forms not only for the delivery of feelings which require them but for the acknowledgement of the feelings the forms provoke. The energy flows in both directions. Two brushes are needed for Davitt and Parnell, but brushes come in pairs anyway and a lady with symbols at heart would choose two heroes to meet the proprieties of the occasion. It would be harsh to maintain that Stephen is merely a function of the codes which engage him, despite Barthes's *sillage,* or that the codes are always aggressive. The codes yield to him as much as he to them. But it is certainly an advantage to think of the speaking voice as mobile and suggestible rather than fixed in its determinations; this prompts us to think of the relation between speaker and codes as transitional and indeterminate at every moment. It is also an advantage to think of the poet as engaged not with the self but with language, turning anxieties of self-expression into fulfilments of linguistic possibility. The process of "making himself" would then be construed more impersonally as that of solving linguistic problems. In any case there is no clause in the Romantic contract which binds us to interpret the self as fixed, we are only forbidden to think of it as enslaved to its environment of objects. Presumably it may constitute itself as it wishes. The theory of the mask which we associate with Wilde and Yeats depends upon that freedom; indeed it is the standard theory of the Romantic imagination translated into theatrical terms, as though the artist were to make a play with every character established from himself by a series of fictive acts. I find the position endorsed, too, in a sentence from the *Biographia Literaria* where Coleridge's theme is self and the consciousness of self, an act by which subject and object, like being and knowledge, are rendered for the moment identical. "In other words," Coleridge says, "it is a subject which becomes a subject by the act of constructing itself objectively to itself, but which never is an object except for itself, and only so far as by the very same act it becomes a subject."[36] The only substantial difference between this account and the structuralist version of the creation of a subject is that Coleridge's description applies to the reflexive act, the act of self-consciousness, and the structuralist version would apply it to every act of the self. In fact, it would not be difficult to make peace between Coleridge and the structuralists but for one consideration, his insistence upon the fusion of subject and object as the characteristic act of imagination. Self-consciousness would always remain a difficulty, structuralists disapprove of assertions based upon introspection, their claim to objectivity depends upon the application of an ostensibly scientific model to mental transactions, and they are often culpably reductive in that application. But they require the subject to authenticate itself rather than to assume that it is the universal ground of authenticity; the subject must not assume that it is already complete but must, by engaging with codes and systems, construct itself as a subject. This is an attractive proposition if only because it takes the mystery out of intellectual actions while leaving them lively enough to command sustained attention. One of the merits of structuralism is its urbanity; shrillness and terrorism are discouraged by the claim that most situations can be analysed.

It would be improper, then, to level a charge of crass positivism against structuralists who try to show that even something as rarefied as the imagination may be understood as a formal act applied to a series of elements already given. The Lockean origin of this approach to mind may be an embarrassment, but it is not fatal to the enterprise; there is nothing in principle against the proposition that the imagination may be understood as a modification of items according to processes susceptible to formal description. Take, for instance, a situation in linguistics. Descartes and even Saussure saw the speaker's ability to make new utterances as an example of the creative power of mind, but when we ask how these utterances are created we qualify the autonomy of the subject. A generative grammar makes the creation of new utterances a process governed by rules which escape the subject, though he has assimilated them and they can only be grasped through his practice of them. In the case of imagination the rules which permit genuine creativity are certainly more difficult to formulate than those Noam Chomsky has defined, but it would be grossly dogmatic to deny that there are such rules, or that they may yet be discovered. Suppose we describe the position in some such terms as these: the creative products of imagination are made possible by operations which the subject has not (or at least not necessarily) invented. In that sense the operations escape the subject. Furthermore, their intelligibility depends upon their being a shared possession, widely understood. Within this framework the question of freedom and its limits still arises: is the production of this particular image on this occasion free or determined? The question, like that of generative grammar, can be answered either way with a show of reason. If an act is performed in a given scene, you can choose to emphasize any of its elements, in Kenneth Burke's terms, act, scene, agent, agency, and purpose.[37] If you emphasize the scene at the expense of the other factors, you favour determinism; if you make everything depend rather upon the agent, throwing the other elements into subsidiary positions, you vote for freedom.

But it is only reasonable to consider not merely the terms, individually, but the several ratios between them. Chomsky's account of the use of language emphasizes the linguistic agent, and refers to "this still mysterious ability":[38] his dispute with B. F. Skinner turns upon the fact that Skinner emphasizes the scene rather than the agent and therefore supports the determinists. And so forth; the situation is clear enough. Other questions may be derived from the same source: is the imagination continuous with perception, or is it a spectacular power, *sui generis?*

Still, it would be unfortunate if all power were deemed to reside in codes, systems, and grids, with nothing left for acts of feeling or even for whim and vagary. We should retain subjectivity and freedom, even if a particular reader thinks that there is more power in the big battalions, the social and political forces, than in the embattled self. We need to represent the situation in terms which sponsor debate and research rather than venom. The imagination is a genuine ability; we know it by knowing its products. If we cannot account for it, we should confess our failure rather than assert that it is unaccountable. May I make a suggestion? The offensive element in Barthes's account of the subject as the wake of all the codes which constitute the "I" is the implication that the subject is merely the sum of his occasions. This figure does not allow any initiative to the subject. But suppose the self were to be related to its codes as the future is related to the present; that is, let the imagination be taken to mean the act of a mind concerned to ensure the freedom of its future. A mind could act in that spirit without troubling itself much with other responsibilities, knowing that it would sustain those in its other roles—perception, conception, and so forth. There is only one mind, but it has several capacities to which we give different names. Imagination would then mean the act of a mind determined to keep open every possibility of creation, freedom, play, and pleasure. Grammatically, the imagination would correspond to the imperative mood, saying, "Let there be light, pleasure, joy, and freedom above all." Or

we can use Austin's word "exercitive," meaning that the act is
prescriptive and creative, the word involves "advocacy that it
should be so, as opposed to an estimate that it is so."[39] The
future is not a beast in the jungle, lying in wait upon the present;
it is still a realm of possibility, the code is not yet closed. There
is a passage in Eliot's "Little Gidding" which speaks to this
purpose in describing a meeting with a "familiar compound
ghost," a wise if stringent master:

> So I assumed a double part, and cried
> And heard another's voice cry: "What! are *you* here?"
> Although we were not. I was still the same,
> Knowing myself yet being someone other —
> And he a face still forming; yet the words sufficed
> To compel the recognition they preceded.[40]

It is salutary that the effective words come as though from a
double speaker rather than from a single identifiable self, and
that the face of the familiar compound ghost is "still forming."
The ghost has something of the impersonal force ascribed to
"monstrous familiar images" in Yeats's "Meditations in Time of
Civil War." The words which suffice to compel the recognition
they precede are those which make a future of such recognitions,
words into which the imagination has projected itself as need,
desire, and creative intention; the animation of the words is a
sign of freedom. In any case the words do not come after the
event, transcribing an event already concluded without their aid,
they press toward a future consistent with their force.

IX

I have been speaking of two rival positions on the imagination.
In the first the imagination is taken for granted, like God in
traditional theologies, it is what one starts from, the ABC of
being, the single creative source. It is natural then to suppose
that the imagination organises experience in its own subjective
terms. This supposition fosters the notion of the mind as the
artistic principle which works to a lesser degree, in ordinary

lives; it includes among its activities the appreciation of what is
given as well as the partly fictive act we call intelligence. In the
second rhetoric the world or reality is taken for granted as the
primary fact, the scene of operations, and the natural supposition is that the energy of the world is brought to a certain degree
of organization in the structures and codes which society has
devised for its continuance. The problem then is to find a place
for the imagination. One answer is to refute the old distinction
between mind and body, and ascribe every experience to the
resultant unity: this has the merit of replacing mystery by a
philosophical biology, an enterprise we have no right to discourage by a presumption that it must fail. Another answer in this
tradition is Barthes's *sillage,* though it does not allow for the
subject's critical power, his propensity for saying "no." If the
question is presented in these stark terms, it appears a matter of
choice, we choose one position and defend it against the other.
But a rhetoric grossly in favour of either position would be a
poor thing. Stevens's poem "The Comedian as the Letter C"
offers the possibility of holding both arguments in the mind if
not simultaneously then at least as two positions between which a
reasonable mind may swing, doing no harm to itself in the
process. The poem begins with the comic hero announcing the
familiar Romantic doctrine that in a world otherwise without
imagination the imagination intervenes through man. Man is
therefore "the intelligence of his soil," in other words "the
sovereign ghost."[41] The comedian goes through the world,
imposing orders as he thinks of them. He is happily employed,
except that he is deluding himself, the reality on which he
imposes his imagination is too weak to count, it has no force to
set against the comedian's imperatives. At this stage the comedian is a facile Romantic mind, his strutting amounts to
nothing. When he comes upon reality in a violent form his
doctrine collapses. Two or three hundred lines later he gives up
the pale Romantic position and becomes a realist, announcing
that "his soil is man's intelligence," in other words "the natives of
the rain are rainy men." Reality is the god of things and of man,

man's spirit is merely a function of the spirit of the world. The comedian travels on, still dissatisfied, reality is too much or not enough, so he keeps going until he ends in sheer scepticism, and beyond that point there is nothing worth saying. But let us keep to his two earlier positions. The Romantic concept of imagination is dear to us when we want to invent or control experience according to our own terms and we think ourselves capable of the assignment. It is full of doubt, but its charm arises from man's sense of the world as tenable and of experience as moving around a centre in the self. Man feels himself capable of understanding and even of transcending whatever experience he is offered, because he has placed himself at the centre. It is not easy, but it is possible, and when it is realized the proof is, in Coleridge's sense of the word, "joy." The realist position is dear to us in two moods; when we feel ourselves rich in the world's riches and we want to rest upon that largesse; or when we feel ourselves overwhelmed by the world and we want to talk ourselves into accepting defeat with good grace. In face of defeat there are many possible responses, mostly strident, apocalyptic. There is also the possibility of good manners. Structuralism may well be most important not for grand truths it is in a position to announce but for the decorum with which it raises a question of the defeat of man; at least it does not cultivate the Romantic whine of self-pity. It assumes that subjectivity, self, imagination, and all such terms are of secondary moment in the world at large, and that man's spirit is merely a function of certain codes. But it offers these ideas with good grace. Perhaps Michel Foucault dances on man's grave, but he is alone in the dance. In general, structuralists avoid the note of terror, they prefer to represent the human condition in terms which leave it open to research and argument, they encourage us to think that the important questions can be stated and analysed. Indeed it is edifying to come upon structuralists trying to make a place for man in a scheme of things in which he does not appear to be a necessary presence: he is at least allowed to construct himself, if he can.

My sense of the situation makes me hope that rival positions will not be regarded as a battlefield. The mind is a moody contraption and, as Emerson says in "Circles," "our moods do not believe in each other." Notional assent is often as much as any proposition can expect to receive from us. Sufficient for the day is the mind's motto. If I were required to make a leap of faith, only one leap being allowed, I would aim for the Romantic assumption which features imagination and subjectivity as primary terms. But I would try to present the "x" factor without making it aggressively gnomic. There is much to be said for the Euclidean procedure of letting ABC be a triangle and pushing forward from that concession without bothering ourselves about the metaphysical problem of justifying it. But in any case I am not persuaded that we have come to the stage of a single choice and battle stations. If Structuralism were to insist upon its insights, it would leave the transcendental subject empty, or at best scattered among its properties, to be reconstructed by interrogation. This is Stephen Heath's idiom in *Vertige du déplacement:*

> On pourrait dire que l'apport de la linguistique saussurienne et de ses prolongements, à travers divers champs d'étude, par "le structuralisme," est précisément d'avoir vidé ce sujet, d'en avoir fait le point de recoupement des structures qui l'agissent (c'est l'*action* de la structure). . . . Il ne s'agit pas—précisons—le contre tout malentendu —de nier le sujet mais de le déplier dans ses dépendances, de l'interroger justement dans sa mise en séance, sur les lieux de sa production.[42]

I am not sure how fiercely such a programme is to be pursued. It may be that those who have an interest in preserving subjectivity and protecting it from the scattering of its properties will be satisfied, so long as their cherished value is not entirely denied. It then becomes a question whether the subject is placed at the commanding centre, with whatever degree of force, identical with itself at every moment, or diffused throughout the structural scene, waiting to be reconstructed from its attributes. Before the dispute can be resolved, structuralists must somehow

come to terms with contingency and history, by which I mean all
the things we cannot help knowing and all the burdens we
cannot help feeling. It is not sufficient that structuralists are
prepared to deal with history as a residue or *sillage* of codes, or
that they are concerned with structural rather than causal
explanation. Too much is at stake. Structuralists must also
reckon with the fact that many of the most powerful codes which
govern our lives are contemptible; we deal more often with
advertising agents than with apostles. There is also the problem
of justifying the linguistic paradigms. It could be argued that
Structuralism replaces the old positivism of objects with a new
positivism of language. Perhaps the rival idioms may be reconciled in the sense in which freedom may be reconciled with
destiny. Structuralism emphasizes destiny, Romanticism freedom.
If the tension between these terms is to be fruitful, we need
something like Hegel's reconciliation of self and universal in the
form of drama, which renders compatible — as Jean Hyppolite
has said — "the liberty of the self and the objectivity of the
world."[43] According to Hegel the imagination is sustained by the
Spirit of the Universe which it partially embodies. The two are
reconciled in whatever consists of parts while being more than
their sum — the family, the State, the work of art. So the dispute
between Romanticism and Structuralism may be resolved not in
theory or in principle but in practice, as in the work of art, the
poem. Each disputant sees the elements congenial to him and is
somewhat blind to the remainder. The saving analogy is drama,
the form in which rival voices express not only their conflict but
their formal need of one another.

There is another way out; to consider that the concept of
imagination is still permitted, but that different interests are now
assigned to it. This possibility is suggested by a passage in
Derrida's *L'écriture et la différence*, where he distinguishes
between two interpretations of structure — the distinction can be
extended:

> L'une cherche à déchiffrer, rêve de déchiffrer une vérité ou une
> origine échappant au jeu et à l'ordre du signe, et vit comme un exil la

nécessité de l'interprétation. L'autre, qui n'est plus tournée vers
l'origine, affirme le jeu et tente de passer au-delà de l'homme et de
l'humanisme, le nom de l'homme étant le nom de cet être qui, à
travers l'histoire de la métaphysique ou de l'onto-théologie, c'est-à-
dire du tout de son histoire, a rêvé la présence pleine, le fondement
rassurant, l'origine et la fin du jeu.[44]

The first interpretation, according to this distinction, accords
with the Romantic doctrine. The imagination is a mysterious
power given to us by an even greater mysterious power and
therefore concentrated upon clues, keys, words to disclose the
Word. It begins and ends in mystery, its fictive power is an
essay in possibility, its cry is nostalgia for a lost place. Yearning
for the original Presence, it cultivates presence, including most
particularly self-presence: consciousness is only the greatest
means of presence, the subject's presence to itself. In the second
interpretation, which Derrida associates with Nietzsche, Freud,
and Heidegger, the imagination has given up one set of interests
in favour of another: it is no longer concerned with truth,
origin, the divine Word, the good original place, the subject as
centre. Its current interests are not grand, a metaphysician
would find them puny. Indeed, I sometimes think they amount
to one: to keep itself agreeably occupied. Certainly it has given
up heroic ambition. The new style is cool, however rueful its
occasions. The great questions of life and death are placed in
parentheses, indefinitely postponed, metaphysical nostalgia is
discredited. Not necessarily the "death of man," but at least or
most a change of style, a nuance, a tone. A man, "that is to
say a head abandoned to its ancient solitary resources" (Beckett
in *The Unnamable),* does not abandon his resources but puts on
the shelf for the time being their age-long crying needs. A
further list of pairings is now offered:

Presence	Sign
Process	Discontinuity
Metaphysics	Ethnology
Plato	Nietzsche
Centre	Free Space

Point of View   Plurality
Line   Labyrinth
Mastery   Play

X

Naturally, our three types of imagination favour corresponding figures of speech and thought. The first, taking pleasure in
recognition and appreciation, favours the image as its characteristic act. The image, in that sense, is a response to a natural
event, it marks the act of a mind determined to rise to the
given occasion, to celebrate in its own life the life it feels in the
natural forms. As a response, it seeks only the fulfilment of being
adequate to the forms appreciated. The second imagination,
which delights in rivalry and is jealous of its own creative power,
favours as its attendant form the metaphor. Metaphor has always
kept company with freedom, expansiveness; we say that it is
heuristic when we mean to praise its self-engendering powers.
The precise relation between tenor and vehicle in metaphor is a
matter of dispute, but it is not our dispute; for our purpose it is
sufficient to say that the relation may be of nearly any disposition, it does not matter in principle, only in practice on specific
occasions. The rivalry may be modest or extreme in one degree
or another. The third imagination, which acts in the form of
negation, has of course its own grammatical form, the negative
imperative, but it also features nearly everything we think of
when we think of irony. It is an act of judgment, and it delights
in critique often to the limit of subversion, the end of a line
which Hegel called infinite, absolute negativity. Of course it is
not required to go to the end. If it has a civic use, it is to
accustom us to live in uncertainty and to feel free while doing
so: if the therapy worked, it would render nothingness domestic,
help us to set up house in the void. Irony is always unofficial
when an official interest is present, it insists upon mentioning the
possible other case when the official spokesman wants to stick to
one official theme. Kierkegaard has a glowing passage in *The*

Concept of Irony where he says that when irony gets wind of the fact that there is something concealed behind the official phenomenon, it reports the discovery by asserting that the subject feels free, "and so the phenomenon never acquires any reality for the subject." "With irony," he continues, "the subject constantly retires from the field and proceeds to talk every phenomenon out of its reality in order to save himself, that is, in order to preserve himself in his negative independence of everything." This is the ironist's way of protecting himself. "With irony, when everything else becomes vain, subjectivity becomes free. And the more vain everything becomes, so much the lighter, more vacuous, more evanescent becomes subjectivity. Whereas everything else becomes vain, the ironic subject does not himself become vain but saves his own vanity. For irony everything becomes nothingness . . . but the ironic nothingness is that deathly stillness in which irony returns to 'haunt and jest'."[45] Surely this restores us to the boy Stephen Dedalus, talking Mr. Vance's sticks and threats into nothing, or rather chanting them into rhyming verses. And the *curriculum vitae* ascribed to the ironist restores us to the *Portrait* as a whole and to the young man Stephen, all else vain, saving his own vanity. He does not apologise to anyone: to Mr. Vance, the reader, or God. Instead, he composes an *apologia* of startling verve and impudence.[46]

XI

I have spoken of Structuralism rather than of structuralists because I am concerned with a tendency, a mood of our time if not the dominant spirit of our age. If I were to debate the merits and limitations of a particular structuralist, I would merely engage in a local argument. By Structuralism I have in mind a body of theory concentrated upon the works of Saussure, Jakobson, and Lévi-Strauss; in the background there are the works of the Russian Formalists generally and of Propp in particular; in the foreground, there is Valéry, the barely acknowledged origin of much French structuralist criticism. The disproportion between theory and practice in structuralist criticism is a commonplace, but the practical work is increasing: a short list, merely to indicate more precisely the activity I have in mind as structuralist commentary on particular texts, would include these: Jakobson and Lévi-Strauss on Baudelaire's "Les Chats" *(L'Homme,* I, 1962), Kristeva on Mallarmé's *Un Coup de dés* (in A. J. Greimas's collection *Essais de sémiotique poétique),* Lévi-Strauss on Bororo myth in *Le Cru et le cuit,* Barthes on Balzac's *Sarrasine* in *S/Z,* Greimas on Bernanos in his *Semantique structurale,* Todorov on *Les Liaisons dangereuses* in *Littérature et signification* and on Boccaccio in *Grammaire du Decameron,* Cesare Segre on Machado's *Soledades* in his *Semiotics and Literary Criticism,* Umberto Eco on the James Bond novels *(Communications* 8, 1966), Christian Metz on Jacques Rozier's film *Adieu Philippine (Image et Son,* January 1967), and, merging into the general context of theory, Genette's studies of Proust in his *Figures III* and *Figures II* and Claude Bremond's "Le Message narratif" *(Communications* 4, 1964). Is there a spirit common to these practical works?

In a rather loose sense, yes: for one thing, these commentaries tend to subordinate *parole* to *langue* and subject to object. The two subordinations act together. I would maintain, against the structuralist position, that *langue* is merely permission to speak, *parole* is the speech itself. Lucien Goldmann seems to me entirely right in saying that the difference between *langue* and *parole* is that *langue* is necessarily "non-significatif" and *parole* is "significatif": the first has as its function to permit the expression of all meanings, the second to perform a signifying act on each of its occasions.[47] The point is not blunted by the fact that the expression of all meanings in a particular language is, even in theory, impossible; presumably there are meanings which have never found a linguistic form. I find it odd, too, that structuralists ignore some of the fundamental problems involved in both *langue* and *parole;* the opacity of *langue,* the Fall by which it lost an original transparent relation to the things it designated; and therefore in every act of *parole* the inescapable error, the "inquietude transcendantale" which Derrida describes in *La Voix et le phénomène.* Structuralists still refer to language as if it were securely based upon a perfectly adequate foundation in society.

If the debate is to move ahead at this stage, the energy is likely to come from the impingement upon Structuralism of three major emphases. First: current work in hermeneutics, developing from Heidegger's *Being and Time* and Gadamer's *Truth and Method.* This work would resuscitate the arts of interpretation, the text as the sacred object of intelligence, and reading as the secular form of divination. There is a passage in Virginia Woolf's novel *To the Lighthouse* which seems to me to capture the hermeneutic desire; it is where Lily is struggling with her painting: "Phrases came. Visions came. Beautiful pictures. Beautiful phrases. But what she wished to get hold of was that very jar on the nerves, the thing itself before it has been made anything."[48] In hermeneutics the reader struggles to divine the meaning of the text as though the text were the visible and—more important—audible sign of an original presence, the thing itself before it has been made anything. Second: the current work in the idiom of play and performance. This work would establish the subject as the player of roles in relation to other people, the scene of the drama, without emphasising the potentially decadent forms of self-consciousness. Third, and finally: the general sense of consciousness as owing its privileged status to the possibility of voice, in Derrida's phrase "la vive voix." This is Derrida's theme in his argument with Husserl, and in *La Voix et le phénomène* he glosses the entire phenomeno-logical tradition which Husserl articulated. The gist of the theme is that "no consciousness is possible without voice: voice is consciousness."[49] Derrida argues against the phonological inter-pretation of consciousness and the metaphysics of presence to which he ascribes it. In *La Voix et le phénomène,* as in *De la grammatologie, L'écriture et la différence,* and *Marges de la philosophie* he maintains that presence is not the absolutely original form of being but rather a determination and effect within a system not of presence but of what he calls "la différence." But he is the first to concede that so long as we speak of consciousness at all, whether as cause or effect, we endorse an idiom of breath and voice. I cannot regret either the privileged status of consciousness or the idiom of its privilege; it seems to me to be sustained by our sense of the bodily condition of our lives, and of our relation to time and earth.

Notes

1. W. P. Ker, *Collected Essays*, edited by Charles Williams (London: Macmillan, 1925), p. 280.
2. James Joyce, *Letters*, Vol. III, edited by Richard Ellmann (London: Faber and Faber, 1966), p. 212.
3. Robert Scholes and Richard M. Kain, *The Workshop of Dedalus* (Evanston, Ill.: Northwestern University Press, 1965), p. II.
4. Aristotle, *De Anima*, 427, B, 16-18.
5. John Crowe Ransom, *The World's Body* (Baton Rouge: Louisiana State University Press, 1968), p. 116.
6. Thomas Hardy, *Collected Poems* (London: Macmillan, 1965), p. 694.
7. Allen Tate, *Essays of Four Decades* (Chicago: Swallow Press, 1969), pp. 403-404.
8. Denis Donoghue, *Thieves of Fire* (London: Faber and Faber, 1973).
9. Hart Crane, *Complete Poems and Selected Letters and Prose*, edited by Brom Weber (New York: Liveright, 1966), p. 36.
10. Hegel, *The Phenomenology of Mind*, translated by J. B. Baillie (London: Allen and Unwin, second edition, 1949), p. 99.
11. Tate, *Essays on Four Decades*, p. 595.
12. Wiliam Empson, *Seven Types of Ambiguity* (London: Chatto and Windus, 1953), p. 205.
13. Hegel, *The Phenomenology of Mind*, p. 99.
14. Georges Poulet, *Les Chemins actuels de la critique* (Paris: Plon, 1967), p. 251.
15. M. Merleau-Ponty, *Phenomenology of Perception*, translated by Colin Smith (London: Routledge and Kegan Paul, 1962), p. 57.
16. Ibid., p. 62.
17. Ibid., p. vii.
18. Jean-Paul Sartre, *Imagination*, translated by Forrest Williams (Ann Arbor: University of Michigan Press, 1962), p. 95.
19. Wallace Stevens, *Collected Poems* (London: Faber and Faber, 1955), p. 10.
20. Sartre, *The Psychology of Imagination* (London: Methuen, 1972), pp. 5-8, 13, 210, 213.

21. Stevens, *The Necessary Angel* (New York: Knopf, 1951), pp. 136-138.

22. M. Merleau-Ponty, *The Primacy of Perception, and Other Essays*, edited by James M. Edie (Evanston: Northwestern University Press, 1964), pp. 60, 74, 164.

23. Ibid., pp. 82-83.

24. James Joyce, *A Portrait of the Artist as a Young Man* (London: Cape, reprint, 1954), pp. 7-8.

25. Paul De Man, *Blindness and Insight* (New York: Oxford University Press, 1971), p. 100.

26. William H. Gass, *Fiction and the Figures of Life* (New York: Knopf, 1970), pp. xi, 171.

27. Roland Barthes, *S/Z* (Paris: Editions du Seuil, 1970), pp. 16-17.

28. Jacques-Alain Miller, "Action de la structure," *Cahiers pour l'analyse* No. 9, p. 95: "Structure donc: ce qui met en place une expérience pour le sujet qu'elle inclut."

29. Julia Kristeva, "The System and the Speaking Subject," *Times Literary Supplement*, October 12, 1973, p. 1250.

30. I. A. Richards, "The Interaction of Words" in Allen Tate (editor), *The Language of Poetry* (Princeton: Princeton University Press, 1942), p. 76.

31. Engels expressed this idea on several occasions, notably in his *Ludwig Feuerbach and the End of Classical German Philosophy* and his letter of September 21-22, 1890, to Joseph Bloch. Also Marx in *The Eighteenth Brumaire of Louis Bonaparte* and the *Theses on Feuerbach*.

32. R. D. Laing and D. G. Cooper, *Reason and Violence* (London: Tavistock Publications, second edition, 1971), p. 49.

33. Claude Lévi-Strauss, "Jean-Jacques Rousseau, fondateur des sciences de l'homme" in *Jean-Jacques Rousseau* (Neuchatel, 1962), p. 242: ". . . qu'il existe un 'Il' qui se pense en moi, et qui me fait d'abord douter si c'est moi qui pense."

34. Mallarmé, *Oeuvres Complètes*, edited by Henri Mondor and G. Jean-Aubry (Paris: Gallimard, 1945), p. 473.

35. Ibid., p. 366.

36. Coleridge, *Biographia Literaria*, edited by J. Shawcross (London: Oxford University Press, 1962), Vol. I, p. 183.

37. Kenneth Burke, *A Grammar of Motives* (New York: Braziller, 1955).

38. Noam Chomsky, *Language and Mind* (New York: Harcourt Brace Jovanovich, 1972), p. 100.

39. J. L. Austin, *How to Do Things with Words* (London: Oxford University Press, 1962), p. 154.

40. T. S. Eliot, *Collected Poems* (London: Faber and Faber, 1963), p. 217.

41. Stevens, *Collected Poems*, p. 27.

42. Stephen Heath, *Vertige du déplacement* (Paris: Fayard, 1974), p. 74.

43. Jean Hyppolite, "The Structure of Philosophic Language according to the Preface to Hegel's *Phenomenology of the Mind*" in Richard Macksey and Eugenio Donato (editors), *The Languages of Criticism and the Sciences of Man* (Baltimore: Johns Hopkins Press, 1970), p. 163.

44. Jacques Derrida, *L'écriture et la différence* (Paris: Editions du Seuil, 1967), p. 427.

45. Søren Kierkegaard, *The Concept of Irony,* translated by Lee M. Capel (London: Collins, 1966), pp. 273-275.

46. I am grateful to Jonathan Culler for entering into most helpful correspondence on several issues raised in the preceding pages. These issues are further clarified in his *Structuralist Poetics* (London: Routledge and Kegan Paul, 1975).

47. Lucien Goldmann, *Structures Mentales et création culturelle* (Paris: Éditions Anthropos, second edition, 1970), p. xv.

48. Virginia Woolf, *To the Lighthouse* (London: Hogarth Press, 1927), p. 297.

49. Jacques Derrida, *Speech and Phenomena,* translated by David B. Allison (Evanston: Northwestern University Press, 1973), pp. 79-80.

Nuances of a Theme
by Allen Tate

On April 8, 1943 Allen Tate in a lecture at Princeton University concentrated his mind upon a major theme, the relation of the imagination to the actual world. The lecture has been published under the title "The Hovering Fly." It was not the first or the last occasion on which Tate addressed himself to this question: indeed, I regard it as his characteristic theme, his signature, the motif and motive of his entire work in poetry, fiction, and criticism. It is not my business to speculate upon its origin, or upon the relation in Tate between temper and theory. Richard Blackmur once said of Tate that "his mind operates upon insight and observation as if all necessary theory had been received into his bones and blood before birth."[1] I am content with that, and would add only one remark, that when Tate felt it prudent to add flesh to bones and blood by producing a theory to sustain his practice, he proved himself entirely capable. The phrases and discriminations he received at various times from T. S. Eliot, Charles Williams, Jacques Maritain, and William F. Lynch merely confirmed what he had already discerned in his reading of Dante, that among the several forms or types of imagination there is one which has a special claim to our respect. Tate calls it the symbolic imagination, or alternatively the literal imagination, contrasting it with the unliteral imagination which he dislikes. Under any name it refers to the full human consciousness engaged with the actual world. Tate speaks of "the symbolic dimension rooted firmly in a literal image or statement that does not need the symbolic significance in order to be immediately understood."[2] I put that description beside another one, in which Tate in the course of saying that "it is the business of the symbolic poet to return to

the order of temporal sequence—to *action"* goes on to specify
what that return means:

> His purpose is to show men experiencing whatever they may be
> capable of, with as much meaning as he may be able to see in it; but
> the action comes first. Shall we call this the Poetic Way? It is at any
> rate the way of the poet, who has got to do his work with the body of
> this world, whatever that body may look like to him, in his time and
> place—the whirling atoms, the body of a beautiful woman, or a
> deformed body, or the body of Christ, or even the body of this death.[3]

Tate does not mean to say that the imagination which has such
a burden to sustain must sustain it with its own bare hands. The
imagination is pretentious or otherwise imprudent if it too
flagrantly declares its independence: it should resort for aid to
the natural world, the world's body, and to the sensory powers
which feed perception, and to the poetic image, what Auerbach
calls the *figura*, by which the action of analogy may be realized.
The imagination is not alone, it should not worship a false idol
in the cult of its own isolation.

I shall not rehearse the theory which in Tate's essays is found
running alongside these admonitions; chiefly because the theory,
persuasive as it is, is merely an abstraction drawn from the
experience of certain classic moments in Tate's response to
literature. He has always been more devoted to poems than to
poetry, and to particular achievements in language than to
language itself. He derives his theory from a response to many
practices and an inclination of temper to discriminate between
them. His theory of the symbolic imagination is drawn from
many occasions on which he has seen it at work and delighted
in its manifestations. I will mention three or four of these, giving
the rough sense of Tate's comment in each case, and making an
effort to show that Tate's sense may sometimes be brought a
little further in the same direction. But I should remark, to
begin with, that when Tate speaks of the relation between
imagination and the actual world, he is concerned with the poet
only as a particular instance of a general situation. The poet
differs from the rest of us only in degree, not in kind. To speak

of the poetic imagination is merely to name one of the human possibilities and to deny that it is a freak of nature. Poetry is only in a mechanical sense an exception to a rule, the sense which tells us that relatively few people write verses. It is rather an extreme instance, a faculty more readily visible in extremity than in a norm. Equally, a poet's imagination differs from anyone else's only in degree and bearing. So the symbolic imagination is an extreme instance of something which is available to everyone as an attitude to life, a particular response, a stance of expectation. If Tate sponsors a particular type of imagination, then, it is not primarily for the sake of poets or of poetry.

I shall begin with Dante, the great passage in the *Inferno*, Canto V, in which the poet converses with Francesca and receives the story of her love for Paolo, how it began when they together read of Lancelot's love, and the story ends when the poet out of pity swoons and falls. The lines which Tate quotes are those in which, the wind having died down, Francesca tells the poet her story, beginning with her birth at Ravenna. But she does not name the town: "the city where I was born lies on that shore where the river Po descends to be at peace with its pursuers":

> Siede la terra dove nata fui
> su la marina dove 'l Po discende
> per aver pace co' seguaci sui.   (lines 97-99)

Tate's commentary on this is, in part:

> Without the least imposition of strain upon the firmly denoted natural setting, Francesca fuses herself with the river Po near which she was born. By a subtle shift of focus we see the pursued river as Francesca in Hell: the pursuing tributaries are a new visual image for the pursuing winds of lust . . . as the winds, so the tributaries at once pursue and become one with the pursued; that is to say, Francesca has completely absorbed the substance of her sin—she is the sin.[4]

I would only add to Tate's sentences the footnote that if we mark the internal rhyme of "seguaci" and "pace," and recall from seven lines earlier the line "noi pregheremmo lui de la tua pace" we find Francesca craving peace and sensing the craving every-where, as in the river pursued by its tributaries. In his reference to "the firmly denoted natural setting" Tate is resuming and endorsing a major tradition in criticism which praises a poet for suppressing his own claims in the presence of the natural object or event. The most celebrated statement in that tradition is Keats's distinction, in a letter of October 27, 1818, between two forms of sublimity, the Wordsworthian or egotistical sublime in which the poet suffuses everything he perceives with his own personality until the object becomes a mere function of the subjective imagination, and that other type of imagination which Keats associated with Shakespeare, in which the poet commits himself to the object in question and suppresses himself in its favour. Or, as T. S. Eliot said of Lancelot Andrewes, "he is wholly in his subject, unaware of anything else." For Tate, the great exemplar of this dramatic imagination is Dante, who exerts no claim upon his own behalf and is hardly to be discovered even in his words.

I choose for the second touchstone that passage in Dostoevsky's *The Idiot* in which the fly hovers upon the pillow in Rogozhin's bed, and the Prince and Rogozhin stand together looking at the dead Nastasya. The translation by David Magarshack is some-what richer than the one Tate quotes, and it has a detail of some importance not present at all in Tate's quotation:

> At the foot of the bed some sort of lace lay in a crumpled heap, and on the white lace, protruding from under the sheet, the tip of a bare foot could be made out; it seemed as though it were carved out of marble, and it was dreadfully still. The prince looked, and he felt that the longer he looked the more still and death-like the room became. Suddenly a fly, awakened from its sleep, started buzzing, and after flying over the bed, settled at the head of it. The prince gave a start. "Let's go back," Rogozhin said, touching his arm.[5]

I shall give about half of Tate's commentary, to get the beauty of it as nearly hot as summary will allow:

> The fly comes to stand in its sinister and abundant life for the privation of life, the body of the young woman on the bed. Here we

have one of those conversions of image of which only great literary talent is capable: life stands for death, but it is a wholly different order of life, and one that impinges upon the human order only in its capacity of scavenger, a necessity of its biological situation which in itself must be seen as neutral or even innocent. Any sinister significance that the fly may create for us is entirely due to its crossing our own path: by means of the fly the human order is compromised. But it is also extended, until through a series of similar conversions and correspondences of image the buzz of the fly distends, both visually and metaphorically, the body of the girl into the world. Her degradation and nobility are in that image. Shall we call it the actual world?[6]

I would think it impertinent to add anything to Tate's account of that scene but for the fact that he worked with a translation which does not include the reference to the fly "awakened from its sleep." I think it an important detail because the fly, aroused from the low level of its existence, buzzes around the bed and then settles down again upon the pillow, as if to join the Prince and Rogozhin in watching the dead girl whose life in one perspective amounted to little more than such a flurry. Dostoevsky's imagination did not produce that hovering fly as if to say, with King Lear looking at the dying or dead Cordelia,

> And my poor fool is hang'd! No, no, no life!
> Why should a dog, a horse, a rat have life,
> And thou no breath at all?

The fly comes from its own stillness, shatters the deathly stillness of the room, and then endorses it. I read Dostoevsky's sentence as bringing to bear upon his triptych of human life and death the arbitrary power of chance, which bears the same relation to choice that a low order of life bears to a higher order of life.

Among many examples which Tate has produced, let my third choice be *Madame Bovary*, the scene in which Emma, having received and read the letter in which her lover Rodolphe conveys his rejection of her love, goes upstairs, opens the window, and looks out over the village:

Down below, underneath her, the village square was empty; the stones of the pavement glittered, the weathercocks on the houses were motionless. At the corner of the street from a lower story, rose a kind of humming with strident modulations. It was Binet turning. . . . The luminous ray that came straight up from below drew the weight of her body towards the abyss. It seemed to her that the floor dipped on end like a tossing boat. She was right at the edge, almost hanging, surrounded by vast space. The blue of the heavens suffused her, the air was whirling in her hollow head; she had but to yield, to let herself be taken; and the humming of the lathe never ceased, like an angry voice calling her.

"Emma! Emma!" cried Charles.

She stopped.

"Wherever are you? Come!"

The translation, as Tate remarks, is not good, it fails to convey "the very slight elevation of tone" in the original. But it is good enough to allow us to linger, as Tate does, over Binet's whirring lathe. The effect of the reference is, as Tate says, to give us "a direct *impression* of Emma's sensation at a particular moment . . . and thus by rendering audible to us what Emma alone could hear Flaubert charged the entire scene with actuality . . . the humming vertigo that draws the street towards Emma is rendered audible to us by the correlative sound of the lathe."[7] The Modern Library translation which Tate quotes is unfortunate in another respect; it has Charles calling Emma by name, but Flaubert has him calling out, "Ma femme! ma femme!" Either way, the ceaseless whirring of the lathe becomes Charles's angry voice, but the repetition in the French is more poignant than the English because it calls upon an abused relationship, not merely upon a name. The demand is more specific, the irony more complete. But in any language the whirring of Binet's lathe is again a low order of life, mechanical, repetitive, and therefore invulnerable: it is everything in life that, since it does not care, can never feel rejection. There are some writers, and Flaubert is one of them, of whom we feel that their imaginations are in an extraordinary degree spontaneous, they have only to think and the figures of their thought are immediately animated, established in full relation to themselves and to whatever else they need for their realization and presence. This faculty is never enough, by itself, to make a man happy or a writer genial, because it is likely that demand outruns achievement, whatever the achievement. A writer may find it easy to suppress himself in favour of his characters, and he may endorse his inclination by a theory of the artist as God found only among his creations. But he is likely to find the suppression incomplete, or the creations flimsy, comparing them with his desires in each case. So Flaubert practised an art, as Henry James described it, unconsoled, unhumorous, and unsociable.[8] It is clear that such an artist exercises the privilege of his art on condition that he does not recognise it as a privilege or take pleasure in the exercise.

Joyce's "The Dead" will serve as well as any other touchstone to indicate our theme, and to show its range. Tate's account of it is one of three commentaries, and the other stories appreciated or reflected upon are Poe's *The Fall of the House of Usher* and James's "The Beast in the Jungle." I shall have nothing to say of James's story, because the sharpest relation is proposed between Poe and Joyce. In his critique of *The Fall of the House of Usher* Tate emphasizes "the dominance of symbolism over its visible base: symbolism external and 'lyrical,' not intrinsic and dramatic." And he says of the symbolism in Joyce's story that it "derives its validity from its being, in the first place, a visible and experienced moment in the consciousness of a character."[9] Tate is particularly impressed by Joyce's presentation of Gretta's boy lover, Michael Furey, "standing at the end of the wall where there was a tree," and he says that without the wall and the tree to give him space Michael Furey would not exist. But I think Tate is particularly held by the mobility of Joyce's chief symbol, the snow. We cannot respond to the symbol by translating it into some psychological equivalent, because the symbol changes in the current and the course of the story, it turns round upon itself, achieving its own reversal. "At the beginning," Tate says, "the snow is the cold and even hostile force of nature, humanly indifferent, enclosing the warm conviviality of the Misses Morkan's party":

But just as the human action in which Gabriel is involved develops in the pattern of the plot of Reversal, his situation at the end being the opposite of its beginning, so the snow reverses its meaning, in a kind of rhetorical dialectic: from naturalistic *coldness* it develops into a symbol of warmth, of expanded consciousness; it stands for Gabriel's escape from his own ego into the larger world of humanity, including "all the living and the dead."[10]

I suppose Tate has in mind here the accepted discrimination between symbolism and allegory by which according to allegory a figure means one thing only and may be translated into that thing without much loss, but according to symbolism a figure is a magnetic force attracting to its orbit any elements in the scene which are moved by kinship and affiliation. In "The Dead" the snow is like a clenched fist, at the beginning, and at the end it opens, extending itself like a possibility.

What can we say of these several examples, so far as they define the symbolic imagination? John Crowe Ransom once remarked of the characters who inhabit his poems that "they cannot fathom or perform their natures." We often refer to their predicament as that of the split personality or the dissociated sensibility: it is one of the chief predicaments in modern literature, and therefore Tate has felt it and studied its operation. It is my impression that Tate offers the symbolic imagination as the best way of fathoming and performing our natures; perhaps the only way. He has never permitted us to escape from the responsibility of the human image, and especially from the duties we acknowledge by admitting that we are finite and historical. This does not require us to live as though the daily round were everything; we are not obliged to capitulate before the brash rhetoric of positivism. But it is a condition of our freedom, including the freedom of the imagination, that we acknowledge in the human situation the ground of that freedom and the ground of our beseeching. Henry James remarked of Flaubert "the strange weakness of his mind, his puerile dread of the grocer, the *bourgeois*, the sentiment that in his generation and the preceding misplaced, as it were, the spirit of adventure and the sense of honour . . ."[11] I think Tate would urge us not to be afraid of the grocer, but to register the continuities and rituals which bind together "all the living and the dead."

It is time to remind ourselves that when we speak of the imagination we mean a human faculty; or if it is a superhuman faculty it is lodged in men and given to them, in varying degrees, like divine grace in the Christian dispensation. When we ask how the imagination works, we come upon the secular equivalent of the same question: how do we comport ourselves in the world? Perhaps there are as many ways as there are people, but I think we can get along reasonably well by distinguishing three.

Taking them in no special order, let us call the first Naturalism, and agree to regard it as the assumption that man's fate is his environment, that subjects are functions of objects. "To the naturalist," as Philip Rahv said, "human behavior is a function of its social environment; the individual is the live register of its qualities; he exists in it as animals exist in nature."[12] If we do not hear much about Naturalism these days the reason is that several of its motives have taken up residence in Structuralism. We have naturalistic motives whenever we agree to separate nature from subjectivity and concede to subjectivity a merely secondary role as product or victim. We have the same motives when we agree to the mechanization of politics in the gross form of administration. Tate has a poem about these severances, called "Unnatural Love":

> Landor, not that I doubt your word,
> That you had strove with none
> At seventy-five and had deferred
> To nature and art alone;
> It is rather that at thirty-two
> From us I see them part
> After they served, so sweetly, you —
> Yet nature has no heart:
> Brother and sister are estranged
> By his ambitious lies

> For he his sister Helen much deranged—
> Outraged her, and put coppers on her eyes.[13]

The standard account of this poem runs somewhat along these
lines. The poem takes Landor as perhaps the last poet who could
appeal to the consanguinity of nature and art. In the twentieth
century, they have separated, and nature has taken to playing
the villain. Heartless when separated from his companion, he has
run to lies and driven his poetic sister first blind and then mad.
So much is agreed. But then there is the title of the poem, and
unless we push our reading a little further it is bound to appear
exorbitant. Surely the liaison of nature and art should be
innocent and natural. At this point I should confess that I
cannot now read Tate's poem without associating it with another
moment in his work. There is a famous example of unnatural
love, the love of brother and sister, on which Tate has pro-
nounced with special emphasis. It is of course the relation
between Roderick and Madeline, brother and sister, in *The Fall
of the House of Usher,* another tale of possession and outrage. If
I cannot keep apart the poem and Poe's story and Tate's
commentary on the story, I may at least plead that the conjunction is suggestive. Tate says of the incest of Roderick and
Madeline:-

> The theme and its meaning as I see them are unmistakable: the
> symbolic compulsion that drives through, and beyond, physical incest
> moves towards the extinction of the beloved's will in complete
> possession, not of her body, but of her being. . . . (Roderick's) naked
> sensitivity to sound and light is not "regulated" to the forms of the
> human situation; it is a mechanism operating apart from the moral
> consciousness. We have here something like a capacity for mere
> sensation, as distinguished from sensibility, which in Usher is atro-
> phied. In terms of the small distinction that I am offering here,
> sensibility keeps us in the world; sensation locks us into the self,
> feeding upon the disintegration of its objects and absorbing them into
> the void of the ego. The lover, circumventing the body into the secret
> being of the beloved, tries to convert the spiritual object into an object
> of sensation: the intellect which knows and the will which possesses are

unnaturally turned upon that center of the beloved which should remain inviolate.[14]

I hope it will not be considered a merely baroque gesture on my part to bring these occasions together, and to offer Tate's critique as a gloss not only on Poe's story but upon his own poem. The critique has for me the value of fleshing out the poem's references to heartless nature and his ambitious lies. If I were asked to annotate the ambition, I would have to resort to Tate's critique sooner or later, the conjunction is in my mind, I cannot suppress it or think it beside the point of the poem. If I were to annotate the reference to Helen, I could not do it without saying that she is the spirit of poetry, she has a special care for sensibility, and if she were left to her natural role she would keep us in the world.

The second of our three ways could go by several names, but in Tate's presence we are prompted to call it narcissism or solipsism. If the first way would keep us in the world only as slaves, the second offers us the shortest way out of Manchester, an escape route into the self. Tate has told us that this is what his "Ode to the Confederate Dead" is about, and that it is concerned with "the failure of the human personality to function objectively in nature and society."[15] Modern self-consciousness is merely one of the signs of this failure, and generally it may be called, as Tate calls it, "the locked-in ego," for which in the poem there are two approximate symbols, the crab and the jaguar, the jaguar leaping to devour himself. I suppose the general feeling about Narcissus arises from three phases in his story: his failure to respond to the love of the nymph Echo; Tiresias's prophecy that Narcissus would live only to the moment at which he saw himself; and finally, that, besotted with his own image, he died of languor. This brings together the notion that solipsism arises from a failure, a defect of worthier commitments; that the stage of self-consciousness is pretty nearly inevitable after this failure; and that the appropriate death is insipid rather than heroic. What this amounts to is a narrative sequence. First, the solipsist cannot bear the feeling that he is given over into the power of things, his good taste or high breeding or some other excess makes him unfit to tolerate such a situation. Or he cannot bear the feeling that he is the victim of history or of time, forces for which he is not responsible. So he determines to consort only with things for which he claims responsibility, his own fictions, mirror-images of himself. His mood is not necessarily apocalyptic or strident, it may be urbanely comic, as in Borges, or ironic as in any accomplished aesthete. But he dies of languor; the price he pays for living a life of fracture or self-engrossment is that the atmosphere he breathes is sickly, he knows that his proceedings are both abstract and arbitrary, he can distinguish one moment from another only in terms of arbitrary sensations. Tate's most sustained parable of solipsism and modern self-consciousness is "Last Days of Alice," a ferocious poem which features the grinning cat quivering "forever with his abstract rage," Alice gazing "learnedly down her airy nose / At nothing, nothing thinking all the day," and sundry references to "the weight of impassivity," "incest of spirit," and "theorem of desire." It is an easy and useful rule when reading Tate to hover upon any words which depend for their force upon strategic division or sever-ance, such words as *essence, theorem, abstract,* and *geometry.*

The third way is the best, if Tate is right. We accept the given world as one force in the tense relation between that world and ourselves. We keep ourselves in the world according to an active faith and an active sensibility. We are not overwhelmed by things, we respond to "the violence without" with an equal and opposite violence within. But it is not our ambition to seize the object in nature and turn it to immediate use. Ransom has been our sharpest critic in discouraging the predatory impulse. When he asks "what we are really trying to do with the object" in nature, he answers that "we are only trying to know it as a complete or individual object; and, as a corollary undoubtedly, to protect it against our other and predatory kind of knowledge which would reduce it to its mere utility."[16] If I have interpreted Tate correctly when his theme is the symbolic imagination, I think he means that the imagination seeks an engagement with objects such that the plenitude of the experience will certify the plenitude of each participant, subject and object. Object and feeling are to be reconciled, and for that reason the imagination which promotes the reconciliation is symbolic. Tate's poems, therefore, testify to acts of consciousness as complete as he has been able to make them, the scale of the effort is nearly as inspiring as the record of the achievement. The chief labour of the poems is to establish between Tate's subject matter and its emergence as form a relation adequately serious. The density of his poems is a measure of their responsibility, an indication of what, in the way of consciousness and care, they have been through. What the poems seek is direct access to experience through its occasions and by means of its forms. In "The Mediterranean" Tate writes: "They, in a wineskin, bore earth's paradise." The wineskin is more important than the paradise because it is the means available and paradise depends upon luck and grace. In "To the Lacedemonians" he speaks of "the bright course of blood along the vein," again a given resource, valued because given. Tate's poems invoke things as though he were unwilling to release them from the responsibility of their meaning, that is, the full weight of their implication in place and time. He will not let objects go their own way if it means disengaging them from their pact with men. When things are invoked, therefore, they come not as they are generally taken to be in a time abstract, positivist, devoid of memory, a time in which "the hard eyes look one way," and faces are "eyeless with eyesight only, the modern power." Rather, Tate instructs objects to engage with the perceiver's mind in such a way as to arrive freighted with human value and moment. This is to say that the seriousness of Tate's enterprise depends upon a sustaining continuity of sense, perception, and imagination. The poems are in that respect acts of consciousness. So in thinking of these poems and in responding to them we often remark that Tate's proceedings are the common, ordinary processes, but they are taken up with such care that they are enriched, deepened beyond anything commonly available: if we think of them as forms of communication, we are not satisfied until we have deepened the term and called it communion; if we think of his poems of memory, we deepen the term and call it commemoration.

Let me give an example to show what I mean. In 1799 a traveller to America reported of men he saw:

> Their faces are bony and sharp but very red, although their ancestors nearly two hundred years have dwelt by the miasmal banks of tidewaters where malarial fever makes men gaunt and dosing with quinine shakes them as with a palsy.[17]

In November 1929, Tate, in Paris, sending a poetic message to Andrew Lytle, wrote:

> And the man red-faced and tall seen, leaning
> In the day of his strength
> Not as a pine, but the stiff form
> Against the west pillar,
> Hearing the ox-cart in the street—
> His shadow gliding, a long nigger
> Gliding at his feet.[18]

The relation between these two passages indicates the relation in Tate between imagination and the actual world. Behind each passage there is a world of fact, not to be dissolved by scepticism or fashionable historiography. Tate accepts not only the fact but what the anonymous traveller has made of it: he is grateful for both gifts. What his imagination makes of both may stand not only as the figure of his poetry but as the exemplar of a way of life. The red-faced man is an emblem, but he has been given what the anonymous traveller did not report, a shadow, a second presence, the "long nigger gliding at his feet." Blackmur has written of the expressiveness and the oppressiveness of history—"of what is time out of mind in the movement of the hand or the reservation of the eye—what is present in us of the past and which, being present, we cannot ignore."[19] Tate's imagination has accepted this presence as a scruple, making the work of conscience that much harder.

He likes it that way. Like any other poet, he delights in possibility, amplitude, open spaces and free ranges. He claims the freedom of enquiring how much meaning a proposed situation will bear: this is the side of Tate most dramatically represented by his response to Rimbaud and Eliot, his kinship with Hart Crane. In that mood, the sky is the limit. But Tate has nearly always admitted a scruple: the fact that an effect is linguistically possible does not make it reasonable. There is a question of cogency. Has he not warned us and himself against the gross indulgence of feeling, will, and intellect? The warning is explicit when Tate writes as a critic. When he writes as a novelist or a poet, he concentrates the triple admonition into a scruple of form. It is his sense of form that prevents him from rushing into excess: poetry, he has written, "is the art of apprehending and concentrating our experience in the mysterious limitations of form."[20] The symbolic imagination, as distinct from the essential imagination ascribed to angels, is content with the human range of experience as its substance, and the human range of form as its means. This does not make an aesthetic for slaves but for free men who know that their freedom is not unlimited: it makes an aesthetic good enough for anyone who is neither barbarian nor fanatic.

It does not, of course, make poems. In poetry nearly everything can go wrong, whether it is propelled by good or bad intentions: this is not an argument against making the intentions good. Several elements go to the making of a poem, and if one of them goes askew the damage is done. But the elements are not in any case enough. Events are only potential experience, as the imagination is only potential creation, the will only potential action, and language only potential speech: it is their juncture in achieved form that makes all of them actual. When a poem by Tate falls short of conviction, it is because the experience has been realised and mastered only to the extent represented by its turbulence, and the language has stuck at that point, whirling as in a vortex. The proof of an achieved poem is its song; that is, its rhythm and movement:

> I thought of ways to keep this image green
> (Until the leaf unfold the formal cherry)
> In an off season when the eye is lean
> With an inward gaze upon the wild strawberry,
> Cape jasmine, wild azalea, eglantine—
> All the sad eclogue that will soon be merry:
> And knew that nature could not more refine
> What it had given in a looking-glass
> And held there, after the living body's line
> Has moved wherever it must move—wild grass
> Inching the earth; and the quicksilver art
> Throws back the invisible but lightning mass
> To inhabit the room. . . .[21]

What we respond to here is the elation of cadence, the continuity of feeling as it stretches across the lines, "wild grass / Inching the earth," intelligence transpiring as song.

If we want a poem all conviction, I suggest Tate's "Mother and Son," too long to quote but hardly too long to memorize. Upon a "firmly denoted natural setting" Tate has imagined and brooded to the point at which the experience has been mastered, the language tuned. The mother is given as ferocious and importunate: the phrases attached to her include "hand of death," "fierce compositor," "falcon mother," "harsh command," "dry fury," "black crucifix," and "cold dusk." The substance of the poem is friction, which is another kind of dissociation, and for brevity's sake we can say that the substance is continuous with that of Tate's novel, *The Fathers*. Common to both the poem and the novel is a represented violence of feeling, the characters are immured in their own extremity. Apart from the difference of scale, there is this further difference, that the dissociation in *The Fathers* is only partly categorical and is mostly social and political; in the poem the dissociation is aboriginal, it operates at a level beneath that of cause and effect. I quote the two central stanzas of the six:

> The falcon mother cannot will her hand
> Up to the bed, nor break the manacle
> His exile sets upon her harsh command

> That he should say the time is beautiful —
> Transfigured by her own possessing light:
> The sick man craves the impalpable night.
>
> Loosed betwixt eye and lid, the swimming beams
> Of memory, blind school of cuttlefish,
> Rise to the air, plunge to the cold streams —
> Rising and plunging the half-forgotten wish
> To tear his heart out in a slow disgrace
> And freeze the hue of terror to her face.[22]

"Transfigured" goes both ways; immediately it qualifies the time, beautiful because transfigured, but more distantly it qualifies the sick man, and the possessing light falls about equally on him and the time. Transfiguration is grace, so the second stanza gives the sick man's terrible answer in kind, his own form of possession, the act of slow disgrace that "freezes the hue of terror to her face." "Cuttlefish," because of its habit and power of ejecting a black fluid so as to darken the water and conceal itself from pursuit; what the sick man conceals is the deadly wish, the feeling cast against the mother. There is more to be said about the blind school of cuttlefish and many other details in the poem, but it is not necessary to go beyond the remark that the achieved form, the poem itself, can bear as much weight as we elect to place upon it, because of the denoted natural scene, the human situation itself. It is this consideration which ensures that the fiction is convincing and not arbitrary. If fiction is like statute law, Tate is content to make his fictions continuous with the common law we all acknowledge, even when we disobey it. The poem ends with three notations of the common law by which things are as they are:

> The dreary flies, lazy and casual,
> Stick to the ceiling, buzz along the wall.
> O heart, the spider shuffles from the mould
> Weaving, between the pinks and grapes, his pall.
> The bright wallpaper, imperishably old,
> Uncurls and flutters, it will never fall.

These details are not circumstantial or dramatic like the hovering fly in *The Idiot* or the eyes of Doctor T. J. Eckleburg in *The*

Great Gatsby, details which become portentous precisely because they arise unpredictably from a situation which they at once irradiate. The details in Tate's poem are significant because of the low level of being they share, the death-in-life and life-in-death they share with mother and son. But they have a further purpose. The abused feelings between mother and son are not resolved by anything that is shown to happen, but held in tension by the narrator, the witness who addresses the son in the last stanza, "O heart." The details stand for the narrator's feeling, since they are what he has chosen to notice. Just as the mother and son are types, with enough contingency to be actual, so the details are types because of the categorical relation for which the narrator's feeling requires them. The details, the flies, spider, and wallpaper, are what they are, and they are also what they become, emblems of the narrator's feeling. They are significant not only because he has noticed them but because his feeling is such that he has not noticed anything else.

Notes

1. R. P. Blackmur, *A Primer of Ignorance,* edited by Joseph Frank (New York: Harcourt, Brace & World, 1967), p. 168.
2. Allen Tate, *Essays of Four Decades* (Chicago: Swallow Press, 1968), p. 453.
3. Ibid., p. 428.
4. Ibid., p. 71.
5. Dostoevsky, *The Idiot,* translated by David Magarshack (Harmondsworth: Penguin Books, 1955), p. 652.
6. *Essays of Four Decades,* p. 119.
7. Ibid., p. 140.
8. Henry James, *Selected Literary Criticism,* edited by Morris Shapira (London: Heinemann, 1963), p. 141.
9. Allen Tate, "Three Commentaries" in *Sewanee Review,* Vol. LVIII, No. 1, Winter 1950, p. 12.
10. Ibid., p. 15.
11. *Selected Literary Criticism,* p. 152.
12. Philip Rahv, *Literature and the Sixth Sense* (London: Faber and Faber, 1970), p. 80.
13. Allen Tate, *The Swimmers, and Other Selected Poems* (London: Oxford University Press, 1970), p. 127.
14. *Essays of Four Decades,* pp. 391-392.
15. Ibid., p. 596.

16. John Crowe Ransom, *The World's Body* (Baton Rouge: Louisiana State University Press, 1965), p. 216.

17. Quoted in Tate, *The Swimmers,* p. 10.

18. Ibid., p. 11.

19. *A Primer of Ignorance,* p. 172.

20. *Essays of Four Decades,* p. 613.

21. *The Swimmers, and Other Selected Poems,* pp. 46-47.

22. Ibid., p. 53.

The American Style of Failure

There is a passage in John Crowe Ransom's *The World's Body* in which the poet-critic refers to a poetry which proceeds out of failure. To its poet "the natural world has dispensed too liberally of its blows, privations, humiliations, and silences in answer to his prayers for sympathy." The victim therefore "invents a private world where such injustices cannot be, and enjoys it as men enjoy their dream."[1] The result is a heart's-desire poetry, and Ransom cannot praise it—he thinks it a symptom of illness. But let us suppose a more congenial possibility, that the poet-victim has contrived to preserve a certain scruple from the wreck of his fortune. If the natural world has humiliated him, he sees in that misfortune no sufficient reason for humiliating himself or writing disgraceful verses. Suppose he were to raise himself from his abjection and, taking failure as his given content, transfigure it by the power of his imagination in the form of art. Failure would then appear only as the origin of his art and not at all as its final condition. There is a proverbial wisdom which informs such a man that the best way of dealing with necessity is by making a virtue of it: the virtue is a work of art which transcends its mere occasion and its mere content. Even when the slings and arrows of circumstance have struck their mark, the victim may call upon certain lively forces for aid: these are mostly the aesthetic forms and ceremonies which always help, in a painful situation, by taking some of the stress of the occasion and assimilating it; they can do this because they have done it so often before, they are well tried in such exigencies. These ceremonies enable a writer to take some of the venom out of the situation by encouraging him to approach it indirectly; he does not rush upon it—he delays, allowing the forms to do their best work. The writer survives his practical failure by the validity of his style; he frees himself from the assault of experience by recourse to a certain pageantry of form. It is as if a poet, speaking bitter words, were to take some of the harm out of them by tuning them to a sweet prosody, as Shakespeare regularly does, while taking care to leave enough harm in the words to make the venom resist the prosody. Resistance is good for both parties, it keeps them alive.

Ransom does not claim that the poetry which proceeds out of failure is likely to be American more often than not: he thinks it a general situation, and does not say Americans are more vulnerable than others. But if we think of the general conditions of failure by contrasting them with those of success, we are likely to find that much American literature achieves its vitality by a conscientious labour to transform the mere state of failure into the artistic success of forms and pageants: it learns a style not from a despair but from an apparent failure. So we have to ask at once what conditions would obtain in his circumstances if a writer's art were to proceed out of success. I think it may be generally agreed that a writer's happiest occasions are those in which there appears to be a sustaining relation between reality and his imagination, between things as they are and that power in himself which delights in a full sense of those things, embodied in their formal relations within the work of art. On such occasions a writer takes pleasure in the sweet confusions of Nature, knowing that they are hospitable to his imagination. The cordiality between imagination and fact is visible in the bright halo which surrounds the fact when the imagination casts its light upon it: at such times the severity of critical discrimination does not think it necessary to assert itself. The congenial relation between imagination and fact is mutually sustaining; there is a productive tension at work between the two forces. The first consequence is that the imagination is likely to understand its own moment in relation to that "pattern of timeless moments" which is history, according to the Eliot of "Little Gidding"; it sees its moment as a point of intersection between time and timelessness. Furthermore it approaches this understanding of

itself in a search for "values and ends." There are other consequences, but we may take them for granted: one felicity leads
to another.

I am not describing the Supreme Good but only those
circumstances and available attitudes which represent the writer's
imagination happily employed. The description is rudimentary,
but it is enough to make the point that American literature
rarely proceeds from such happiness. On the contrary it is more
likely to issue from conditions representing a radical separation
of imagination and reality, a rift between consciousness and
experience, a desperate metaphysic arising from the failure of
the imagination to find answerable substance in the given world.
This is orthodox doctrine on the general nature of American
literature, if it is not already a commonplace. I have not heard
anyone disagreeing violently with Richard Poirier in his assertion
that "American books are often written as if historical forces
cannot possible provide [an environment of 'freedom'], as if
history can give no life to 'freedom,' and as if only language can
create the liberated place."[2] This place is Mr. Poirier's theme,
the "world" which according to the ontology of American
literature must be linguistic and "elsewhere" because it cannot
be historical, social, and "here." The argument is familiar, but
none the worse for that, provided it is true. I cannot speak
against it; it seems true to me, though I hope its acceptance
will not be so complete as to establish a binding premise or a
written Constitution for the Study of American Literature. For
my purpose the argument means that the success of American
literature, in the major books, proceeds from conditions amounting to failure; that is, from conditions which would seem to veto
the traditionally sustaining relations between imagination, society, and history upon which a substantial literature has generally
depended.

I propose to begin by recalling a moment of some fame in the
record of American feeling, that supremely revealing occasion
when one of Henry James's books met in Henry Adams a

remarkably unresponsive reader. The occasion is well known but
perhaps it will bear another recital in at least one respect. In
1914 the second volume of James's autobiography was published
under the title *Notes of a Son and Brother*. James sent a copy to
Adams, and in due course received a letter of thanks. The letter
has not survived, but we can make a reasonable guess that its
general drift was to say, "What's the use?" We can go further:
Adams probably accused James of fiddling while every Rome in
their several worlds was burning. "I have your melancholy
outpouring of the 7th," James replied, "and I know not how
better to acknowledge it than by the full recognition of its
unmitigated blackness." The letter continued:

> *Of course* we are lone survivors, of course the past that was our lives
> is at the bottom of an abyss—if the abyss *has* any bottom; of course,
> too, there's no use talking unless one particularly *wants* to. But the
> purpose, almost, of my printed divagations was to show you that one
> *can*, strange to say, still want to—or at least can behave as if one did.
> Behold me therefore so behaving—and apparently capable of contin-
> uing to do so. I still find my consciousness interesting—under
> *cultivation* of the interest. . . . It's, I suppose, because I am that queer
> monster, the artist, an obstinate finality, an inexhaustible sensibility.
> Hence the reactions—appearance, memories, many things, go on
> playing upon it with consequences that I note and "enjoy" (grim
> word!) noting. It all takes doing—and I *do*. I believe I shall do yet
> again—it is still an act of life.[3]

James does not disagree with Adams, so far as the facts of the
situation are concerned: if it comes to a question of the practical
utility of writing, both writers take failure for granted, they are
survivors living out their lives in a situation which does not admit
of hope. Their sentiments proceed directly out of failure. But
while Adams deals with a bad situation by making the worst of
it, James deals with it by making the best of it, and the best
of it is the same thing as the most of it. James's mind is
thrown upon its own resources, but they constitute a ground for
vitality and force if not for practical hope. Temperamentally
James's mind responds to a dismal situation by creating a verbal
world as rich as the situation is poor; this is what he means by

finding his consciousness interesting "under cultivation of the interest." If the situation were happy rather than dismal, his consciousness might be tempted to sink to rest upon it; but his consciousness becomes most interesting to himself when it is the only promising thing in the situation, the situation in itself being inclined to put a stop to every excitement. There is no harm in thinking of this verbal world as a creation in deliberate rivalry to the given circumstances, if we understand that the rivalry is never so extreme as to repudiate every relation to its occasion.

James's constructions represent life as it ought to be, rich where the original is poor, dense where the original is thin, but they are not Platonic universes. The reason is that James's imagination is incorrigibly related to the given world by its curiosity, its sense of pleasure, its joy even in the presence of gratifications incomplete and transitory. The difference to James between a situation apparently dismal and a situation apparently happy is not as great as it is to common minds, because James sees creative possibility where a common mind sees defeat. A very little reality goes a long way with James, because it is the nature of his mind to push it far afield, to attend upon it under every cultivation of its interest. In the *Notes of a Son and Brother*, speaking of his failure to acquire any mathematical education, he says that he bore the dismal experience no malice—"resorting again to that early fatalistic philosophy of which the general sense was that almost anything, however disagreeable, had been worth while; so unable was I to claim that it hadn't involved impressions."[4] This is the only demand that James makes upon experience; he takes every experience as it comes and asks of it only that it will not positively prevent impressions from issuing, under imaginative cultivation. When we say that James is a man of faith, we mean faith in his own imagination and therefore in the principle of imagination in general, a power capable of making something out of virtually nothing. Blackmur had this meaning in mind when he said that James seems to inhabit another world than ours, "that other

world which has as substance what for us is merely hoped for."[5]
The Golden Bowl is in that light James's most imparadised
fiction because it shows, with proper elation, how much a
qualified heroine can make of an appalling matter, starting out
with every failure and defect in the conditions and with nothing
on her side but that celestial imagination which we recognize as
patience.

In "The Bench of Desolation" Herbert Dodd has been afflicted
with one loss after another so that now, sitting by himself on the
bench, he could almost be said to have been reduced to nothing,
but James gives him "the dignity of sitting still with one's fate,"
and this dignity takes the form of impressions continuous if not
bountiful; so that when Kate Cookham comes back to him at the
end we feel her coming not as a mechanically happy ending but
as the embodiment of impressions which deserve at least that
fulfilment. In "The Beast in the Jungle" James makes John
Marcher feel, to begin with, a grand impression for which there
is as yet no occasion, the occasion being what he is doomed to
wait for, "the sense of being kept for something rare and strange,
possibly prodigious and terrible" that is sooner or later to happen
to him.[6] In the event the something rare and strange turns out
to have been his failure, all along, to recognise in May Bartram
the rich possibilities of life available to him if only he had been
touched by passion sufficient to respond to them. May Bartram
was what he had missed. Near the end, when the conditions
appear to amount only to failure, James gives Marcher for a
moment the blessing of being able to feel the pain of it: he holds
up to the light of his consciousness the desolate fact of his
failure:

> He had justified his fear and achieved his fate; he had failed, with the
> last exactitude, of all he was to fail of; and a moan now rose to his
> lips as he remembered she had prayed he mightn't know. This horror
> of waking—*this* was knowledge, knowledge under the breath of which
> the very tears in his eyes seemed to freeze. Through them, none the
> less, he tried to fix it and hold it; he kept it there before him so that
> he might feel the pain. That at least, belated and bitter, had
> something of the taste of life.

It is characteristic of James that he makes the substance of this knowledge an object so that Marcher, who has been ignorance and egotism all along, may at least see it. This man, who has been watching his own life for years, now at last has something worth watching if only that he may feel the pain of it. It is an impression for which the phrase "the taste of life" has been kept ready. The beast in the jungle leaps out in the form of knowledge, a ferocious epiphany. Marcher suffers his fate without knowing it, till the end; ignorance constitutes his fate by being the essential condition of its leap. If he had only known, he could have baffled his fate. James tries to give him impressions commensurate with such knowledge, but at the end he can only give him impressions commensurate with humiliation. The story is terrible precisely because it reduces Marcher to such penury and because we feel the stress of this necessity in a writer wonderfully reluctant to leave his characters to that dreadful extent impoverished.

It is fair to ask whether or not James gives mere life its due, since his argument is that life is not to be trusted or admired until it has been transfigured by the imagination. In itself, as James wrote in the preface to *The Spoils of Poynton*, life is capable of nothing but "splendid waste"; the imagination is responsible for everything else, when there is anything else. The imagination is responsible for meaning, order, grace, miracle, and redemption, where each of these depends upon a rich "impressional harvest." Mere life gives the artist either too much or not enough; either way it is nothing without the ministry of an answering imagination, intelligent where life is stupid, economical where life makes a waste.

This is as much as we are required to say of James in this context, where the question at hand is the nature of a style which proceeds from conditions amounting to failure, and the style is proof that the writer has taken the harm out of failure, converting penury in substance to plenitude in the realized form. Besides, we are asking James to keep before our minds certain possibilities, temperamental axioms, especially those upon which

Henry Adams directed his scorn. In the *Education* Adams
admits to an ambition "to control power in some form,"[7] the
readiest form being political: he spent ten years trying to
establish an independent party of the centre, and he wrote the
novel *Democracy* partly as an attack upon James G. Blaine, the
Senator Ratcliffe of the novel, formidable because corrupt in
what appeared to him the supremely good cause. In the event
Adams's education became at least in his own eyes a picaresque
narrative of failure in Palmerston's London, Grant's Washington,
and Charles W. Eliot's Harvard. Reading Adams, one often
suspects him of taking pleasure in failure, cultivating it for the
moral superiority to be got from it, since a rueful manner can be
just as successfully protective as an enclosure of plangencies.
Since Adams insists on giving us the history of his failure, we
may as well say in return that his failure was a defect of feeling;
like John Marcher, he failed to seize the day. His concern was
with energy, power, *praxis,* but most of his own expelled itself in
the process of irritating his theme. There is no answer to
objective force except an internal force in the form of passion,
sufficient to rise to every objective occasion if not to overwhelm
it. Instead Adams developed in his style a rueful note to mock
and thereby to hold at bay the gross energy which was his theme.
He was incapable of risking in his own life that passion or
"violence within," commensurate in kind if not in degree with
the "violence without," the gross energy that pushed mind aside
and left will baffled. Adams just as much as James had recourse
to style, so that he might win there while he failed everywhere
else. If he reminds us sometimes of Eliot's J. Alfred Prufrock, it
is because he insists on being the first to put his absurdity into
words. He claims the privilege of sentencing himself. In the
Education he presents his life as a game of cards, being always a
loser, or as a race, in which he loses himself in the study of it.
Only the fact that he has never been enchanted saves him from
disenchantment; he preserves his dignity by knowing the score
and being the first to tell it:

Adams had held no office, and when his friends asked the reason, he could not go into long explanations, but preferred to answer simply that no President had ever invited him to fill one. The reason was good, and was also conveniently true, but left open an awkward doubt of his morals or capacity. Why had no President ever cared to employ him? The question needed a volume of intricate explanation. There never was a day when he would have refused to perform any duty that the Government imposed on him, but the American Government never to his knowledge imposed duties. The point was never raised with regard to him, or to any one else. The Government required candidates to offer; the business of the Executive began and ended with the consent or refusal to confer. The social formula carried this passive attitude a shade further. Any public man who may for years have used some other man's house as his own, when promoted to a position of patronage commonly feels himself obliged to inquire, directly or indirectly, whether his friend wants anything; which is equivalent to a civil act of divorce, since he feels awkward in the old relation. The handsomest formula, in an impartial choice, was the grandly courteous Southern phrase of Lamar: "Of course Mr. Adams knows that anything in my power is at his service." *A la disposicion de Usted!* The form must have been correct since it released both parties. He was right; Mr. Adams did know all about it; a bow and a conventional smile closed the subject forever, and every one felt flattered.[8]

Jean Starobinski has remarked of third-person autobiographical narration in general that it works to the benefit of the event and only secondarily reflects back upon the protagonist the glitter of the actions in which he has been involved; the event as such is italicized, the personality of the protagonist is to some extent suppressed.[9] In Adams's case third-person narration has the further consequence of implying that whatever happens to the protagonist is bound to be in the nature of things rather than in the nature of his personal choice. Adams's failure comes to appear a fault in the system, in the given set of relations; it is "in the cards" rather than a defect merely personal. Ostensibly he puts the blame on himself: as he says of himself in his undergraduate years at Harvard, "He had not wit or scope or force." But his style works against this attribution. The rueful note is directed through the short sentences of the *Education* as if their brevity marked the blunt facts of the situation; it is absurd, Adams appears to say, to pretend that the case would be altered by an increment of personal merit. Handsome formulas, like Lamar's, may be devised to mediate between the facts of the case and the feelings of their victim, but the facts remain unchanged and the victim has only the consolation of knowing that he has been graciously rather than peremptorily set aside. Whatever he can salvage on his own behalf goes to form his manner, his style, which constantly draws attention to the fact that at least he is not indulging himself in grandiloquence. The last word in third-person narration comes in the chapter called "The Abyss of Ignorance" where Adams brings to definition the process of self-immolation which he has been conducting all along.[10] The rhythm is given in a sentence: "After so many years of effort to find one's drift, the drift found the seeker, and slowly swept him forward and back, with a steady progress oceanwards." The sentences which follow do not merely document the drift, they conspire with it: the last evidence of Adams's failure is the conversion of personal will into impersonal force, the merging of a failed self in the forces that ruined it. Adams moves the paragraph toward this mechanical idiom by speaking of will as automotion. The passage reads:

> The process is possible only for men who have exhausted automotion. Adams never knew why, knowing nothing of Faraday, he began to mimic Faraday's trick of seeing lines of force all about him, where he had always seen lines of will. Perhaps the effect of knowing no mathematics is to leave the mind to imagine figures—images—phantoms; one's mind is a watery mirror at best; but, once conceived, the image became rapidly simple, and the lines of force presented themselves as lines of attraction. Repulsions counted only as battle of attractions. By this path, the mind stepped into the mechanical theory of the universe before knowing it, and entered a distinct new phase of education.[11]

Clearly in this passage Adams is preparing us to find that the Dynamo has superseded the Virgin in the history of force: from now on, we should expect to find, however ruefully, that images

drawn from the organic world, natural forms, "honey of generation," and the familial pieties of Adams's eighteenth-century self
have been suppressed; and that increasingly the springs of action
are organized in terms of manmade energies, machines, and
turbines. Theology hands itself over to technology, Chartres is
overwhelmed by Chicago. As Adams says of a dynamic theory of
history, by assigning attractive force to opposing bodies in
proportion to the law of mass it "takes for granted that the
forces of nature capture man. . . . He is the sum of the forces
that attract him . . . ; the movement of the forces controls the
progress of his mind." Adams's style, therefore, is his way of
preparing himself for surrender, with only as much loss of face
as is inevitably involved in the greater loss of self. Darwinism is
the name for a corresponding gesture by which human feeling
consigns itself to the determination of third-person narration.

Mr. Gore speaks of these matters, or of something like them,
in *Democracy* when Madeleine Lee asks him whether or not he is
prepared to believe in the new doctrines, democracy, universal
suffrage, science, and so forth. Gore proclaims his faith in these
forces, mainly because they appear to be in the cards; they arise
inevitably from what has gone before, and therefore he is willing
to try the experiment of having them. When Mrs. Lee asks him
to suppose that his experiment may fail, Gore answers indirectly:

> "I wish, Mrs. Lee, you would visit the Observatory with me some
> evening, and look at Sirius. Did you ever make the acquaintance of
> a fixed star? I believe astronomers reckon about twenty millions of
> them in sight, and an infinite possibility of invisible millions, each one
> of which is a sun, like ours, and may have satellites like our planet.
> Suppose you see one of these fixed stars suddenly increase in bright-
> ness, and are told that a satellite has fallen into it and is burning up,
> its career finished, its capacities exhausted? Curious, is it not; but
> what does it matter? Just as much as the burning up of a moth at your
> candle."[12]

It is understood that Gore speaks for Adams in the novel, and
that his philosophy is neatly given in the same conversation:
"Let us be true to our time, Mrs. Lee!" Gore's problem, like
Adams's, is to discover, preferably by processes reasonable and

systematic, what precisely the time is so that he can be true to it. *The Education of Henry Adams,* and Adams's entire work as an historian, are his attempt to define the spirit of his age, so that his good will may find something to respect. More generally he wanted American intelligence, which showed signs of waywardness, to catch up with American power, which showed signs of running wild. He wanted a fixed star and a planetary sense of the world, and the nearest he came to either, on his own behalf, was in devising a style. It is mostly a low style, if we think of the three Renaissance styles sponsored by decorum, the styles low, mean or middle, and high or grand. Adams's common style is low because it responds to failure by assuming its color, it chooses a low key as particularly appropriate for notes rueful or satirical. Surrounded by circumstances of failure, it claims the merit of not rising above its station; the claim is a rhetorical gesture, of course, because every style that arises from circumstances amounting to failure projects a commensurate symbolic success. The success claimed is not in practice but in decorum, resilience, and tone; it is the merit of doing the right thing when the only fate in store is failure.

Even in a short list of such styles there must be a place for the high style of failure which preserves dignity from the general ruin and gives it an ennobling rhetorical panache. A defeated general looks well on a high horse. I am thinking of a literature which has good reason to know the taste of failure in its circumstances and has therefore practised a talent for transforming failure into a high and lordly style, reaching for aesthetic and moral victories to make up for its defeated army. I refer to the army which General Lee surrendered to Grant at Appomattox, and the literature which, after that surrender, never again surrendered to another, least of all to New York. There is a moment in that literature which we may regard as pretty nearly complete in its recourse to a style of heroic failure, in Allen Tate's *The Fathers* when the Yankee officer about to burn Major Buchan's splendid Virginian house gives the major and his family half an hour in which to leave. The major answers,

"There is *nothing* that you can give to me, sir,"[13] and he goes back into the house and hangs himself: he had not even been a secessionist, though his children went off to the war on the Confederate side. There is a sense in which Major Buchan's gesture bears the same relation to his circumstances as fiction bears to fact: his high style is a projection of his decorum, his feeling for the way things ought to be, the way people of his kind ought to behave, especially in defeat. It is a metaphor which leaps beyond the literal ground of its occasion, and the problem is to define the relation between the two, assuming a relation of some kind.

Allen Tate has pondered this matter in his capacity as a critic. He speaks of the symbolic imagination as that form of it which adheres to the world's body and conducts its action through analogy, "of the human to the divine, of the natural to the supernatural, of the low to the high, of time to eternity."[14] To put the matter much too bluntly: the symbolic imagination is content to live in the daily world and make the best of it by using all the resources of analogy and metaphor. Major Buchan's imagination is symbolic in that excellent sense, because its terms of reference are domestic and historical; his values are feudal, organic, traditional, familial and in those ways entirely honorable; what he despises tends to be mechanical and mercantile. The symbolic imagination is also possessed by Lady Buchan's mother, of whom Lacy recalls that once when a neighbor's bull was brought to the house at Pleasant Hill and some young girls asked the woman what the bull was doing there: "He's here on business," she answered. Looking back on that remark, Lacy says his mother was "a person for whom her small world held life in its entirety, and for whom, through that knowledge, she knew all that was necessary of the world at large." The symbolic imagination is content to remain finite and historical, knowing that this condition allows for as much ceremony as we can well use. In Tate's fiction it adheres to the world and enhances it with certain noble rituals, manners, codes, rites of dignity, actions to which one's mere personality may safely be consigned. The symbolic imagination would allow us to live at ease in the world, if we gave it a chance. But Tate's theme in *The Fathers* is the perversity by which his characters, innocent for the most part, turn violent and evil so that a world of equal ferocity may defeat the world into which they were born.

I read this in association with another phrase of Tate's, where he describes what he calls the angelic imagination. This is the form of imagination which "tries to disintegrate or to circumvent the image in the illusory pursuit of essence." If we need another description it may just as accurately be called the Manichean imagination: under any name it declares itself as an exorbitance. Tate says that it exhibits the hypertrophy of the three classical faculties: feeling, will, and intellect. The hypertrophy of feeling is an incapacity "to represent the human condition in the central tradition of natural feeling." Hypertrophy of will is "the thrust of the will beyond the human scale of action." Hypertrophy of intellect is "the intellect moving in isolation from both love and the moral will, whereby it declares itself independent of the human situation in the quest of essential knowledge."[15] Tate finds all three exorbitances in the imagination of Poe, but Poe is only a particularly extreme example of an exorbitance so pervasive in American literature that it may be deemed to characterize it; it means a desperate scepticism about the validity of the ordinary world as a ground of being and a home for the human spirit. The character who represents this scepticism most defiantly in *The Fathers* is George Posey, and although Lacy Buchan thinks him wonderful as a force he knows that the force is self-destructive as well as destructive of other selves:

George Posey was a man without people or place: he had strong relationships, and he was capable of passionate feeling, but it was all personal; even his affection for his mother was personal and dis-ordered, and it was curious to see them together: the big powerful man of action remained the mother's boy. What else could he have been? . . . He had great energy and imagination and, as Cousin Jack said, he had to keep moving; but where? I always come back to the horseman riding off over a precipice. It is as good a figure as any other. And that is what he gave to Semmes—mystery and imagina-tion, the heightened vitality possessed by a man who knew no bounds.

The word which does most of the work in that passage is "personal"; it is as problematic here as in a famous passage in *The Great Gatsby* where it is used in much the same sense. In both places it refers to that intensity of feeling which has nothing to sustain it but itself, a function of the will in isolation from every ground of reason or value. In Tate's passage it is associated with strength, energy, passion, and imagination, though I am sure the angelic rather than the symbolic imagination is intended. Most of all it is associated with disorder, and consigned to the figure of the horseman riding over a precipice, perhaps to distinguish it from the rational imagination as featured in the *Phaedrus* of Plato by way of the charioteer and the two winged horses. In any event it is wilful and it knows no bounds: none of its feeling is prepared to entrust itself to the publicly available forms; instead it lives on the desperate knowledge available to the man who, whatever else he knows, knows no bounds. Tate picks up the word "personal" again a few pages later:

> But then George was a man who received the shock of the world at the end of his nerves. As to all unprotected persons, death was horrible to him; therefore he faced it in its aspect of greatest horror— the corrupt body. And it is likely that he hated money too; therefore he spent all his time making it. There is no doubt that he loved Susan too much; by that I mean he was too personal, and with his exacerbated nerves he was constantly receiving impressions out of the chasm that yawns beneath lovers; therefore he must have had a secret brutality for her when they were alone. Excessively refined persons have a communion with the abyss; but is not civilization the agreement, slowly arrived at, to let the abyss alone?[16]

I am suggesting that Tate's novel, ostensibly about the defeat of the Old South, is really about the defeat of the symbolic imagination by the angelic imagination. The symbolic imagination is terrestrial, familial, domestic, and historical; it maintains a special interest in the sustaining relation between man and place, a relation embodied in customs, rituals, forms, and civility. The angelic imagination is an act of will, it is alienated from the world and therefore whirls between two worlds, depending upon its own intensity to keep it going; scornful of existence, it makes a direct claim upon essence, and therefore aspires toward every version of ultimacy and the absolute. The critical pressure brought to bear upon the angelic imagination comes not from a demonstration of its failure or even of its practical success, New York defeating Virginia, but from a few instances of heroic style in the defeated, notably in the old major himself, and continuously from the style of the novel, Lacy Buchan's sense of the values at risk. In the passage just quoted the critique is presented through Lacy's steady hold upon the moral issues, as when he says that Posey loved his wife too much, and goes on to explain the judgment, "by that I mean he was too personal."

The narrative style is concentrated upon surrounding the facts of the case with an ambience of moral comment appropriate to the values of a gentleman with Southern blood in his veins. The chief characteristic of the style is that it is willing to surround each proffered act with cause and consequence. The basic sentence is in two parts, the second released by the word "therefore" as an act is followed by its consequence: the cause is given, too. The sentences are organized by a grammar which, reasonable even as it stands, has the further merit of holding the act at a sufficient distance to allow the reader to apprehend it along with its cause and consequence. The style treats each act as if, for complete understanding, the reader must resort to an historical sense lively enough to move from Monticello or Bull Run to Greece, Rome, and Troy. In "Religion and the Old South" Tate says that "images are only to be contemplated, and perhaps the act of contemplation after long exercise initiates a habit of restraint, and the setting up of absolute standards which are less formulas for action than an interior discipline of the mind."[17] Tate's sentences about George Posey are prologomena toward precisely that discipline: they give us the events, but in such a way as to prevent us from laying hold upon them immediately or violently. Style is therefore an absolute standard, like honour in the Old South or conscience anywhere: that it may fail in every practical sense, like honour in the Old South, is not a reason for living otherwise or preferring another code.

So we have three versions of a style proceeding from conditions amounting to failure; three, and we might have more. It is not my business to estimate how many more would be required to make a valid typology of American literature and the ways of the American imagination. James stands for hyperbole, meaning the imagination that delights in making the most of a situation in itself niggardly and unpromising, knowing that what it makes is disproportionate to its mere substance, and taking pleasure in the disproportion. Adams stands for irony, a figure which enables the ironist to place himself at a reasonably safe distance from his general experience if not from its worst disasters. Tate has described irony as that arrangement of experience "which permits to the spectator an insight superior to that of the actor; it shows him that the practical program, the special ambition, of the actor at that moment is bound to fail."[18] It shows us, incidentally, why the Southern critics were so much concerned with irony that they made it an almost universal principle of poetry. Whether they called it irony, tension, or wit, they had in mind a process by which the poet renders himself invulnerable, taking all his risks knowingly in the form of his poem. Meanwhile the piquancy of Adams's *Education* arises from the fact that he is at once actor and spectator, and must in the second capacity make himself invulnerable to the fate of the first. As for Tate, his style is curial, meaning that it issues not only from conditions of defeat but from ancestral places of law and formality, and bears the mark of a grand mythology: it judges every action according to the majesty of precedent, honour, and discipline, while knowing full well that the common world has forgotten those pieties.

I began with a moment in which one of James's books met a singularly gruff response. If I end with a moment in which one of his sentences met a response so lively that the reader copied it out and sent it to a friend in Havana, it is partly to suggest that such congruities testify to the fact that the Jamesian ensemble of circumstances is not, for once, limited to James. Suppose a poet were to feel that reality, without the intervention of the imagination, is monstrously impoverished, indeed that it

virtually constitutes poverty and destitution: he would then feel
that poetry is the only way of redeeming reality and that
metaphor is the readiest form of miracle. I think it was in some
such mood that Wallace Stevens, coming upon a sentence of
James's, was impelled to transcribe it. He reported to his Cuban
friend that "in the world of actuality . . . one is always living a
little out of it." He continued: "There is a precious sentence in
Henry James, for whom everyday life was not much more than
the mere business of living, but, all the same, he separated
himself from it. The sentence is . . . 'To live *in* the world of
creation—to get into it and stay in it—to frequent it and haunt
it—to *think* intensely and fruitfully—to woo combinations and
inspirations into being by a depth and continuity of attention
and meditation—this is the only thing.' "[19] Stevens thought
James's sentence precious because it spoke to his condition and to
his aesthetic sense; it is what Stevens himself would wish to say in
his own behalf. Both writers exert their imaginations upon
situations amounting to failure. James made the most of those
situations by exerting his consciousness upon them, or in the
fiction another consciousness equally forceful, in the avowed
hope of transcending them. Stevens's method was extensive rather
than intensive; his favorite process was that of developing a
theme not by complicating it but by supplying it with several
variations, not only to show what the imagination can do in a
good cause but to redeem an otherwise blank object in the light
of an appropriate transcendence. He was fond of variations
because they allowed him to live a little out of the official theme;
it is a relief to have thirteen ways of looking at a blackbird.

This is merely an instance, but it implies the possibility that
each specified style, if pressed a little beyond itself, may set up
certain affiliations worth attending to. A relation between James
and Stevens cannot be regarded as unreasonable. I am merely
illustrating an interest on my part, and fearing to claim too
much for the method. Ideally one should woo these relations and
combinations instead of leading them by the nose. I am not sure
what form the wooing would take if it were to start with Adams

or Tate, though it seems reasonable to expect that these writers would also, like James, establish themselves in fruitful relation to their colleagues, cousins in style, under cultivation of the interest.

If we were to press upon Adams's style with a view to its possible and useful relations, we would begin by recognising in him a genuine self-distrust converted thereafter into a style which consorts most happily with irony, a rueful note, and a local wit directed against his own bewilderment. We should expect to find a style of this kind, or at least a family likeness of that style, when a mind tries to confront forces which it cannot hope to defeat but which it has some hope of understanding. In American thought we are likely to come upon such a style when a sensitive mind engages with such forces as technology, big business, advertising, the "military-industrial complex," and so forth, forces in themselves unworthy as a general rule but, worthy or not, successful in practice. In those circumstances an ironic style would testify to the fact that the writer understands the forces at work but cannot hope to defeat them. Irony would be related to its occasion, then, as thrift to conspicuous consumption; a man may exercise thrift as an opposing principle or because he refuses to compete with predatory affluence in its own terms; either way his style is his sign, his badge. In using Veblen's idiom at this point I have sufficient justification in his style; like Adams's it is an ironic style issuing from an accepted failure to change the symptoms it examines. In such books as *The Instinct of Workmanship* and *The Theory of the Leisure Class* Veblen goes out of his way to avoid giving the impression of launching a direct attack on the forces which determine the social and personal world. What he says of these powerful forces is said in a style ostensibly neutral; the style appears to say that it would be indecorous to expend any visible emotion in attacking these forces. The speaker in Veblen's books is represented as superior to the foibles of the machine process precisely in the degree to which he sees them for what they are, but he does not pretend that to see through them in a book is the same thing as to defeat them in the world. The irony of this vision enables Veblen to withhold rage from its natural objects; so he calls the lust for money "pecuniary efficiency," and salesmanship "business enterprise." When he uses such words as "waste" or "exploit" he pretends to do so without recourse to their odious sense; he uses them as morally neutral counters while knowing full well that in practice they are nothing of the kind. He allows his reader to supply the censure which he pretends to have withheld. This enables him to protect himself against a charge of sour grapes; he is writing as an economist concerned with causes, not as a moralist concerned with judgments. In the chapter of *The Theory of the Leisure Class* called "Modern Survivals of Prowess" Veblen insists that he is dealing with his various topics with sole reference to their economic bearing, that is, "to their direct action in furtherance or hindrance of a more perfect adjustment of the human collectivity to the environment."[20] In the same breath he sets aside everything that might be said of such topics from other standpoints, moral, aesthetic, and so on. His rhetoric is a matter of withholding outrage from outrageous occasions, bringing a cool style to bear upon forces which, but for the style, would drive a man to rage. By holding moral outrage in abeyance, he makes his reader supply what is missing from a style apparently self-contained. That it should be self-contained is the chief demand Veblen makes upon his style, since it testifies to the fact that the centre of his being is still in place even if elsewhere mere anarchy is loosed upon the world. The self-possession of the style is consistent with an origin in either pride or vanity, in righteousness or in that wounded form of righteousness which can hardly be distinguished, in its visible marks, from malice.

Finally the curial style relies for its cogency upon its relation to certain grand values which are in danger but which for that reason retain the beautiful feature of being vulnerable. If we start from its employment in Tate's fiction, poetry, and criticism, we can proceed by easy steps to find it, however diversely, in Ransom, Warren, and the Southern writers generally. But it is not confined to the South. We may expect to meet it when a writer, sensitive to the zeitgeist, refuses to grovel before it, when he insists upon invoking certain values which he reveres and which he knows to be in trouble. The curial motive makes him ground his entire work upon those hallowed terms, and he means to save them by reciting them with irresistible grace. In practice these values are likely to be lost, so they are often recited in an elegiac spirit as if to maintain the decency of the occasion.

I am thinking again, as in Chapter I, of Lionel Trilling's work in fiction and criticism, work propelled by the desire to maintain as living values certain forces at present under strain. Each of Trilling's books represents a determination to redeem and enforce the values consecrated in such words as reason, mind, sincerity, pleasure, society, self, and order. Witness the attempt to speak up for mind in *Beyond Culture,* self in *The Opposing Self,* idea in *The Liberal Imagination,* virtue in *The Middle of the Journey.* A classic occasion was Trilling's defense of reason, maintained in *Sincerity and Authenticity* in direct opposition to the cult of madness as "the paradigm of authentic existence and cognition," one of the most dismal marks of a current ideology. Trilling's rhetorical method is to surround his god term with a halo as a mark of its presence in history and an indication that he means to assert its continuing validity despite the fact that the time is unpropitious. Sometimes he argues directly and trenchantly in favour of his god term, sometimes he draws upon its ancestral reverberations in the hope that these will be enough, and sometimes he recites the holy word as if it had never been desecrated. There is always a temptation to assume that because a god term is holy to its celebrant it must be holy to everyone; a writer may make the mistake of thinking that he does not need to establish the sanctity of the word, that he has only to invoke it. In "Mind in the Modern World," as I have remarked, Trilling is distressed by the "disaffected relation to mind which has come to mark our culture"; he means American culture, but he knows that whatever happens in America is likely to happen soon in other countries. He refers to "the ideological trend which rejects and seeks to discredit the very concept of mind." Merleau-Ponty has spoken of those great books in this century which have expressed "the revolt of life's immediacy against reason."[21] Trilling knows these books and admires them, as he discloses in *Beyond Culture,* but he does not think we can blame *The Birth of Tragedy, The Golden Bough,* or *Notes from Underground* for that loss of confidence in mind which is one of our present discontents. He speaks up in behalf of mind, but he does not argue the case directly; rather he surrounds mind with a number of terms which have a familial likeness to it, such terms as order, coherence, inclusiveness, and objectivity. Mind is to be known by the company it keeps and the objects it serves. Trilling recites these several terms as Arnold recited sweetness and light in *Culture and Anarchy,* hoping to make them persuasive by the radiance they cast upon the entire scene. He does not try to convince R. D. Laing or David Cooper that mind is still to be preferred to madness or that the ideology of madness is so much cant: instead he represents the life of mind in such terms that a reader of goodwill could not think of disavowing it. Trilling approaches an ethic by way of an aesthetic: a thing is likely to be felt as good if it is first felt as beautiful. Trilling is alive to the risk involved in this rhetoric; he has a fine ear for the hum and buzz of current feeling, and a gift for defining it, as in the conflict between Laskell and Maxim in *The Middle of the Journey.* But he is unyielding in his moral preference. He does not permit the reader to construe mind in any other terms than those endorsed by order, coherence, objectivity, and inclusiveness; that is one part of his rhetorical verve. Gradually the reader comes to feel that values so graciously expounded must be splendid in themselves and that their failure in an ostensibly civilized society would be monstrous.

Henry James said of Hawthorne that he had become an artist "just by being American enough." American writers generally have pursued the same object by the same method, accepting the state of being an American on principle as well as at heart. It is not a question of chauvinism, but of style. I have spoken of style without defining it. There is no definition, unless we repeat what everyone believes, that style is "saying the right thing," its characteristic marks being exactitude, verve, and nonchalance. If we say that style is a principle of persuasion and that we recognize it by its propriety, we say little. Like Wallace Stevens's river of rivers in Connecticut, style is not to be known beneath the appearances that tell of it. The appearances that tell of it in American literature are mostly signs of risk and strain. We say of the literature that it engages the reader by its turbulence, the immense strain required to make the work declare itself. It is thrilling to see risks taken by others. Of "style as risk" there is much to be said, beginning with the fact that it is impure in its affiliations: it incorporates the meretricious as freely as the heroic. So it is necessary to discriminate between styles, since risk is not enough and there is a difference between heroism and folly. When we speak of style we speak of nearly everything, the poem and the style of the poem are one (Stevens, again). It is common to say that literature is an achievement of style: when we say this of American literature, we mean to go further and say that it is characterized by the precarious achievement of style in conditions nearly desperate and against nearly all the odds.

I offer, for what it is worth in its bearing upon the situation of the American writer with the conditions of failure in his bones, a final sentence from *Notes of a Son and Brother* where James, pondering the death of Minny Temple, wonders what would have become of her and of other similarly defeated persons if they had been granted the "ampler experience" of living a normal span of life. James refers to "the naturalness of our asking ourselves what such spirits would have done with their extension and what would have satisfied them; since dire as their defeat may have been we don't see them, in the ambiguous light of some of their possibilities, at peace with victory."[22] The sentence admits a double emphasis: that such spirits would never have known victory, even if they had lived an age; and that even if they had lived long enough to know it, they would not have been at peace with it. There is at least a possible application of the sentiment to American writers, for whom it was never intended. Do we not feel that American literature thrives upon the conditions of failure and that it would lose its character, if not its soul, were it given the conditions of success? If there is now a tradition of American literature, it starts from penury of circumstance and achieves, at enormous personal cost, a style never secure in the possession of itself but always pursuing its best and most difficult self.

Notes

1. John Crowe Ransom, *The World's Body* (Baton Rouge: Louisiana State University Press, 1968), p. ix.
2. Richard Poirier, *A World Elsewhere* (New York: Oxford University Press, 1966), p. 5.
3. Henry James, *Selected Letters*, edited by Leon Edel (London: Rupert Hart-Davis, 1956), pp. 204-205. (Letter of March 21, 1914).
4. Henry James, *Autobiography*, edited by F. W. Dupee (London: W. H. Allen, 1956), p. 241.
5. R. P. Blackmur, *A Primer of Ignorance*, edited by Joseph Frank (New York: Harcourt, Brace and World, 1967), p. 180.
6. Henry James, *Complete Tales*, edited by Leon Edel (London: Rupert Hart-Davis, 1964), Vol. XI, p. 359.
7. Henry Adams, *The Education of Henry Adams* (Boston: Houghton Mifflin, 1961, Sentry Edition), p. 36.
8. Ibid., p. 322.
9. Jean Starobinski, *La relation critique* (Paris: Gallimard, 1970), pp. 88-89: "L'effacement du narrateur (qui assume alors le rôle impersonnel d'historien), la présentation objective du protagoniste à la troisième personne, fonctionnent au bénéfice de l'événement, et, secondairement, font rejaillir sur la personnalité du protagoniste l'éclat des actions dans lesquelles il a été impliqué."
10. Cf. Kenneth Burke, *A Grammar of Motives* (New York: Braziller, 1955), pp. 120f.
11. *The Education of Henry Adams*, pp. 426-427.
12. Henry Adams, *Democracy* and *Esther* (New York: Anchor Books, 1961), p. 45.
13. Allen Tate, *The Fathers* (London: Eyre and Spottiswoode, revised edition, 1960), p. 305.
14. Allen Tate, *Essays of Four Decades* (Chicago: Swallow Press, 1968), p. 427.
15. Ibid., pp. 403-404.
16. *The Fathers*, pp. 185-186.
17. *Essays of Four Decades*, p. 571.

18. Ibid., p. 467.

19. Stevens, *Letters,* edited by Holly Stevens (New York: Knopf, 1966), p. 506. Stevens transcribed the sentence from F. O. Matthiessen, *Henry James: The Major Phase,* it appears in an entry for October 23, 1891, in F. O. Matthiessen and Kenneth B. Murdock (editors), *The Notebooks of Henry James* (New York: Oxford University Press, 1947), p. 112.

20. Thorstein Veblen, *The Theory of the Leisure Class* (London: Allen and Unwin, 1957), p. 266.

21. M. Merleau-Ponty, *Sense and Non-Sense,* translated by Hubert L. Dreyfus and Patricia A. Dreyfus (Evanston: Northwestern University Press, 1964), p. 3.

22. James, *Autobiography,* p. 528.

The Eye and the Mind's Eye

I: The Eye as Benevolent Despot

There is a moment in one of Robert Duncan's meditations on reality and language when the poet says: "To see a table, to converse with a table: that is a daily wonder."[1] I choose this moment not because it is remarkable but because it is common: any poet of goodwill might say such a thing. Duncan begins with a common phrase and hopes to redeem it by placing beside it a second phrase like the first in grammar, though otherwise more rarefied. The second verb has the same object as the first, so it sends us back to the first and makes us find there the values emphasized by the transition. Seeing a table and conversing with a table are identical, if the seeing is in the right spirit. If it is not right, it makes the table an indifferent object because we are an indifferent subject. The relation depends upon our goodwill. Poetry proposes to turn monologues into dialogues, lest the world remain a lonely place. But there is a question: must the table be rendered human, assimilated to our sense of it or to our need of it, for our gratification? One of Emily Dickinson's poems reads:

> Perception of an object costs
> Precise the object's loss—
> Perception in itself a Gain
> Replying to its Price—
> The Object Absolute—is nought—
> Perception sets it fair
> And then upbraids a Perfectness
> That situates so far—[2]

Perception takes the harm out of the Object Absolute, its perfection, and renders it available to our sense of it. The object does not suffer, presumably, but by its new relation to the

128

perceiver it has lost its independence, it has become relative to the perceiver's history. Duncan's table remains what it was because it was never absolute, as soon as it became a table it became part of human experience, though a neglected part. When seeing is acknowledging, the perceiver makes up for the neglect. In John Osborne's play *A Hotel in Amsterdam* the writer Laurie says that a swimming pool is a terrible thing to look into: no past, no future. I suppose he means that it is terrible because translucent, entirely devoid of the shadow which testifies to history and value; nothing in itself, it makes everything depend upon the perceiver. Mirrors are often considered terrible for the same reason: no history, commitment, or preference. We like to think that it is possible to translate every object of our experience into terms at least provisionally subjective, but we do not want the translation to come too easily. A few objects ought to remain intractable, lest we too easily transform reality into our own culture and gratify ourselves with a sense of power. It would be terrible to live in a world utterly impenetrable, a planet indifferent to our adventure—a fate observed in many fables from Kafka's *The Castle* to Frost's "The Most of It"—but it would be specious satisfaction to regard the translation of nature into culture as a simple and entirely satisfactory process.

Duncan's sentences refer to a morality of sight, not merely because sight has long been regarded in Western thought as the first and greatest of the senses but because modern poets especially consider the act of seeing as the best indication of a man's sense of life. To see in the right spirit is to live well. Marianne Moore's poems make sight an acknowledgement of nature, a compliment rather than an intrusion: perception of an object is a form of civility, poems make a grammar-school of courtesy, they exercise one's good manners. Objects are known by our seeing them, and we are known by the way in which we look at them. Miss Moore's poems display a mind moving with proper decorum and passion through intelligibles: the items observed are diverse becasue they testify to the range of the mind's encounters. Success in these experiences is indicated by the tone of our meetings and transitions: Miss Moore's superiority is conveyed by the gusto and elegance of her grammar. In any case the act of sight has as much responsibility to ethics as to optics. "As a man is, So he Sees,"[3] Blake told Dr. Trusler. The principle is that an act depends upon a prior stance, an attitude, the act is contained implicitly in the attitude, the dumb show, the gesture. Lionel Johnson said to Yeats, trying to cheer him up, that God asks nothing from the human soul but attention. Modern poets assume that the quality of attention, indicated by the quality of sight, is a sufficient criterion; by their vision we shall know them. This is one reason among many to explain how the aesthetic question is deemed to include the moral question. In Wallace Stevens's poems the most pressing questions of life and death are formulated in aesthetic terms, the moral and metaphysical nostalgia which we feel in the poems is assuaged by the nuances of perception which it provokes. Seeing in the right spirit becomes the most available form of virtue. Stevens is thrilled to discover that there are at least thirteen ways of looking at a blackbird, and that each way is right; a discovery congenial to a man who resents what he regards as the totalitarian nature of a strictly religious or doctrinal belief. Seeing may or may not be believing, but Stevens circumvents the question of a specific religious belief by revelling in the diversity of seeing, the productive powers of imagination, his poems enliven the common experience of sight with rainbows of glowing detail far beyond the routine of sensual eyes. I shall leave aside for the moment a troublesome question: how much of the power we casually ascribe to the eye depends rather upon the brain. Those who praise the eye often evade the question, and their opponents who argue that the eye is helpless without the brain are more concerned to praise the brain than to deride the orb. It is easy to show that a man's senses rarely act independently or separately, like a channel on a TV set, but it does not follow that all his senses work simultaneously at full stretch. Senses differ in their codes as in the speed of their functions. Some experiences are mainly dependent upon a predominant sense: it is not necessary

to assume with Marshall McLuhan that the other senses are then
annulled, it is enough to consider them for the moment more or
less idle. Hans Jonas has argued that sight is properly considered
the most excellent of the senses, "the measure of the other
senses" as well as "the model of perception in general." He also
remarks that among the senses sight has the special power of
simultaneous presentation: one glance discloses "a world of
co-present qualities spread out in space, ranged in depth,
continuing into indefinite distance, suggesting a direction away
from the subject rather than toward it." The special bias of
sight is that it gives the present moment a character of its own,
not as the precarious intersection of past and future but as a
dimension sustaining its own content: it clears a space in which
the present moment asserts itself. Jonas maintains that sight
"provides the sensual basis on which the mind may conceive
the idea of the eternal, that which never changes and is always
present," it enforces the character of the self-contained object
confronted by the self-contained subject. Again it secures "that
standing back from the aggressiveness of the world which frees
for observation and opens a horizon for elective attention." But
it achieves this "at the price of offering a becalmed abstract of
reality denuded of its raw power."[4] By sight, the subject imposes
distance upon the object, and the enchantment which distance
lends is that of detail, up to a point, and, beyond that point,
composition and proportion, an impression of natural kinship
between one thing and another. But there are writers who resent
the implications of distance, and not least its safety; they do not
want to think of subject and object as separate entities. Often
these writers resort to the sense of touch, they insist on knowing
the world by contact. Whitman and William Carlos Williams
are cases in that point. There are other writers who try to evade
the distancing force of sight by altering its normal character;
as Wordsworth speaks of "an eye practised like a blind man's
touch," an extraordinary perception, by the way, and entirely
characteristic of Wordsworth, since it ascribes to the eye what it
is conventionally not supposed to need—a continuous history of

practice and effort—and what it rarely exhibits in its dealing
with objects—misgiving, fear, hesitation, scruple, and local
successes achieved only by trials and errors. For a similar reason
Yeats distinguished between two kinds of seeing, the glance and
the gaze, and for the most part favoured the gaze. The glancer
looks out upon a world utterly separate from himself, maintaining a safe distance from objects and approaching them only with
bureaucratic intent. Yeats associated him with those who merely
administer a world to which they feel no attachment or responsibility, like civil servants or Roman emperors, nothing but power
in mind. Gazers are a different nation, their force is internal,
they have no design upon the world, in Yeats's terms they are
subjective rather than objective. Gazers seek first the kingdom of
their own imagination, their fictive place, their soul. To the
gazer the given world may be alien or charming, but in any
case what is given is merely an occasion to lead the mind
beyond the evidence toward its own fictions. The true Rome is
always what is gazed upon beyond the primary Rome which is
merely visible. The only important limitation in Jonas's account
of sight in *The Phenomenon of Life* is that he ascribes to the
eye only one skill, one character, one propensity: it is Rousseau's
"l'oeil vivant," the eye as guardian of a mind determined to
survive, invulnerable to experience.

Of the metaphors which arise from the experience of sight, the
most resourceful is the book of Nature. The book is separate
from the mind that reads it, but reading is interpretation, the
reader cannot be passive, he must construe the words and turn
them into experience. Words are offered to him with this
freedom, and it is understood that he deals with them on those
terms. The book of Nature is a picture-book of natural forms,
but their syntax must be divined, and it cannot be as obvious as
the splendour of the forms. Nature provides the words, the
diction, but syntax is occult. Often the best hope is supposed
to arise from innocence, the purity of the source. Emerson says,
in the major essay on Nature, that "a life in harmony with
nature, the love of truth and of virtue, will purge the eyes to

understand her text." The text is reliable, a book of Revelation, and if it opaque to us, the fault is in ourselves, as Emerson says, "the ruin, or the blank, that we see when we look at nature is in our own eye." That the metaphor is still alive is clear from the later *Cantos* in which Pound endorses the emergence of truth as crystalline form, "ubi amor ibi oculus est" (Canto 90) and the praise of John Heydon as "Secretary of Nature" (Canto 91). It is part of the Christian tradition that God provides us with two books, the Bible and Nature, and the idiom of revelation is supposed to apply to both.

The common understanding of perception, then, is that it is a visual act, we come to know something as we come to see it. The perceiver is separate from the object of perception, he has an impression of the world as "an extended, spatially continuous, variously coloured and shaded field, which is presented as a finite but unbounded whole."[5] The light by which we see is deemed to come from the sun, and in that case truth is felt to be an independent fact; or from ourselves, our inner light, identified with soul or intelligence, and in that case truth is a creative act of the mind. According to common understanding, everything in the field of vision is seen as the material of a possible or metaphorical order, on the analogy of the picture and its frame. Perception is fulfilled when the picture is sufficiently stable to be contemplated. This view of perception is particularly congenial to early eighteenth century literature and it accounts for Augustan concentration upon the coherence of the picture rather than the details of which it is made. In *The Dunciad* Pope scorns "the critic Eye, that microscope of Wit" which "sees hairs and pores, examines bit by bit":

> How parts relate to parts, or they to whole,
> The body's harmony, the beaming soul,
> Are things which Kuster, Burman, Wasse shall see,
> When Man's whole frame is obvious to a Flea.[6]

Pope is appealing to one of the cardinal analogues of unity, the body's harmony, and it is a sign of his bravado, and of his wit, that he enforces unity in the idiom of division, the division of body and soul. Soul is beaming because its inner light responds to the outer light of creation, the harmony of man and nature in visual terms. We are to place ourselves at a vantage point from which "Man's whole frame" is visible; not too near, not too far. If too near, we are in bad taste, inquisitive; if too far, we see nothing. As Pope says in the introductory sentences to the *Essay on Man*, "It is therefore in the Anatomy of the mind as in that of the Body; more good will accrue to mankind by attending to the large, open, and perceptible parts, than by studying too much such finer nerves and vessels, the conformations and uses of which will for ever escape our observation."[7] This admonition is in keeping with the spirit of satire which Wyndham Lewis expressed in *Men Without Art* when he declared an interest in the ossature rather than the intestines of an animal organism. To Pope and Lewis the good life is an achievement of perspective. In Swift, distortions of perspectives are based upon the understanding that truth is what survives them. Swift employed by genius what Shaftesbury offered as a method: there is a passage in the *Characteristics* where he recommends that truth be discovered by subjecting possible truths to the strain of ridicule; whatever survives the strain is genuine. Johnson thought the method monstrous presumably because he was unwilling to take its risk. The Augustan writers sought in the field of Nature a significant relation between one thing and another, and between each and the whole. The Newtonian light which Pope and Thomson celebrate, however diversely, falls upon a world supposed to be mechanical and particulate: matter consists of particles which, to begin with, are homogeneous, differences of substance are caused by forces between the particles which drive them into heterogeneous combinations.[8] It was easy to reconcile this view of things with Christian belief: if original matter is passive, its activity is caused by a divine spirit diffused throughout the universe. God's love for His creatures is revealed in the animation of natural forms, the works of Creation, and the Incarnation.

The Augustan theory of imitation supposes that there is a common, objective world to which man stands in apposition. Reality is there, in front of one's eyes, reliably present. The Augustan writer does not look for signs and wonders but for evidence of intention in given objects, he receives pattern as proof of divine purpose. This stance governs the force of Augustan wit which commands the relation between one thing and another. The grammatical equivalent is a sequence of diverse images controlled by a verb. The verb does the work of survey, and the images denote a multiplicity of experiences enclosed within a single frame. John Shade, Nabokov's poet in *Pale Fire,* quotes an apposite passage from Pope's second Epistle of the *Essay of Man* where the theme is man's adherence to his nature:

> See the blind beggar dance, the cripple sing,
> The sot a hero, lunatic a king;
> The starving chemist in his golden views
> Supremely blest, the poet in his Muse.[9]

Shade feels that the lines "smack of their heartless age": his editor Charles Kinbote does not comment on the age but on Pope's failure to find a monosyllable to replace "hero" so as to accommodate the definite article before "lunatic." Neither Shade nor Kinbote mentions that the magnificence of the passage arises from tension between the several phrases and the single verb that controls them. I think it wonderful that the verb comes as the first syllable of the first line and that it is the verb "to see," challenging any number of visible objects. The figures in that landscape make an arrested dance of life and death, a dance of gargoyles which would be overwhelming but for the power of survey featured in the verb. Strain between the power of sight and what it sees is exhilarating because of the human capacity engaged. In the "Epistle to Burlington" Pope addresses the great man, "Bid the broad Arch the dangerous Flood contain": it is Pope's typical line, beginning and ending with a verb of control, the mood imperative, supporting at each end the broad arch poised against the flood. Whatever is, is right in Pope because the force of existence joined to the force of perception is irrefutable, enabling him to convert negative into positive terms even when the ostensible justification is slight. The validity of final causes is unquestioned: that is, Pope does not question it, and it is endorsed by the harmony of mediate causes. Hence in the *Essay on Man* chance is converted to "direction which thou canst not see," and discord to "Harmony, not understood." Man sees so much that what he does not see will not trouble him, he hopes, his survey is limited but limitation is its strength. Satire, the strongest form of survey, gains strength again by its detachment from the objects of survey. The satirist sees more than other men because he remains detached, unintimidated by the spirit of the age.

But it is not enough to say that Augustan literature is concerned with the relation between one thing and another, between parts and whole: it is assumed that each thing is complete and fixed in its nature, or at least there is an official conspiracy to act upon that assumption and to declare intimations of fluidity suspect. The objects of sight are what they are seen to be in the moment of perception, and that is the limit of the reality conceded to them. The best comparison is drawn from photography. Susan Sontag has remarked that a camera is a device for taking possession of space in which one is otherwise insecure. Objects transfixed lack the power to hurt, their nature becomes merely virtual to us, our relation to them is a symbolic form of imperialism, token of affluence and possession. Pope's verbs are cameras; doing the work of a lens, they prescribe the conditions on which he is willing to receive the objects of his experience. Walter Benjamin has said that a camera focussed upon us records our likeness without returning our gaze: to the camera we are pure objects, and we stay in that condition even if we say "cheese" and wave to the photographer. A comparison between *The Dunciad* and Antonioni's *Blow-Up* in this respect would not be fanciful, since in both cases the effect depends

upon possessing the human image as a mere thing, a pure
object, frozen or congealed. For the sake of simultaneous
possession, sight removes the images of its attention from history,
or rather from their own possible history. Whatever their nature
at the moment of sight, it is the only nature they are allowed to
have, so long as they remain in that frame of reference. Blind
beggar, cripple, and sot are transfixed, arrested in their natures
like figures in a photograph, they will never be more or less than
they are, because their being has ceased to be historical in the
process of becoming picturesque. They may participate in the
photographer's history, the history of his feeling, but not in their
own freedom and possibility. The force engendered in their
relation to each other is not a force of becoming, as in history,
but of being, as in morality: they are moral absolutes now. We
are not allowed to attend upon these figures individually. The
prosody directs us swiftly from one to the next, concentrating our
attention upon their latitude, not their depth. We are not
allowed to be curious about the reality lying "beneath the
appearances that tell of it": instead of depth, intricacy of visual
relation is offered as the proper study of mankind. Philip
Larkin's poem "Lines on a Young Lady's Photograph Album"
says of the flowers, the gate, "these misty parks and motors,"
that they lacerate the heart "simply by being over," and the
girl contracts the speaker's feeling "by looking out of date." Of
the figures congealed in the photograph album Larkin writes:

> Yes, true; but in the end, surely, we cry
> Not only at exclusion, but because
> It leaves us free to cry. We know *what was*
> Won't call on us to justify
> Our grief, however hard we yowl across
> The gap from eye to page.[10]

Larkin is sensitive to the gap between eye and page, a token of
other severances, and to the "faithful and disappointing" art
which removes the sitter from the life of becoming and possibility:
it is an exorbitant price to pay for the precision of a "hold-it"

smile. The gap from eye to page affects *what is* just as much as *what was,* since each is equally congealed, equally removed from its part in historical movement.

There is a passage in Merleau-Ponty's *The Primacy of Perception* where the theme is Matisse's art and Merleau-Ponty says of the women in the paintings that they are not immediately women but they become women. Presumably the force which gives them that life is the feeling engendered between perceiver and painting, as earlier between painter and paint, a collaboration in the adventure of form. In neither case is the relation fixed; the problematic nature of the relation arises from what Merleau-Ponty describes as a certain disequilibrium maintained within the indifference of the canvas. "The line," he says, "is no longer the apparition of an entity upon a vacant background, as it was in classical geometry":[11] it registers the adventure of form which corresponds to the fluidity of feeling. Matisse keeps the women in their history by giving them a future in which they are to become themselves. The disequilibrium to which Merleau-Ponty refers is harmonised, steadied at a late stage in the perceiver's experience; the women become women when the perceiver has made his peace with the restlessness of the painting itself. Matisse ensures for his women a life of becoming, since that is what formal restlessness means, the women are not transfixed. But the pressure by which Augustan literature acts is entirely different, it excludes suspect objects or neutralises them, it does not welcome risk or adventure, it insists upon a definitive order. Augustan literature depends upon a declared positivity of objects, they are allowed to look neither before nor after. Women who enter an Augustan poem are fixed in their being, they have ended their lives to become what Augustan language forces them to become, objects seen across the gap between eye and page. If we have any misgivings about personification as an Augustan trope, they arise from the same feeling, that the personified term has had its life removed from history and congealed as a moral absolute. The term is held at whatever point it has reached, and that is the end of its development, it has been removed from history to act among forces and relations within the static field of sight. There is no objection to personification unless we yearn to give such words a future as well as a past. As moral absolutes they are imposing, and the capital letter awarded them by the printing press is recognition of that status, but it is hard to forget that a different language might have released them for a further life in history and consequence. This applies generally, even where there is no personification:

> The watchful Guests still hint the last Offence,
> The Daughter's Petulance, the Son's Expence,
> Improve his heady Rage with treach'rous Skill,
> And mould his Passions till they make his Will.

Empson quoted these couplets from *The Vanity of Human Wishes* as an example of the ambiguity (third of his seven) arising when two ideas, connected only by being both relevant in the context, are given in one word simultaneously. He made much of the puns in "heady" and "will," though not of "improve" meaning severally "employ to advantage, invest, enlarge, and aggravate." His general point about Augustan poetry and eighteenth-century poetry at large is that "what oft was thought" has a merely delusive simplicity, and the things which were "ne'er so well expressed" turn out to be, even in a compact antithesis, those "shifts and blurred aggregates of thought by which men come to a practical decision."[12] Right; but there are two further points. The special Augustan quality in Johnson's couplets is that the daughter is totally sunk in her petulance, the son in his expence, the equation of person and offence in each case is so complete that the persons are not allowed to exist beyond the point of representing their ruling vices, they have nothing but their vices. The impression of power so ready in Johnson's poetry depends upon a language which takes pleasure in congealing its objects, turning them into things even if they are not things. This kind of poetry refuses to allow the daughter to change or to become anything but her petulance. The shifts and blurred aggregates of thought which Empson has in view are there, and often arise from the sources he describes, but Augustan diction likes to anticipate the practical decision the poetry will reach by being as far as possible decisive to begin with. The language has already made up its mind about those daughters and those sons.

The sensory equivalent of this practical decisiveness is the "despotism of the eye' to which later poets refer, the eye's demand for immediate clarity, since it doesn't like changing its mind. Of course it is a good question to what extent Pope, Swift, and Johnson were convinced by their aesthetic preferences, or merely suppressed their misgivings. They thought the procedures good enough for social, moral, and political purposes, and they took the line of fending off metaphysical questions on the ground that they were merely a function of curiosity. Locke and, even more so, Hobbes were useful to these poets because they encouraged them to conduct their intellectual lives upon a simple picture of man and nature. When Hobbes writes, in the later chapters of *Leviathan,* of the kingdom of darkness, or when he attacks the scholastic doctrine of abstract essences, he speaks not only for "natural Reason" but for a simple diagram of life. The dominant sense offers as true that which may be seen, the rest is matter of faith or obscurity. If these writers were terrified of fluidity and vagueness, it was because these qualities were an offence to the eye. Charles Tomlinson has a poem about binoculars, or rather about our exorbitant demand for clarity at any price, which speaks of definition becoming clear-cut but bodiless:

> To see thus
> Is to ignore the revenge of light on shadow
> To confound both in a brittle and false union.[13]

The poem speaks of binoculars as vehicles of madness, invoking that sense of manic intensity with which we enforce such gross lucidities. I think Tomlinson's imagination was stirred not so much by the deathly picture we see through binoculars but by the feeling we have when we put them down again and return to a plain sense of things, willing to be duped if necessary by ordinary appearances and immensely relieved to be restored to the common world. The poem has much to say of the congealed object,

but not much of the equally congealed perceiver. In Augustan
literature the perceiver, to command what he sees, standing back
from the field, must be prepared to give up many other possibilities for the immediate boon of sight, he is not allowed to take
satisfaction in the range of his subjectivity so long as his official
role is that of control and possession. The fiercest Augustan
satire is vented upon those perceivers who run beyond these
limits; like the sublimists and enthusiasts ridiculed by Pope,
Swift, and Gay. In "The Mechanical Operation of the Spirit"
Swift defines Enthusiasm as "a lifting up of the soul or its faculties
above matter," and however we interpret that work generally
we cannot doubt that Swift is attacking spiritual arrogance. I
have some sympathy for those wretches, browbeaten, constantly
ordered to keep their eyes on the finite object. In the third Book
of *The Dunciad* the Goddess of Dulness transports the King to
her temple:

> Him close she curtains round with Vapours blue,
> And soft besprinkles with Cimmerian dew.
> Then raptures high the seat of Sense o'erflow,
> Which only heads refin'd from Reason know.
> Hence, from the straw where Bedlam's Prophet nods,
> He hears loud Oracles, and talks with Gods:
> Hence the Fool's Paradise, the Statesman's Scheme,
> The air-built Castle, and the golden Dream,
> The Maid's romantic wish, the Chemist's flame,
> And Poet's vision of eternal Fame.[14]

The sins are pretty venial, as sins go. Pope's wit is mischievous,
making all these delusions the same. Of course he knows that men
do not and cannot live by reason alone, and to be fair he does
not encourage anyone to try. One of the remarkable features of
the *Essay on Man* is the value it puts on instinct and self-love.
Reason and self-love are good, it says, only in their mutual
bearing:

> Self-love stronger, as its objects nigh;
> Reason's at distance, and in prospect lie:
> That sees immediate good by present sense;
> Reason, the future and the consequence.[15]

Reason is first among equals, then; if it can see the future and the consequence by standing well back from the sensory excitement of the occasion, it has something of divinity in its nature. Later in the *Essay* when Pope speaks of "light and darkness in our chaos join'd," he calls the power that distinguishes them "the God within the mind."[16] There is nothing pre-Romantic in the phrase. To Pope, the divinity that sees our consequences is the communal eye; it is like the human eye in its sense of reality, but it rebukes the vanity of that eye, its personal idiosyncrasy. The communal eye is the common sense of society, and it is like Tradition in literature and feeling. If we know more than our fathers, it is for Eliot's reason, that they are what we know. If we see more, it is because they are what we see. But we are restrained by the eye of society, which augments the work of nature in moral and cultural terms, seeing things in grand perspective.

The danger in this idiom is that a man may be dazzled by surfaces. Pope hopes that the opacity of appearance is reliable, but rather than dazzle himself with surface glitter he would prefer to let the mind run beyond appearance. If the soul does not accept the discipline of his own reason, or the better reason of society, there yet remains the admonitory eye of God. This is the situation in Pope's Imitation of the sixth Epistle of the first Book of Horace, the "Nil Admirari":

> This Vault of Air, this congregated Ball,
> Self-centr'd Sun, and Stars that rise and fall,
> There are, my Friend! whose philosophic eyes
> Look thro', and trust the Ruler with his skies,
> To him commit the hour, the day, the year,
> And view this dreadful All without a fear.[17]

Philosophic eyes are endorsed, but only because the situation imposes extreme choice, either to be overwhelmed by dreadful appearances or to send the mind through and beyond them. These eyes do not pretend to see anything profound beyond appearances, the world to them is translucent, they resist dazzle and trust God. This is what Aristotle does when he appears in Pope's "The Temple of Fame":

His piercing eyes, erect, appear to view
Superior worlds, and look all Nature through. . . .

But Aristotle has the advantage of hindsight; dead, he is among the gods. The nearest mundane equivalent is the sage of "Windsor Forest" who, retired from the busy world, can safely play the mental traveller. Such a man can "look on heav'n with more than mortal eyes" because his free soul willingly comes home to the "sequestered scenes" of time and place. It is often said that the Virgilian retirement-poetry of Pope and other Augustan writers demonstrates the ease of their relation to the natural world, but the tradition of the happy man is complex and it rarely features a direct engagement of man with the full life of his time. Retirement-poetry appeals to rhythms of natural life which the daily rote of personal and public life merely affronts, so the poem tells more of need than of ease. "The Deserted Village" and "Windsor Forest" entertain as much life as they can, but between the lines we feel the venom of daily life which they cannot assuage or control. The mind does not engage with its occasions directly; daily life is allowed to come into these fictions of accord only as an "absence in reality." The relation between mind and occasion is construed by analogy with the relation between eye and object. In such poems the mind chooses not to look at the whole scene of things. The relation between mind and occasion is static, whether strong or weak according to the visual analogy. According to the "philosophy of five senses" which Blake ascribed to Bacon, Newton, and Locke, reality is what the senses deliver to the mind; mind waits for the delivery, but takes no part in it other than by reflection upon its own processes. This is the "single vision" which Blake and Yeats in their different voices denounced, a sense of reality as utterly independent of consciousness; it is naturalism, or the Roman glance.

But the real problem is that sensations are understood in Augustan literature as images, and images as little pictures, visual events separated from an external source. Image as a literary term is relatively recent; it became popular when the Royal Society demanded a perspicuous language free from rhetorical and metaphysical pretention.[18] It was hoped to establish words upon a relation to things and to pictures of things, a word could appeal to its corresponding object in nature. An image was understood as the sign of its external source. The fear of words, so strong in Augustan literature, could only be stilled in available terms by recourse to things as their guarantors. This notion of the image remained intact, despite Burke's objection in the *Origin of the Sublime and the Beautiful,* until late in the nineteenth century; indeed, it still represents a general understanding of imagery and its relation to consciousness. So long as consciousness was understood in visual terms, this understanding of the image was secure, but it was threatened when Darwin presented life in terms of evolutionary movement; when Bergson introduced the note of movement into every act of the mind; when Sartre argued that the image, far from being objective, is that which cannot succeed to objectivity, it is subjectivity itself. I mention these events not to do them justice but to suggest that the Augustan concept of consciousness cannot easily deal with the mind as agent. Knowledge to Augustan writers is the power of survey, and it finds Nature as a picture-book, most congenial when the pictures stand still, waiting to be seen: it is not happy with movement, either in object or subject. In *The Will to Power* Nietzsche said that the eighteenth century tried to forget what it knew of man's nature in order to assimilate him to its utopia. I assume he means the Augustan dream of producing communal man, a dream of uniformity. This dream is so alien to us that we respond to Augustan writers in the degree to which they deny themselves. *The Dunciad* touches us because we feel that Pope has been drawn into complicity, despite his official role, with the objects of his attack. If the fourth Book is a dance of death, we feel that Pope is participating in it, as if for once and desperately he longed to release himself from the severe light of intelligence and cast himself upon that darkness which, increasingly, he conceived as universal. The *Essay on Man,* by comparison, seems too orthodox to reflect our own divisions. I have argued on another occasion that Swift's power is engendered in the vigour of his negations, but in the *Tale of a Tub* the forces he denies avenge themselves by erupting into the work through the violence of parody. Officially, parody negates what it parodies, but in the *Tale* Swift registers the force of sinister figures and in a measure conspires with them; one form of violence responds to another. We rejoice in these subversions and infidelities, and feel that a writer should be his own most capable enemy: all the better if his imagination registers what his official role would reject. At the least we read these Augustan masterpieces to feel the tension between an enforced orthodoxy of sight and mind and, beneath the surface, the aboriginal violence officially denied.

II: The Purer Eye

The fourth Book of *The Dunciad* appeared in 1742, and in the same year Edward Young published the first three books of *Night Thoughts*. Young gives Pope a few crumbs of praise, but he thinks his work on the whole misguided. Instead of concerning himself with the Grub Street of daily life, Pope should have taken as his theme "immortal man," should have sung man's genius, his immortality, the Supreme Fiction (to use Stevens's phrase) of man as such. Since a different style certifies a different sense of life, Young's poem rushes to declare it: imagination, genius, immortality, sublimity, Man not men. Night thoughts are deemed more profound than day thoughts because they are not limited by the prosaic requirement of lucidity and precision. The mind is its own place and may be sufficiently lighted from within.

It is customary to say that the first critical reaction to empiricism in the early eighteenth century came in Addison's essays on the pleasures of the imagination. Those essays are often superficial, but they are important as revealing a sensibility which found the direct engagement of Man and Nature too harsh. Addison felt intimidated by a blunt encounter between a self-possessed subject and an independent object in the full light of day. The mind, in that relation, is committed to a strict account. In *The Spectator* (June 30, 1712) Addison said that "because the

Mind of Man requires something more perfect in Matter, than
what it finds there, and can never meet with any sight in Nature
which sufficiently answers its highest Ideas of Pleasantness; or, in
other Words, because the Imagination can fancy to itself Things
more Great, Strange, or Beautiful, than the Eye ever saw, and is
still sensible of some Defect in what it has seen; on this account
it is the part of a Poet to humour the Imagination in its own
Notions, by mending and perfecting Nature where he describes
a Reality, and by adding greater Beauties than are put together
in Nature, where he describes a Fiction."[19] There is nothing
remarkable in the programme: so far as it goes, it can be found
in Bacon's *Advancement of Learning,* Sidney's *Defence of Poetry,*
and many other meditations on the poet as a constructive liar.
But Addison's tone is different. Neither Bacon nor Sidney urges
that it is a sufficient criterion that a fiction be psychologically
congenial. Any day-dreamer knows that he can release himself
from nature, dreaming away the given world, but the point of
Addison's essays on the imagination is that they convert aesthetics
into psychology and turn it away from politics and morality.
Sensations and impressions are considered important as food for
the psyche; their nature in other respects, and their origin, are
not considered important. Distinctions between visible and invisible impressions are considered of little account. Impressions
from any source are available to the imagination. Addison
deflects the moral analogy which distinguishes between daylight,
darkness, and twilight: they are all one to him, the only criterion
is freedom of fancy. In "The Pleasures of Melancholy" Thomas
Warton prefers Spenser to Pope because Spenser encourages the
pensive mood while Pope's descriptions are harsh and "cold." The
idiom of feeling is invoked to supersede the idiom of knowledge,
because the criteria of knowledge are strict while those of feeling
are free and easy. There is in the eighteenth century an evan-
gelical movement not only in Christianity but in poetry, and it
defines itself as a movement of terminology from wit to genius,
perspicuity to vision, knowledge to feeling, the reasonable to the

sublime. Imagination is construed as the power which transcends reason, alters sensory evidence in favour of a psychologically ideal state, and responds rather to desire than to morality. Reality is changed by a flick of feeling, and this process is regarded as the essential act of imagination. Two hundred years later Stevens speaks in *Notes Toward a Supreme Fiction* of "false flick, false form, but falseness close to kin."[20]

The question hovers upon the relation between man and nature, or the perceiver and landscape. Marshall McLuhan in *The Gutenberg Galaxy* ascribes to *The Seasons* a major discovery in the definition of these relations. Landscape could be invoked in such a way as to render it susceptible to the perceiver's sense of it, without scandalising the empiricists. He did not mean that landscape is to yield to his feeling, but that it offers men a moral analogy which they are well advised to consult. God has disposed the natural forms according to an art of Nature: men, reading the signs, comport themselves in that light, as Queen Anne did, thereby ensuring the peace of the Augustans. Men are susceptible to landscape, and they may improve the natural setting in accordance with a taste well instructed by nature and the purest examples, like Pope in Twickenham, but the idiom of sight does not encourage Pope to find his merely local and personal feeling registered in the landscape. The connotations of landscape are moral, not psychological. Much of this attitude survives in *The Seasons,* but Thomson's sense of landscape is more accommodating than Pope's, and what it accommodates is a far more generous recognition of the range of human desire. In "Spring" he invokes "the purer eye" which has the faculty of seeing the Divine Author in His works. The purer eye has something of an angel's power of apprehending essence directly, a meta-instinct to be deployed upon the visible forms:

> What is this mighty breath, ye curious, say,
> That in a powerful language, felt, not heard,
> Instructs the fowls of heaven, and through their breast
> These arts of love diffuses? What, but God?

> Inspiring God! who, boundless spirit all
> And unremitting energy, pervades,
> Adjusts, sustains, and agitates the whole.
> He ceaseless works alone, and yet alone
> Seems not to work; with such perfection framed
> Is this complex, stupendous scheme of things.
> But, though concealed, to every purer eye
> The informing Author in his works appears:
> Chief, lovely Spring, in thee and thy soft scenes
> The smiling God is seen—while water, earth,
> And air attest his bounty, which exalts
> The brute-creation to this finer thought,
> And annual melts their undesigning hearts
> Profusely thus in tenderness and joy.[21]

This is provisional, merely one moment of many in the rhythm of *The Seasons,* but it fairly represents the new sensibility. "Purer eye" goes with "finer thought." God's divinity manifests itself not only in His smile but in the form and intention of his energy; set against the "undesigning" heart of the brute creation. The key term is "exalts," going with "melts" and "profusely." Josephine Miles has remarked of this kind of poetry its need "to increase the terminology of observed qualities" rather than to enlarge the idiom in which moralities and actions are defined.[22] There is particular emphasis on words which generalise upon the qualities common to man and nature as privileged occupants of a divinely ordained space—such words as Thomson's exalts, melts, profuse, breast, love, soft, tenderness, and joy. In "Winter" the natural forms tower over men not to overwhelm them but to sublimate their passions, and everywhere men are reminded of the powers and values which draw them together as a privileged species. The range of human feeling is taken seriously because it responds to the scale of a divinely created universe. Psychology is natural science employed upon man's feelings; every new discovery requires a further development of descriptive vocabulary, mainly adjectival since qualities are in question, and—as Miss Miles has shown in *Eras and Modes*—a cumulative, phrasal language in which a rich internal organization of sound testifies to a correspondingly rich structure of relationships between man, nature, and God. Such poetry proceeds under auspices which can be described by their affiliation to the Protestant Bible, Longinus, Pindar, Milton, and the Whig voice of feeling. In Thomson, Nature "wears to the lover's eye a look of love," and the love is a divine invention. Thomson's celebration of Newton shows that the idiom of light is still felt as valid, the God of Light hospitable to human feeling. There is a wooing both ways between the rhythm of seasonal forms and the rhythm of human feeling: the forms are not merely moral emblems but token of responsiveness at large. They do not merely instruct men, they receive and entertain them.

Thomson's poetry obviously requires a delicate balance of motives if the presentation of feeling is to embody a mutual relation between man and nature. There is bound to be a temptation to lean in one direction or another; either to find in the natural forms a divine force to which man merely responds, or to suggest that these forms are psychologically neutral, waiting upon man's spirit before moving in any direction. Naturally enough, the poetry of the period has its indeterminate moments. At the end of the third Book of his *Pleasures of Imagination* Akenside defines imagination as God's energy acting within us: to respond to the natural forms is to "hold converse" with God. This is orthodox, but there are strange passages in the poem:

> O! teach me to reveal the grateful charm
> That searchless nature o'er the sense of man
> Diffuses, to behold, in lifeless things,
> The inexpressive semblance of himself,
> Of thought and passion.[22]

"Searchless" means inscrutable, but not in the sense of forbidding search. As in Watt's "Great God, how searchless are thy ways," we are free to search, but not if we indulge the vain pretention of taking God's measure or plucking the heart of His mystery. But Akenside's "lifeless" pulls "searchless" into the suggestion of a closed book which no one can open or read. It is difficult to square Akenside's orthodoxy on other occasions with the assertion here that the only thing man can find in these natural forms is the inexpressive semblance of himself. Such a discovery would testify either to gross self-delusion or the morbidity of egotism which Hawthorne attributes to Dimmesdale in *The Scarlet Letter,* egotism extended "over the whole expanse of nature, until the firmament itself should appear no more than a fitting page for his soul's history and fate." Henry James thought the passage too much of a good thing, but its bearing is indisputable, Dimmesdale's morbidity of egotism is the dark side of the sentimentality which Akenside and other writers practise upon inoffensive landscapes. Such paradises are artificial.

The question is the participation of sense and mind in experience, the difference it makes to literature when the auspices under which these enterprises proceed are what they are and not other. The Romantic poets had these questions in view in their comments on Locke and Newton and Hartley. Coleridge praised Newton for his scientific discoveries but disapproved of the cause they were made to serve. "Newton was a mere materialist," Coleridge maintained, " — *Mind* in his system is always passive — a lazy Looker — on on an external World. If the mind be not *passive,* if it be indeed made in God's image, & that too in the sublimest sense — the Image of the *Creator* — there is ground for suspicion, that any system built on the passiveness of the mind must be false, as a system."[23] If the mind is passive, the senses must be guilty of placing it in that humiliating state, and the chief culprit must be the eye. Elsewhere Coleridge speaks of "that Slavery of the Mind to the Eye and the visual imagination or Fancy under the influence of which the Reasoner must have a *picture* and mistakes surface for substance."[24] Yeats speaks in *A Vision* of a new naturalism that leaves man helpless before the mere contents of his mind, and elsewhere of Locke sinking "into a swoon" induced by the separation of primary from secondary qualities and the postponement of mind. The situation of man, the perceiver, stationed in front of a fixed scene, a mere spectator of life, marked a puny fate for one who supposed himself a son of God. To Romantic poets, and to such poets as Thomson, Akenside, and Collins, man's dependence upon knowledge, lucidity, and the boundaries of daylight consciousness was a grave restriction of his possibilities: helpless before the darkness that rendered his primary sense null, he could not deal with forces that revelled in obscurity, those old moles in the cellar. When Augustan writers enforced an orthodoxy of man, a set of attitudes and values, they did not provide for the marginal or subterranean forces in man which cannot be destroyed merely by being rebuked: those forces went underground, or stayed there, or drove men mad.

The perennial problem is to define a relation between man and nature at once free and legal, free enough for consolation and ease of bearing, legal enough for order and discipline. There is another problem only less majestic, to discover the god-term in whose auspices man's richest life may be conducted. The possibilities are not endless: a list which includes knowledge, being, and action is nearly complete. Wordsworth claims to see into the life of things at certain canonical moments, but he does not claim to find his own semblance there or that the moments would be exalted by such a discovery, if nothing more were discovered. We take the claim seriously because his vision is mediated through the natural forms and certified by the quality of his attendance upon them. His poems translate the relation between man and nature into domestic terms, the guiding analogies are personal and filial. The substance of each occasion is feeling. In one of the most remarkable passages of the Preface to *Lyrical Ballads* he speaks of "our continued influxes of feeling" as "modified and directed by our thoughts, which are indeed the representatives of all our past feelings." Thoughts and feelings are not different things, or different in kind, the substance in each case is feeling but thoughts are familes of feelings, feelings brought to a higher degree of organization and kinship. Thoughts are the feelings we have already had, so far as they remain with us in the form of kin. Wordsworth's idiom is Idealist in cast, as we see from its congruence with Susanne Langer's programme in her study of mind, to consider "the entire psychological field—including human conception, responsible action, rationality, knowledge— as a vast and branching development of feeling."[25] Coleridge represents the development from the opposite direction. In

Chapter XII of *Biographia Literaria* he speaks of sensation as "vision nascent, not the cause of intelligence, but intelligence itself revealed as an earlier power in the process of self-construction." At this point Coleridge wants to repair the breach between sensation and mind by bringing mind forward and making it an early rather than a late arrival in the enterprise, he has an interest in representing the whole process as a process of knowledge, so that every stage in it becomes a stage of knowledge.

The differences between Coleridge and Wordsworth are real, but they do not alter the determination of both poets to declare the unity of man's life, under fortunate conditions. When Wordsworth says that in rural life "the passions of men are incorporated in the beautiful and permanent forms of nature," he invokes a version of Natural Law which declares that there is a relation between men and the world in which they live, and that the relation is not arbitrary but natural. The law is clearest in childhood, Time's Utopia, so the child is "best Philosopher," "thou Eye among the blind." In "Tintern Abbey" he celebrates the "mighty world of eye and ear" and he allows that it is composed of two parts, what the senses "perceive" and what they "half create." That "half" represents Wordsworth's scruple, he does not release himself from evidence of the senses or the gift of nature. He is not, like Coleridge, a metaphysician; his favourite words are certified by their participation in a tangible world, "this green earth." Even when he rises to high occasions in *The Prelude,* he mediates them through the terms of time and place. The happiest times are those in which the senses appear to be enough and the human spirit is possessed by

> a feeling and a love
> That had no need of a remoter charm,
> By thought supplied, or any interest
> Unborrowed from the eye.

I take this to mean that the sensations were so continuously lavish that he did not feel it necessary to supplement them by reference to other, past sensations, families of sensations already established and held in the memory; it was sufficient merely to live in such immediacy. But there is a notable passage in Book XI of *The Prelude* where he recalls a state

> In which the eye was master of the heart,
> When that which is in every stage of life
> The most despotic of our senses gain'd
> Such strength in me as often held my mind
> In absolute dominion.

Presumably the only difference between the two occasions is that the first meant pure enjoyment, a holiday in sense, and the second was spoiled or at least complicated by the intrusion of a scruple. He found himself carried off on a holiday when he ought to have been at work, so he couldn't enjoy it. Mind called to him like an ode to Duty. In the next lines he recites, but briefly, the various means

> Which Nature studiously employs to thwart
> This tyranny, summons all the senses each
> To counteract the other and themselves,
> And makes them all, and the objects with which all
> Are conversant, subservient in their turn
> To the great ends of Liberty and Power.

Unfortunately be breaks off at that point, "this is matter for another Song," though he gives himself time for a word of confession:

> Here only let me add that my delights,
> Such as they were were sought insatiably,
> Though 'twas a transport of the outward sense,
> Not of the mind, vivid but not profound:
> Yet was I often greedy in the chase,
> And roam'd from hill to hill, from rock to rock,
> Still craving combinations of new forms,
> New pleasure, wider empire for the sight,
> Proud of its own endowments, and rejoiced
> To lay the inner faculties asleep.

Clearly Wordsworth is confessing sin, the wilful indulgence of "outward sense" at the expense of the "inner faculties," and quite properly he presents the sin as a mixture of greed and pride. His

ethic depends upon a certain hierarchy among the faculties, even
though their substance is entirely feeling. One sense should be
curbed by another, any one of them by the several senses
together, like a strong trade union; and the senses by the highest
structure of feeling, the mind. This is what Yeats, too, had in
view in the lines

> Locke sank into a swoon;
> The Garden died . . .

because the Garden cannot mean anything else but the entire
concert of the senses, or the entire faculty which culminates in
mind. Wordsworth goes one step further, because he has the
mind controlled by "the heart," presumably the organ of man's
humanity which registers the whole moral history of the race. In
this discipline the present moment is reconciled to the past, to
time and history, the living person to the dead and those yet
unborn; becasue these, too, are families in which the present
moment is a new-born child. The sequence in Wordsworth from
sensation to heart includes so much that it stands as the perennial
discipline. I find it again in Rilke's poem "Wendung" which
begins with victories of the eye; stars collapse under the strain of
that scrutiny, even the gods are forced to acknowledge it. The
perceiver looks so hard at towers, he terrifies them; and suddenly,
showing his power, rebuilds them. Or, in the evening, with calm
perception he receives animals, lions, flowers. "Birds flew straight
through him"; the flowers looked back to him as if to children.
But he soon realises that his glance, so powerful, is without love,
and the more the world is looked at, the more it wants to grow
in love. At this point the work of the eye is finished: "Denn des
Anschauns, siehe, ist eine Grenze." It is time for the work of
heart, "Herz-Werk," heart must work upon the sensations which
the eye has captured. The images have been subdued, but they
are not known, because they have not been loved:

> denn du
> überwältigtest sie: aber nun kennst du sie nicht.[26]

Rilke offers these waiting images in personified form as a girl, a creature whom the perceiver has wrung from a thousand natures. She is possessed but not yet loved, therefore not yet known. The epigraph to the poem is taken from Kassner: "the way from intensity to greatness leads through sacrifice." What is sacrificed is the human will. In the first lines of the poem the eye is powerful but wilful and predatory, it has Wordsworth's empire of sight. At the end, the will is transcended: calm perception, corresponding to love, makes the transition in the middle lines from power to acknowledgement. The purer eye has freed itself from the greed of the sensual eye and is transfigured in affection. Traditionally, sense is controlled by mind, but in Rilke as in Wordsworth the final arbiter is the heart. Mind is not defeated: rather, heart is the name given to energy or feeling when its dealing with sensations is such as to consider at the same time the claims of emotions, passions, persons; its dimension is time, its motion not merely the stream of consciousness (a libel upon mind) but the bloodstream in which everything is acknowledged. Under fortunate conditions the complete consort would be found dancing together, but Wordsworth is alert to those experiences in which an impression of unity, from whatever source, is dominant. He is most Wordsworthian, however, on those occasions when the separation of man and nature seems least to obtrude. In this, too, he differs from Coleridge, as Coleridge recognised in that handsome poem in which he congratulated his friend on the completion of *The Prelude,* where he speaks

> of moments awful,
> Now in thy inner life, and now abroad,
> When power streamed from thee, and thy soul received
> The light reflected, as a light restored.[27]

Coleridge recognises that it is a mark of Wordsworth's character to give the experience in its domestic form, a labour of love; light reflected, received as if it were bestowed. Wordsworth turns these events to human purpose by continuities of feeling, the gift ennobled by its source. Once received, gifts enter the inner life in the form of feeling, a blessed agitation answering the vitality of nature's forms; it need never be lost, since care acts through memory. Memory is ultimately heart-work, but it is more locally work of the mind's eye, a second sight related in complicated ways to the first: it restores to the mind what the senses once held and then released or disowned, but the sensations recalled in memory are not identical with those first impressions. Memory may be a ball-and-chain, but it may also be a transfiguring power, and in any event the recalled sensations, entering a new context of feeling, have come from afar, it is not to be supposed that they are their original selves or even carbon copies. For one thing, sensations recovered in memory have what the originals never had, a history. But again we distinguish between two kinds of memory. The first is simple, merely the power of recall, with an implication that what is recalled is required for use; a name, perhaps, or an occasion. This is the mnemonic power discussed by Frances Yates in the first chapters of *The Art of Memory*. Memory in that character uses the mind's eye to find what is lost, searching its memory-places for signs deposited along the way. The faculty is satisfied when it has found what it needs. Memory in Wordsworth and Rilke is different because its motive is different. Conscious or involuntary, memory is valuable to such poets because it enriches the life of feeling, sustains the imagination as a form of freedom. Involuntary memory is like fancy, satisfied with casual relations and conjunctions: voluntary memory corresponds to imagination in choice and freedom. The purpose of memory is to give sensations what they would otherwise lack, historical weight and density, narrative plenitude. Intensity is not in question: immediate sensations may or may not be intense, they may be more acute than those retained in the second life of memory, but they cannot have the same weight of time and feeling. Wordsworth was just as susceptible as any other poet to the fascination of immediacy, as the confessional lines quoted show, but he valued most the continuity of feeling as it is embodied in memory. Indeed, he often gives the impression of distrusting the intensity of the present sensation and of wishing to have it calmed and authenticated in memory, as in tranquillity. He wanted images to justify themselves according to criteria of "the heart" and to bring with them the resonance and distance of years:

> While with an eye made quiet by the power
> Of harmony, and the deep power of joy,
> We see into the life of things.

Only Wordsworth would have hit upon "quiet" as the word to draw the eye away from its greed and clamour toward the depths of harmony and joy before restoring it to its own idiom, deepened. The situation resembles the art of the storyteller by which, in Walter Benjamin's account, the object of the story is not to convey an event but to show the event embedded in the storyteller's life so that he may pass it on as experience to those listening. In Wordsworth, memory takes part in this work, turning into experience what is otherwise merely information. The eye is cleared of its despotism.

There is a corresponding passage in *The Notebooks of Malte Laurids Brigge* where Rilke speaks of memories:

> And still it is not yet enough to have memories. One must be able to forget them when they are many and one must have the great patience to wait until they come again. For it is not yet the memories themselves. Not till they have turned to blood within us, to glance and gesture, nameless and no longer to be distinguished from ourselves—not till then can it happen that in a most rare hour the first word of a verse arises in their midst and goes forth from them.[28]

The phrase "no longer to be distinguished from ourselves" marks the moment at which memory becomes insight; or rather at which sensations recovered and enriched in memory enter the stream of feeling to constitute the power we call insight. Insight is the consanguinity of feelings which, coming from many sources, enter and become the single state of man. At that point the eye and the mind's eye have collaborated, like perception and memory, to form a single stream in which feeling and thought are indistinguishable. This is Wordsworth's special power; he is

uniquely sensitive, among English poets, to those impressions
which are no longer to be distinguished from ourselves, and to
the occasions which provoke them. His sensual eye was not, in
fact, especially acute. When an incident is related both by
William and by Dorothy, her account is generally more vivid,
more precise, than his. But his special power consists in the
liaison of eye and mind's eye, the double power provokes his most
heartening and heart-rending poems. His characteristic theme is
not feeling but the history of feeling, the narrative hazard, the
whole process by which sensations become indistinguishable from
one's self. All is well with him so long as direct continuity is
maintained by an eye made calm and a mind's eye made deep,
but a crisis arises when these modes are separated and the circuit
of feeling is broken; a common predicament in Romantic poetry,
as in the "Dejection" Ode when Coleridge says of the natural
forms, "I see, not feel, how beautiful they are." "Blank" is the
word Coleridge uses, especially in his Notebooks, for the condition in which the circuit of feeling is broken and the imaginative
or moral impulse dies: it is the dreadful opposite of his "joy" or
"hope" because it testifies to an agnosticism directed against life
itself. "Existence itself gives a claim to Joy," he wrote.[29] Sight is
important to Coleridge and other Romantic poets only as a
productive means of feeling, but when the writer confesses that he
sees, not feels, the beauty of natural forms he means that the
circuit of feeling is broken by the exorbitance of sight, its refusal
to see itself as a member of a family. So long as sight remains
exorbitant, the experience cannot have the subjective glow which
Romantic writers value. To feel, as Susanne Langer says, is to do
something, not to have something; it is subjective because "felt
as action." The exorbitance of the eye imposes upon the experience the alien idiom of possession. Something more intimate is
congenial to Romantic writers. In *The Philosophy of Symbolic
Forms* Cassirer speaks of "transforming the passive world of mere
impressions, in which the spirit seems at first imprisoned, into a
world that is pure *expression* of the human spirit."[30] The same
desire obtains even when the spirit, subject confronting object,

feels its dominance and subjectivity can only take the form of force. When the eye is felt as a despot, however benevolent, the subject longs to release himself from the strain, preferably by converting the work of the eye to his inner purposes. Impressions can be registered as expressions only when the eye is calmed in a narrative life, a history, and the final stage is the conversion of its power; mind exerts itself as energy, transforming external into internal power. The despot is persuaded to join at last in a common purpose.

It appears that the spirit can never be satisfied, but at least we can say what form the satisfaction would take. It is not a choice of subject or object. Subject may be fixed, as in Augustan poetry, or free, as in the new sensibility and Romanticism: in any case it is easy to despise such freedom by calling it fluidity or chaos. Samuel Beckett remarks in his meditation upon Proust that "exemption from intrinsic flux in a given object does not change the fact that it is the correlative of a subject that does not enjoy such immunity: the observer infects the observed with his own mobility."[31] The mind is mollified, presumably, by a situation in which natural forms seem hospitable to feeling; or alternatively a situation in which those forms, despite their independence, make among themselves harmonies and congruences so complete as to appear human to human eyes. We allow, too, for a mind like that of Alain Robbe-Grillet's which insists upon assuming that the relation between man and the world is entirely arbitrary, merely the relation between a box and whatever it contains. The list of variant readings is incomplete. But we ought to emphasize a situation in which the external world seems so well-formed that the intervention of subjectivity in any form is felt as a vulgar intrusion. There is a passage in this spirit in one of Rilke's notebooks where the poet describing a Spanish landscape says that, far from finding release in it, he found it made new demands upon him:

> because there the external thing itself—tower, mountain, bridge—
> already possessed the unheard of, unsurpassable intensity of those
> inner equivalents by means of which it might have been represented.

Everywhere appearance and vision came, as it were, together in the object, in every one of them a whole inner world was exhibited, as though an angel, in whom space was included, were blind and looking into himself.[32]

It is an extraordinary passage, clairvoyant in perception. We are used to situations in Romantic poetry in which appearance and vision are felt as coming together in the subject, the normal confluence of such forces. But Rilke's testimony refers to such a condition of objectivity in the landscape that he concedes to it the intensity we generally reserve for subjectivity. However, the perfection of an absolute object requires a corresponding perceiver, who must be equally perfect if he is to qualify himself for such a task. The poet makes him an angel, who can register absolute being at once by looking into himself. The angel is essential subjectivity, the only "being" capable of receiving essential objectivity. Rilke's mind is extraordinary sensitive to those moments in which subject and object become so much at one that it is impossible to separate the physical and metaphysical elements. Or rather, extraordinarily sensitive to occasions on which objects in space appear to have done for themselves what, according to Idealist arguments, can only be done for them by the human imagination. Rilke's angels attend upon those moments. There is a glowing letter of August 1921 in which he ascribes the work of imagination in nature not to the natural forms of a landscape but to the air between them. He is speaking of the Valais, "this perhaps greatest valley of Europe," in which "a decorative group of beautifully cultivated and wooded hills enacts the richest changes of scene, landscapes compose themselves before one's eyes as if they were just created — and such objects (houses and trees) as there are within this purview have the same distances and tensions in relation to each other that we know from the rising constellations: it is as though space were created by this magnificent unfolding and interrelations of the details — an effect that could not be enjoyed so fully were it not that the air participates in an extraordinary way in each object, enveloping it and joyfully making every intervening space, even

into the backgrounds, the source of so many, one would almost
think, *felt* transitions."[33] The feeling Rilke finds in the Valais is
not presumed to be his own; it is as if the objects, incited by the
air between them, aspired to the most composed forms of
themselves.

An easier situation arises when visible objects seemed so certain
of themselves that they "resist the imagination almost successfully," in Stevens's phrase. Henry James has a meditation on
Rome in which he proposes a sense of the city and recognises
the advantage practised by the spirit of the place over the spirit
of the person. The theory of the Sublime is much concerned with
this advantage, but James's idiom is his own. Pondering the
advantage, he comes upon his old sense of making "a mere Rome
of words, talking of a Rome of my own which was no Rome of
reality." James attends to the Rome of words because it is the
Rome of feeling, it is what we make of something when, trying to
make sense of it, we let ourselves go some distance beyond that
exercise. James knows that the object to be perceived can easily
be overwhelmed by the perceiver, at least in his own mind: it is
our dearest modern conviction that perception is more glorious
than its occasion, the thing perceived. James knows that we
delight in this superstition. So he sets over against our Rome of
words the other Rome, the "enclosing fact" of the city, a place
resistant to our fictive greed, it cannot be dissolved in the spirit
of our consciousness. He has a quaint way of acknowledging the
second Rome; he does not verify it by recourse to its history,
architecture, or mass. James's evidence for the second Rome is a
fact of decorum and morality, that everyone who came to the
city "bore himself with the same good manners."[34] A mind is
satisfied when, having one Rome, it ensures the possession of
two; as Stevens in his poem to Santayana speaks of the historical
Rome and that "more merciful Rome / Beyond," the two cities
"alike in the make of the mind."[35] It is well that they are alike in
one respect, being otherwise different. It cannot be bad to have
two Romes for the tension between them: it would be bad if the
Rome of words gorged itself on the other so that nothing of the

palpable city remained in our minds. There is always a danger that perception may undermine the very content of perception, and all our techniques become ways of confounding ourselves. There should be a day in every year when consciousness allows itself to be suspended by fact in a Mardi Gras of mere reality. Perhaps Rilke had such a day in view when he wrote his great sonnet of the archaic torso of Apollo. The statue is broken, head and limbs have fallen away, but in another sense it could not be more complete. The eyes are lost, but the torso glows like a candelabrum, then like a star. The curve of the chest blinds the perceiver by the radiance of its presence. In fact, the roles of subject and object are reversed: it is not a case of an integral perceiver looking at a broken statue. The statue seems so complete that its authority is concentrated as if in an eye. For here on the torso, as Rilke writes, there is no place that does not see you: "denn da ist keine Stelle, / die dich nicht sieht." The sonnet ends, you must change your life, "Du musst dein Leben ändern," as if to say that to be worthy of the experience you must become, like the broken torso and despite the evidence, whole, complete, shining.

To revert to the purer eye: let us suppose that in moving from the harsh confrontation of subject and object the imagination is willing to live among doubts, confusions, half-lights, velleities. The risks are psychological, the imagination wants to enrich the mixture of its experiences and knows that it is likely to irritate ontologists and epistemologists alike by letting its procedures run wild. Subjectivity is likely to become inordinate and unruly. The texts from Rilke stand for the scruple which may attend upon subjectivity when it comes upon objects dazzlingly complete, requiring for perfection nothing that a mere perceiver can give. Generally, the scruple of subjectivity is not too strict, it lets the subject run loose if not wild. I end this section with an illustration of the liberties a subjective imagination is likely to take, and of its self-imposed limits. On September 30, 1949, Wallace Stevens received from Paule Vidal a painting by Tal Coat, a still-life featuring a Venetian glass bowl and various domestic bottles, glasses, and terrines. He was charmed by the picture, and within a few days he found himself thinking of the Venetian bowl as an angel and the domestic things as peasants. A few days later he wrote a poem of the picture, calling it "Angel Surrounded by Paysans," a meditation on the relation between this angel and those peasants. The angel says to one of the peasants:

> Yet I am the necessary angel of earth,
> Since, in my sight, you see the earth again,
> Cleared of its stiff and stubborn, man-locked set . . .[36]

More than two years later he commented on the poem, repeating that the angel is the angel of reality:

> This is clear only if the reader is of the idea that we live in a world of the imagination, in which reality and contact with it are the great blessings. For nine readers out of ten, the necessary angel will appear to be the angel of the imagination and for nine days out of ten that is true, although it is the tenth day that counts.[37]

The point of the illustration is this: we may assume that Stevens, charmed by the picture as a whole, was especially charmed by the suggestive difference in bearing between the Venetian glass and the other pieces, an aristocratic presence surrounded by common people. Letting his mind play upon the forms, Stevens made a distinction of class or caste between its objects, and from the distinction he made a relation between them in which the peasants find themselves capable of experiences aesthetic and spiritual; in the presence of the angel they see the earth again and truly. This is a description of the purer eye in the peasants as in Stevens: in Stevens, the Tal Coat picture is not dissolved but transfigured, it provokes a sense of relationships other than those it merely painted: in the peasants, it is as though a landscape of Burgundy were seen with Venetian eyes. The earth is seen "cleared of its stiff and stubborn, man-locked set"; it is my impression that this is how Thomson proposed to see it in *The Seasons.*

III: The Mind's Eye

What the purer eye sees is a situation compounded of man and nature, each term genially disposed toward its neighbour. There is a mutual convention by which conclusions are postponed and strict definitions are avoided. Wordsworth's compromise is based upon a corresponding assumption that a familial relation obtains between man and nature. The poet takes landscape and the visual forms as equivalent to the world because they are deemed the most permanent part of it and because landscape is blessedly indeterminate, its forms amenable, suggestive rather than assertive. Poetry becomes a token of peace on earth. Language, as Wordsworth says in the "Essay on Epitaphs," "if it do not uphold, and feed, and leave in quiet, like the power of gravitation or the air we breathe, is a counter-spirit, unremittingly and noiselessly at work, to subvert, to lay waste, to vitiate, and to dissolve." Language could uphold and feed because its proper analogies are paternal; it is a member of the family of man and nature. In *The Excursion* Wordsworth marvelled "how exquisitely the individual Mind . . . to the external World / Is fitted" and how exquisitely, too "the external World is fitted to the Mind." But Blake wrote in the margin of that treaty: "You shall not bring me down to believe such fitting & fitted. I know better & please your Lordship."[38] What Blake knew better is a story of eye, mind, and nature told in terms of energy and stress. Part of it may be recalled in his annotations on the *Discourses* of Reynolds. When Reynolds, speaking of colour, told young artists to "have recourse to nature herself . . . in comparison of whose true splendour the best coloured pictures are but faint and feeble," Blake answered, "Nonsense! Every Eye Sees differently. As the Eye, Such the Object."[39] It is the difference between seeing with and seeing through the eye. Blake insists upon withdrawing content and value from the object to the eye, and then from the eye to the mind; he refuses to compromise with matter or the senses, his cardinal term is imagination or vision. Fredric Jameson has spoken of "that instinctive idealism which characterizes the mind when it has to do with nothing but spiritual facts."[40] Blake insists, in theory more than in practice, upon turning material facts into spiritual facts, his syntax hastens the process by which perception turns objects into knowledge. In his comments on Berkeley he drives the philosopher to the end of the line, leaping the gap between man and God, extending the human imagination until it encompasses divinity: ignoring the fact that Berkeley insisted that the gap is absolute distance. The ground of the case is Blake's assertion that "man's perceptions are not bounded by organs of perception; he perceives more than sense (tho' ever so acute) can discover."[41] The argument is close to Santayana's in *The Sense of Beauty,* except that Santayana's version is far more urbane and it reserves for art and hypothesis the faculty which Blake ascribes to the mind itself. "Most things that are perceivable are not perceived so distinctly as to be intelligible," Santayana argues, "nor so delightfully as to be beautiful":

> If our eye had infinite penetration, or our imagination infinite elasticity, this would not be the case; to see would then be to understand and to enjoy. As it is, the degree of determination needed for perception is much less than that needed for comprehension or ideality. Hence there is room for hypothesis and for art.[42]

Santayana goes beyond Blake's answer to Locke: man's perceptions are greater than the sum of his impressions, even if reflection and self-consciousness are added to that side of the scale. Blake's quarrel with Locke amounts to three related arguments: first, that Locke grossly reifies the objects of knowledge; second, that he refuses to concede that a man's perceptions are in any respect increased or qualified by his mind; third, that he makes perception a closed rather than an open system.

There is a passage near the end of the sixth Book of Plato's *Republic* where Socrates is quizzing Glaucon about the senses, pointing out that while nothing more is required for the purpose of hearing than voice and the power of hearing, in the case of seeing a third thing is necessary, not only the object and the sense of sight but light. Light as the third requirement raised a question of God as its source, and therefore a question of the relation between man, the world, and the God of Light. The eye, Socrates says, is "the most sun-like of all the instruments of sense."[43] There is, however, a more daring passage in the *Theaetetus* where Socrates argues that sensory perception cannot make the whole of knowledge, for much of what is called knowledge consists of truths involving terms which are not objects of perception. In fact, Socrates maintains, sensory perception is not knowledge at all, knowledge consists in our reflection upon sensory impressions, not in the impressions themselves. Besides, the mind contemplates some things through the bodily faculties, but other things through its own instrumentality. Plato's denigration of the senses has been invoked in diverse causes, but normally to support an argument for the definition of man as spirit or soul. Meister Eckhart has a beautiful passage in which, quoting St. Gregory, "we cannot see the visible except with the invisible," he says that "the eye sees nothing corporal, lacking the a-corporal thing which quickens it to sight." "Subtract the mind," he says, "that is, the soul which is invisible, and the eye is open to no purpose, which before did see." Soul is, he continues, "the mean between God and creature. . . . If she prefers the inferior powers of her five senses to her higher ones whence comes her knowledge of celestial things, then she grows ignoble and base."[44] Those who speak of the senses in these terms have an interest in representing the relation between eye and mind as that of instrument to power. Power exceeds any one of its instruments, vision depends upon the cooperation of eye and mind, but it is the mind that quickens the eye to see: "whatever we see is seen *with the mind.*"[45] Bereft of the mind, the eye is in the predicament ascribed to Lady Macbeth in the sleep-walking scene. "She has light by her continually," we are told, and the doctor says, "you see her eyes are open," but the waiting-woman answers, "Ay, but their sense is shut." Mystics and Christian Platonists speak of the mind or soul; when Blake and Coleridge refer to imagination, we receive the word as secular equivalent of soul and register the supernatural aura felt in that idiom. Sustaining such language there is

the "self-creating word of God" to which Coleridge refers in
Biographia Literaria. St. Augustine speaks of the spirit's vision,
visio spiritalis, active even in darkness, as though the divine Light
were mediated through the human imagination.[46] It is part of the
same tradition that a thing may be felt as a presence precisely
in the degree to which it is excluded. A few months ago in
Dublin I saw a sequence of paintings by Charles Birchfield, mostly
domestic exteriors, a small town, houses, horses standing outside.
The paintings were meticulous, each object was given as though
it were imprisoned in its nature. There was every form of life
except the human form, the houses were like coffins, the horses
stood harnessed to carts as though they had long since given up
expecting their masters to arrive. The streets looked as though
they were awaiting some human attention that would never come.
Gradually, however, as one looked at the paintings, one found
the humanity, ostensibly excluded, suggesting itself in the measure of its exclusion. The mind insisted upon peopling the houses,
sending traffic through the streets, picking up the horses' reins.

Blake's attack upon the philosophy of five senses turns upon
the assertion that in practice the five are reduced to one and the
act of the mind is confounded. "Five windows light the cavern'd
Man," he sings in the mocking song of *Europe*, but more soberly
later in the poem:

> when the five senses whelm'd
> In deluge o'er the earth-born man; then turn'd the fluxile
> > eyes
> Into two stationary orbs, concentrating all things.[47]

The passage is concerned with the loss of visionary power, the
mobility of fluxile eyes directed by the imagination: now the eyes
are stopped, transfixed before their objects. By this single vision
all things are concentrated, at the cost of their lives, and the mind
is defeated. It cannot be far from that concentration to Locke's
swoon. In Coleridge the attitude is more devoutly Platonic. "We
should lose no opportunity of tracing words to their origin," he
advises, so that "we will be able to use the *language* of sight

without being enslaved by its affections." The point is that a word may be tied to sight and the thing seen, especially in a corrupt age, but the history of the word releases us from attention to surface meaning, allows us to think with the mind's eye of memory and, better still, imagination. Etymology is wiser than local meaning because it is free from the tie of surface. By pursuing a word to its origin, Coleridge says, we secure ourselves "from the delusive notion, that what is not *imageable* is likewise not *conceivable.*" Further: "to emancipate the mind from the despotism of the eye is the first step towards its emancipation from the influences and intrusions of the senses, sensations and passions generally." Our best hope in this way, Coleridge continues, is the faculty of abstraction, by which I assume he means the power of considering each fact in the light of a corresponding idea, the form in the light of form itself, as in the Platonic archetype. The superiority of one man over another consists in his greater power of abstraction: among the resources of language, those are best in which the power of abstraction is certified. "Hence," Coleridge says, "we are to account for the preference which the divine Plato gives to expressions taken from the objects of the ear, as terms of Music and Harmony, and in part at least for the numerical symbols, in which Pythagoras clothed his philosophy."[48] This is the point at which Coleridge, moving away from Wordsworth, approaches his own poetry: his characteristic theme is not the relation of man and nature, for natural forms are merely some of the occasions of human feeling, they are not important in themselves but as provocations. Coleridge's theme is the relation between man's immediate feeling and its ideal, permanent form; and then, in the love poems especially, the situation that arises when such a form is identified with a beloved image, as in "Constancy to an Ideal Object." The comic version of this constancy is given, incidentally, in *Tom Jones* when Tom, false to Sophia in her mere empirical nature, leads her to the mirror so that she may see the ideal object to which, he protests, he will henceforth prove constant. Coleridge's poem ends:

> And art thou nothing? Such thou art, as when
> The woodman winding westward up the glen
> At wintry dawn, where o'er the sheep-track's maze
> The viewless snow-mist weaves a glist'ning haze,
> Sees full before him, gliding without tread,
> An image with a glory round its head;
> The enamoured rustic worships its fair hues,
> Nor knows he makes the shadow, he pursues![49]

The fact is here considered in the light of an idea, and it is a question how much of the fact survives. The survival of the idea is guaranteed, since it is a function of the mind. Of Coleridge's supreme fiction, as of Stevens's, the case is clear: it must be abstract. But the idea is considered, too, under the sign of fact, the fact cannot be easily set aside, Coleridge acknowledges it as a presence in "full" — "sees full before him, gliding without tread." Feeling adheres to the fact, however subjective its composition. Officially, the poem tries to separate Coleridge from his feeling by consigning it to the enamoured rustic, but the separation cannot be complete, Coleridge's irony turns upon himself. The poem exerts upon his feeling the abstractive power which Coleridge recommends in the handling of language, but there is no question of a complete emancipation from the despotism of feeling: feeling moves between fact and idea, but it is not dissolved. Coleridge's theme is the scruple which attends upon the simultaneous possession of fact and idea, it must be abstract because the mind's power must be declared.

I have remarked the supernatural aura which surrounds the imagination in Blake and Coleridge; it is also present in Stevens when abstraction is the theme. "The abstract does not exist," he concedes, "but it is certainly as immanent; that is to say, the fictive abstract is as immanent in the mind of the poet as the idea of God is immanent in the mind of the theologian."[50] Obviously a belief in God cannot be refuted if its ground is the propensity of the believer's mind. Coleridge is one of those poets in whom the fictive abstract is to an unusual degree immanent, and when Stevens says that the ravishments of truth are fatal to the truth itself, he speaks pure Coleridge but translates his metaphysics into secular, that is to say into psychological, terms. "How clean the sun when seen in its idea," Stevens writes; that is, when seen as if in an original heaven at once abstract and accessible. Sustaining that desire there is Stevens's fundamental motive, to find the power of God active in man rather than in nature. To the Augustan poet God's power is chiefly manifest in the created, visible forms of nature: to Wordsworth, in a sense of the fellowship of man and nature: to Blake and Coleridge, in man's imagination, his divine part. There is a passage in the *Hexameron* of St. Ambrose where man is declared to be made in the image of God, *ad imaginem Dei,* by virtue of his mind, and especially by virtue of his ability to imagine things he has not seen; the mind, "quae considerando spectat omnia."[51] Erwin Panofsky has shown that in the work of Federico Zuccari, "without contesting the necessity of sensory perception, the Idea was reinvested with its apriori and metaphysical character by deriving the ideational faculty of the human mind directly from divine knowledge: the dignity of genius is justified by its origin in God."[52] In such a tradition the transaction between a man's eyes and the visible surface of things is bound to appear superficial, unless its mere instrumentality is in question. True vision is an internal power, divine in origin, equally active in darkness as in light.

Even in less Platonic traditions we find a desire to make the experience of sight more profound, seeing through the surface of the object; the desire to see with something of the depth and fullness of the mind's activity. The history of modern painting discloses a desire to make eyes do the work of the mind, or appear to do so, accepting the standards of mind. I think it also accounts for Stevens's desire to represent a clairvoyance of perception in which organic limitations are transcended. "Perhaps there is a degree of perception," he says, "at which what is real and what is imagined are one: a state of clairvoyant observation, accessible or possibly accessible to the poet or, say, the acutest poet."[53] It may also explain why Yeats and other poets of "the tragic

generation" engaged in psychical research, hermetic writing, and
magic, out of a desire to attach once again to phenomena, as
apprehended by the mind, the halo of presence torn from them
by science and positivism. In "In Memory of Major Robert
Gregory" Yeats writes:

> We dreamed that a great painter had been born
> To cold Clare rock and Galway rock and thorn,
> To that stern colour and that delicate line
> That are our secret discipline
> Wherein the gazing heart doubles her might.

The secret discipline is the contemplation of one's own mind;
Yeats admired it especially in Shelley's Cythna. If a reader asks
why the landscape of Clare and Galway is necessary, the answer is
that such imaginations need an obstacle. The end of the process
may be a state of trance or revery, but the process itself requires
stimulation, obstacles, provocations on which energy may expend
itself. The gazing heart doubles her might because it sees with
the mind's eye: energy from that source bounces back from its
ostensible object. "Gaze" is Yeats's word for the internal power
which Blake calls "vision": the internal light finds itself reflected
in the landscape, and the light returning to the mind is in that
way doubled. It is the visual equivalent of the perfection for
which Eliot chose an aural figure in "The Dry Salvages":

> music heard so deeply
> That it is not heard at all, but you are the music
> While the music lasts.

An empiricist would say that Yeats's landscape is not seen at all
but cheated out of sight. In Canto 83 Pound mocks Yeats in
this way:

> and uncle William dawdling around Notre Dame
> in search of whatever
>   paused to admire the symbol
> with Notre Dame standing inside it[54]

— an incident which has its counterpart and perhaps its origin in
The Tragic Muse when Nick Dormer, replying to Gabriel Nash's

"interest in the beautiful," directs that interest toward the Notre
Dame: "Ah, the beautiful—there it stands, over there! I am not
so sure about yours—I don't know what I've got hold of. But
Notre Dame *is* solid; Notre Dame *is* wise; on Notre Dame the
distracted mind can rest."[55] Nick's case is that the mind's
distractions are self-induced, wilful, corrupt, they need to be
taken out of themselves, startled into a true sense of proportion
by seeing irrefutable solidity and wisdom. This makes the general
case against Symbolism that it merely projects the poet's will upon
an inoffensive landscape, and then deems significant what is
merely, as a result of corrupt attention, portentous. According
to Pound, Yeats sees the symbol first because it is a function of
his grossly symbolizing imagination; some time later, perhaps, he
adverts to a cathedral trapped inside the aura. "Yeats had bad
eyes, saw nothing": Robert Lowell's version in *The Dolphin;* but
Yeats's eyes were good enough to see, in "Meditations in Time of
Civil War,"

> The stilted water-hen
> Crossing stream again
> Scared by the splashing of a dozen cows

—where "stilted" proves that eye and mind's eye are in focus.
Pound thought of Yeats as if he were Gabriel Nash, of whom
Richard Blackmur wrote that he was "the namesake of incentive
and possibility and unaffixed freedom, and indeed everything
good unless by chance you took it seriously."[56] Pound disapproved
of Symbolism because he spoke for values embodied in the
cathedral, its texture and line, independent of the perceiver:
Symbolism spoke for itself, with cathedrals for incentive and
excuse. But his teasing of Yeats ignores an entire dimension of
Yeats's art which transcends the limitations of Symbolism by
recourse to an imagination essentially dramatic. Pound thought
of form in strongly visual terms. Form is that which comes into
view and establishes itself before our eyes, we recognise it in mass
and line, the clearer the better. He disapproved of Impressionism
in painting because its pictures gave so much to the eye in colour

and texture that they neglected the visual aspect of line. He resented any art which blurred the demarcation between form and matrix, event and setting.

In such a quarrel the empiricist is in a strong position, nine days out of ten, unless he defeats himself by denying perception altogether. But there is a difficult moment when the argument cannot be settled in Johnson's stone-kicking way. There is a remarkable chapter in Foucault's study of madness, where he considers the status of what a madness sees; and presents the Cartesian stance of doubt as the great exorcism of madness. "Descartes closes his eyes and plugs up his ears the better to see the true brightness of essential daylight; thus he is secured against the dazzlement of the madman who, opening his eyes, sees only night, and, not seeing at all, believes he sees when he imagines. In the uniform lucidity of his closed senses, Descartes has broken with all possible fascination, and if he sees, he is certain of seeing that which he sees. While before the eyes of the madman, drunk on a light which is darkness, rise and multiply images incapable of criticizing themselves (since the madman *sees* them), but irreparably separated from being (since the madman sees nothing)."[57] Foucault is referring to that part of the third *Meditation* in which Descartes abjures the evidences of his senses and turns the mind's eye upon himself. "Holding converse with myself," he says, "and looking deeply within, I shall try to become more familiar with myself, and know myself better." In effect, he tries to discover within, by force of self-consciousness, the plenitude which empiricists claim to see in the world at large. The only requirement is that objects of perception are now determined by their source in the imagination that produces them; a relation to an externally valid world is not proposed. Speaking of ideas, Descartes says that if they are considered in themselves and not in relation to something else, they cannot be false, "for whether I imagine a goat or a chimera, it is as true that I am imagining the latter as that I am imagining the former." I am not sure that modern literature could have gone very far in the theory and practice of fiction if Descartes had not pointed in this direction. Stevens says in *Notes toward a Supreme Fiction,* "Adam / In Eden was the father of Descartes," presumably because Adam thought himself into being, or at least into human being. Much of modern poetry depends upon a similar act of the mind, with only as much dependence upon other things as is inevitable in the nature of the case: if it is considered in itself and not in relation to something else, the most blatant fiction cannot be refuted, any more than Descartes's chimera or Husserl's flute-playing centaur. It is difficult to consider fictions in relation to something else in the world because evidence in such cases is hard to establish, and there are writers who delight in undermining it. Borges, for instance, whose mind revels in gargoyles and griffins: has he not described a place called Tlön, a planet congenitally idealist, for whose citizens the world is not a concourse of objects in space but a heterogeneous series of independent acts, successive and temporal but not spatial? Borges brings to ironic conclusion the creed that divinity resides within ourselves: whatever we create is created just as evidently as the natural forms created by God, perhaps more evidently than those if subjective criteria are enforced. Another part of the irony consists in the demonstration that language, conventionally regarded as safely sustained by its relation to things, is just as idealist as its master.

The question turns upon the character of imagination, its disposition to alter an old world or raise a new one. There is a charming passage on this theme in the commentary on Blake by Yeats and Ellis. Blake's teaching, they say, may be given in a few words. One: "Nature is merely a name for one form of mental existence. Art is another and a higher form. Nature—or creation—is a result of the shrinkage of consciousness—originally clairvoyant—under the rule of the five senses, and of argument and law." Two: "In Imagination only we find a Human Faculty that touches nature at one side, and spirit on the other. Imagination may be described as that which is sent bringing spirit to nature, entering into nature, and seemingly losing its spirit, that nature being revealed as symbol may lose the power to

delude."[58] Presumably nature loses the power to delude when its
reality is not identified with its appearance but rather with the
halo of radiance which surrounds it when seen by the mind's
eye, the impression of depth which sustains it, or the mind's
double might in its presence. Reality then appears not as surface
but as act, the act of imagination, stimulated by the given world.
This explains why Blake repudiates memory. Annotating Wordsworth, he writes that "Imagination is the Divine Vision not of the
World, or of Man, nor from Man as he is a Natural Man, but
only as he is a Spiritual Man. Imagination has nothing to do with
Memory."[59] The reason is, as Yeats and Ellis observe, that art
rises to its true place only when it is set free from memory "that
binds it to Nature." To Blake, memory is like Locke's reflection,
a leisurely indulgence after the fact of sensation, the fading of
perception: like reflection, it inserts itself in the gap between
subject and object, thereby keeping each in its separate place.
Memory is to Blake what sight was to Stevens on a dismal occasion, merely "a museum of things seen."

The essential power of imagination, a quality of spirit, is
the power of making fictions and making sense of life by that
means. Fiction is the most available form of freedom, freedom of
feeling and action. The theory of fiction is as interesting as the
theory of transformational grammar, and for the same reason,
because both procedures testify to our freedom. We quarrel
about innate ideas, but we defend innate fictions. It is not
necessary to suppose that our freedom, even in making fictions,
is unlimited, we do not create from nothing. Writers accept the
limitation of words at least in theory, though they struggle to
circumvent it in practice; they know that words serve two masters,
the purity of the work of art and the impurity of common use.
Words used with pure intention drag impure allegiance into the
sanctuary of art; there is no help for this situation. The novelist
makes his fiction, and the normal means is by reciting a story,
because stories, like lives, are temporal and they begin and end.
If he wants something more subtle, the novelist secretes it in the
texture of his story. In return for the story, the available part of

fiction, the novelist claims the right to qualify his report, insinuating doubts and hesitations where the story would run boldly from one episode to the next. Conrad's narrator confesses that his western eyes failed to see what eastern eyes would have seen at once: we take this as saying that fiction is a mixture of freedom and necessity in various proportions. In the major novelists the strain between freedom claimed and necessity acknowledged is a sign of the depth from which the feeling comes. Sight being the standard medium of knowledge, such fictions are often inhabited by ghosts, and ghosts have two qualities, they have only visual existence, and they speak only when spoken to. Since they can be seen but not encompassed by sight, they testify to what lies beyond knowledge.

Fictions are an outrage to empiricists when they appear to be sustained chiefly from within by the act of imagination. Santayana has spoken of "the sphere of significant imagination, of relevant fiction, of idealism become the interpretation of the reality it leaves behind."[60] A reader of modern fiction often finds himself thinking of novels in this way as commentaries upon a superseded text. We say that the fictive imagination makes its own laws without censorship from nature or society, but secretly we hope that the laws it makes will turn out to be congenial to the laws of nature. For the same reason we welcome new discoveries in form and expression, but secretly we hope they will turn out to have as much continuity as change in their characters. We hope that the novelist will find it desirable if not necessary to work with beginnings, middles, and ends, principles and destinies, the counterparts if not the equivalents of their companions in organic life. It is a comfort to know that the most accomplished fictionist must compromise, and that compromise is inscribed in his materials, paint, stone, sound, words. It is hoped that fictions will seem less threatening when we have lived with them for a while and grown used to their blatancy: that gradually they will come to appear natural, making a treaty with the vernacular ways of language.

If fiction moves between freedom and compromise, prophesy lives between personality and fate. The prophet is more than a person, but by fate rather than arrogance. To Blake, prophesy is the chief form of freedom, imagination, energy. "If it were not for the Poetic or Prophetic character," he says, "the Philosophic & Experimental would soon be at the ratio of all things, & stand still, unable to do other than repeat the same dull round over again."[61] What the prophet speaks is wisdom because it does not rest upon individual perception; he commands past, present, and future. The freedom of tone we find in the prophetic poems of Blake or of Smart depends upon the feeling that in these voices the common distinction of subject and object is dissolved. Visual analogies no longer apply. The conventional relation between word and thing is overwhelmed: the word suffuses the thing to the point at which the world as a concourse of objects is superseded by language as a sequence of sounds, there is nothing in reality that has not become verbal. But the words do not rely upon subjectivity, in any limiting sense, for their force, they are words in a ritual. Power has been transferred to the words as though the imagination, fleeing the world of given forms, were to secrete itself in the lexicon, issuing without warning as prophesy. In Smart's *Song to David* nothing in the world is explicated as though its nature were stable, given once for all, but rather as though it had now to be given its nature by a poet speaking the right words. The world, in that poem, is invoked rather than observed, it is called to the eye of the mind, as Yeats says in several plays. The assumption upon which it is invoked is, as Cassirer says of the idealist position in language generally, "that the world of things and the world of names form a single undifferentiated chain of causality and hence a single reality."[62] The poet is a mage of language.

We have lived with these assumptions a long time now. Perhaps we are tired of them. We repeat, as in a daze, that the mind creates reality by its own act. Modern literature is moving from the idiom of knowledge, subject and object, to the declared immediacy of action, freedom, and gesture. The advantages are felt at once: a more direct sense of life, the old gaps transcended. But we face many difficulties. Action is often subverted from within, we fall from the grace of action to the ignominy of motion, accident, caprice. Many of our acts have lost the name of action and are stretched across a void. Perception loses value when it has come to the point of threatening the very object and content of perception. Richard Blackmur has spoken of our new knowledges as "techniques for finding trouble in ourselves and in the world" so that "it is almost as if to make trouble had become the creative habit of the general mind."[63] As action, anything goes. I think this accounts for the impression of ennui in Samuel Beckett's recent work and for the recoil from intelligence so evident in many intelligent writers. In that respect Lionel Trilling is right: we have lost confidence in mind, though to say that it is not, as we have seen, to dispose of the question. To Beckett, individual perceptions are "puny exploits," these treaties between man and nature merely enact "the farce of giving and receiving." The most sensitive writers today find themselves in the predicament of Eliot's Gerontion:

> I have lost my sight, smell, hearing, taste and touch:
> How should I use them for your closer contact?
>
> These with a thousand small deliberations
> Protract the profit of their chilled delirium,
> Excite the membrane, when the sense has cooled,
> With pungent sauces, multiply variety
> In a wilderness of mirrors.

But we cannot rest in that predicament. It is still a question of using whatever old and new skills we have in the hope of finding not only actions but principles of actions. Stevens, inquisitor of structures, found himself asking in the "Esthétique du Mal":

> One might have thought of sight, but who could think
> Of what it sees, for all the ill it sees?

It is a happy concession, but perhaps premature. We resort to Rilke again. His panther, imprisoned, paces round and round the circle of the cage, eyes weary of the geometry of the bars. But every now and then, the poem says, the shutter of the panther's eyes is lifted, and an image rushes in, moves through the stillness of his limbs to end in his heart: "und hort im Herzen auf zu sein." Rilke does not say why the shutter lifts now and then drops down again upon the panther's eyes: the exhilaration of change, perhaps, is sufficient explanation. Not every image that enters rushes to the heart: we may concede that many sensory events are wasted, even when the mind participates in them. Rilke's poem seems to say that every image is wasted unless it ends in the heart. Wordsworth says as much. In both poets the criterion is not knowledge, consciousness, or even action in itself; it is the "heart-work" by which sensory and intellectual events become part of our affections and are no longer to be distinguished from ourselves.

A final point. We have been considering several attitudes to experience and many different versions of the imagination, but two seem to assert themselves with particular force. There is, for the first, a form of mind which enforces upon experience the fixity of a visible form, preferably that of print in a book. There is, for such a mind, no moment too soon for the intervention of intelligence: experience has hardly begun before it is forced to answer to a demand for clarity, precision, and visible form. This is what defines "Augustanism"; the fact that the paradigm of imperial Rome was already stationed above experience had the effect of making the intelligence intervene, if anything, pre-maturely; the official form which experience ought to take was already inscribed, authority preceded its occasion. Augustanism is an art of observation and it discriminates mainly in terms of truth and vanity, but the defect of its merit is that it has little interest in other discriminations or other relations between one thing and another. At the other extreme there is a form of mind which postpones the intervention of intelligence in the hope of offering hospitality to more and more experience. This brings together such writers as Addison and Thomson. There is a passage in Thomas Pynchon's novel *The Crying of Lot 49* where Oedipa Maas speaks of wanting to believe "that the unconscious would be

like any other room, once the light was let in." Addison wanted to
believe the same thing, and to open the room kept shut by
Augustanism and labelled as dangerous. Hawthorne is acting in
the same spirit when he refers to the moon, when Robin is waiting
on the steps of the church in "My Kinsman, Major Molyneux,"
"creating, like the imaginative power, a beautiful strangeness in
familiar objects." The question of truth does not arise, the
strangeness is welcome because beautiful; the imaginative power
is willing to postpone the anatomy of truth in favour of immediate
plenitude of sensation. The categories are subjective, psychological, sensory rather than epistemological in any strict respect:
what is deemed important is the richness of impression. Clearly
in such a mood the intelligence is kept in suspense, it is not
allowed to intervene lest it curb the flow of feeling. The two forms
of mind do not necessarily differ in the quantity or the quality of
intelligence but rather in the degree of patience which each
exhibits: one form is more willing than the other to defer
judgment, lest its application be premature and exorbitant.

Notes

1. Robert Duncan, *Derivations* (London: Fulcrum Press, 1968), p. 102.
2. Emily Dickinson, *Complete Poems*, edited by Thomas H. Johnson,
(London: Faber and Faber, 1970), pp. 486-487.
3. Blake, *Complete Writings*, edited by Geoffrey Keynes (London:
Oxford University Press, 1969), p. 793.
4. Hans Jonas, *The Phenomenon of Life* (New York: Harper and Row,
1966), pp. 136f.
5. C. D. Broad, *Examination of McTaggart's Philosophy* (Cambridge:
Cambridge University Press, 1938), Vol. II, Part I, p. 64.
6. Pope, *Poetical Works*, edited by Herbert Davis (London: Oxford
University Press, 1966), p. 562.
7. Ibid., p. 239.
8. Cf. Robert E. Schofield, *Mechanism and Naturalism: British Natural
Philosophy in the Age of Reason* (Princeton: Princeton University Press,
1970), p. 23.
9. Pope, *Poetical Works*, p. 257.
10. Philip Larkin, *The Less Deceived* (Hessle, Yorkshire: Marvell Press,
1955).
11. Maurice Merleau-Ponty, *The Primacy of Perception*, edited by James
M. Edie (Evanston: Northwestern University Press, 1964), p. 184.

12. William Empson, *Seven Types of Ambiguity* (London: Chatto and Windus, third edition, 1953), p. 68.

13. Charles Tomlinson, *The Necklace* (Fantasy Press, 1955).

14. Pope, *Poetical Works*, p. 526.

15. Ibid., p. 252.

16. Ibid., pp. 25-26.

17. Ibid., p. 357.

18. Cf. R. Frazer, "The Origin of the Word 'Image' " in *English Literary History*, Vol. XXVII, pp. 149-161.

19. *The Spectator,* edited by Donald F. Bond (Oxford: Clarendon Press, 1965), Vol. III, p. 569.

20. Wallace Stevens, *Collected Poems* (London: Faber and Faber, 1955), p. 385.

21. Thomson, *Poetical Works,* edited by J. Logie Robertson (London: Oxford University Press, 1965, reprint of 1746 text), pp. 35-36.

22. Akenside, *Poems* (London, 1772), p. 82.

23. Coleridge, *Collected Letters,* edited by Earl Leslie Griggs (Oxford: Clarendon Press, 1956), Vol. II, p. 709. (Letter of March 23, 1801.)

24. Coleridge, *Philosophical Lectures 1818-1819,* edited by Kathleen Coburn (London: Pilot Press, 1949), p. 434n.

25. Susanne K. Langer, *Mind: An Essay on Human Feeling, Volume I* (Baltimore: Johns Hopkins Press, 1967), p. 23.

26. Rilke, *Sämtliche Werke,* Vol. II (Inel-Verlag, 1963), pp. 82-84.

27. Coleridge, *Poetical Works,* edited by E. H. Coleridge (London: Oxford University Press, reprint, 1969), pp. 404-405.

28. Rilke, *The Notebooks of Malte Laurids Brigge,* translaged by M. D. Herter Norton (New York: Capricorn Books, 1958), pp. 26-27.

29. Coleridge, *Notebooks 1815-1816,* No. 4292.

30. Ernst Cassirer, *The Philosophy of Symbolic Forms,* translated by Ralph Manheim (New Haven: Yale University Press, 1953), Vol. I, pp. 80-81.

31. Samuel Beckett, *Proust* (London: John Calder, reprint, 1965, p. 17.

32. Rilke, *Briefe aus den Jahren 1914-21,* quoted in *Duino Elegies,* translated by J. B. Leishman and Stephen Spender (London: Hogarth Press, 1939), p. 18.

33. Cf. Hans Egor Holthusen, *Rainer Maria Rilke,* translated by J. P. Stern (Cambridge: Bowes and Bowes, 1952), p. 48.

34. Henry James, *William Wetmore Story and his Friends* (London: Thames and Hudson, 1963), Vol. II, pp. 208-209.

35. Stevens, *Collected Poems,* p. 508.

36. Ibid., pp. 496-497.

37. Stevens, *Letters,* edited by Holly Stevens (New York: Knopf, 1966), p. 753. (Letter of May 29, 1952).

38. Blake, *Complete Writings,* p. 784.

39. Ibid., p. 456.

40. Fredric Jameson, *The Prison-House of Language* (Princeton: Princeton University Press, 1972), p. 103.

41. Blake, *Complete Writings,* p. 97.

42. Plato, *The Republic,* translated by Paul Shorey (London: Heinemann, 1935), Loeb edition, 508B, Vol. II, p. 101.

44. Franz Pfeiffer, *Meister Eckhart,* translated by C. de B. Evans (London: Watkins, 1924), pp. 288-289.

45. Agnes Arber, *The Mind and the Eye: A Study of the Biologist's Standpoint* (Cambridge: Cambridge University Press, 1954), p. 115.

46. Augustine, *De Genesi ad litteram,* PL, XXXIV, 458, Lib. XII C.vi: "ubi nihil videntes oculis corporis, animo tamen corporales imagines intuemur, seu veras, sicut ipsa corpora videmus, et memoria retinemus; seu fictas, sicut cogitatio formare potuerit. Aliter enim cogitamus Carthaginem quam novimus, aliter Alexandriam quam non novimus." Quoted in Peter Clemoes, "Mens absentia cogitans in *The Seafarer* and *The Wanderer"* in D. A. Pearsall and R. A. Waldron (editors), *Medieval Literature and Civilization: Studies in Memory of G. N. Garmonsway* (London: University of London, Athlone Press, 1969), pp. 62-77.

47. Blake, *Complete Writings,* p. 241.

48. Quoted in Alice D. Snyder, *Coleridge on Logic and Learning* (New Haven: Yale University Press, 1929), pp. 126-127.

49. Coleridge, *Poetic Works,* p. 456.

50. Stevens, *Letters,* edited by Holly Stevens (New York: Knopf, 1966), p. 434. (Letter of January 12, 1943).

51. Quoted in Clemoes, *supra.*

52. Erwin Panofsky, *Idea,* translated by Joseph J. S. Peake (Columbia, south Carolina: University of South Carolina Press, 1968), pp. 91-92.

53. Stevens, *Opus Posthumous* (New York: Knopf, 1957), p. 166.

54. Pound, *Cantos* (London: Faber and Faber, 1954), p. 563.

55. Henry James, *The Tragic Muse* (London: Rupert Hart-Davis, 1948 reprint of 1890 edition), p. 139.

56. R. P. Blackmur, Introduction to *The Tragic Muse* (New York: Dell, 1961), p. 9.

57. Michel Foucault, *Madness and Civilization,* translated by Richard Howard (London: Tavistock Publications, 1967), pp. 108-109.

58. Edwin John Ellis and W. B. Yeats (editors), *The Works of William Blake* (London: Quaritch, 1893), Vol. I, p. xii.

59. Blake, *Complete Writings,* p. 783.

60. Santayana, *Interpretations of Poetry and Religion* (New York: Harper and Row, reprint, 1957), p. 290.

61. Blake, *Complete Writings,* p. 97.

62. Ernst Cassirer, *The Philosophy of Symbolic Forms,* translated by Ralph Manheim (New Haven: Yale University Press, 1953), Vol. I, p. 118.

63. R. P. Blackmur, *Anni Mirabiles 1921-1925* (Washington: Library of Congress, 1956), p. 14.

"The Word Within a Word"

The publication of the first drafts of *The Waste Land*[1] has not greatly eased the difficulty of reading the poem. We now know that the poem issued, however circuitously, from the unhappiness of Eliot's first marriage—though certain lines and passages in the first drafts were written before 1915—but we hardly know what to make of that fact, unless it prompts us to say that the dominant feeling in the poem is not universal despair but particular guilt, and that the specific movement of feeling through the words corresponds, however obscurely, to the act of penance. Some readers of *The Waste Land* feel that Eliot is saying: "God, I thank thee that I am not as the rest of men, extortioners, unjust, adulterers, or even as this small house-agent's clerk." But this sense of the poem is unworthy, false to its spirit as a whole, though there are a few passages which support it. The area of feeling which the poem inhabits is the general provenance of guilt, fear, dread; the presence of disgust, including self-disgust, is not surprising. The first drafts show, and this is more to the point, that the poet's original sense of his poem made it, even more than the final version, a medley. Pound's criticism tightened the poem, but did not otherwise alter its movement. One characteristic of the poetry remains. Eliot's poems often try to escape from the emotional condition which incited them, not by willing its opposite but by working through a wide range of alternative conditions. The poems find safety and relief in numbers. One mood is answered not by another, equal and opposite, but by a diversity of moods. It is the diversity that saves. The medley of poems which eventually became *The Waste Land* was designed, it appears, with this diversity in view. To the charge that Eliot's poem is the work of a Pharisee, therefore, I would not reply that on the contrary it is the work of a publican, but rather that it effects a movement of feeling to make penance possible. Diversity, number, and allusion are the auspices under which the poem moves.

I want to suggest now that this sense of the poem is related to our recognition of its character as a distinctively American work. Specifically, the poem is, in Hawthorne's terminology, a romance. In the Preface to *The House of the Seven Gables,* Hawthorne distinguished between romance and novel. The novel aims at minute fidelity to the probable, but the romance, claiming "a certain latitude," proposes to present "the truth of the human heart" under circumstances "to a great extent of the writer's own choosing or creation."[2] There has always been an implication, in later comments on the romance, that it is the form of fiction most congenial to those feelings for which social correlatives are not available; or, if available, seriously inadequate. It is a commonplace that the romance, in Hawthorne's sense, holds a special position in American literature and that it is particularly serviceable to the writer who feels his imagination driven back upon its own resources. One of the tenable generalizations we continue to make about English literature is that its position is not desperate in this regard. The English writer generally thinks himself ready to establish his feeling in a particular setting and to let it develop and take its chance there. He declares a certain confidence in representing the life of feeling in terms of man, nature, and society. Nearly everything is allowed to depend upon the relation of man to the society in which he lives, the relation of person to person and to place. We say that English literature is personal, meaning that it is social, historical, and political. We do not say this of American literature. The question of locality is important to American writers, not least to Hawthorne in *The House of the Seven Gables,* but in American literature generally, and especially in the literature of the nineteenth century, a shadow falls between person and place. The feelings in the case are rarely entrusted to that relation, or indeed to any other: there is an impression that such feelings cannot hope to be fulfilled in such relations. There is a remainder of feeling which cries for release in dream, nightmare and fantasy. I want to pursue the notion that *The Waste Land* is best understood as an American romance.

It may be useful to recall Eliot's sense of American literature. He rejected the assertion that there is an American language distinct from English: in his view, both languages use the same notes, even if the fingering is sometimes different. He was not of Mencken's party in that argument. As for the literature, he registered New England as a moral presence, a regiment in the army of unalterable law, but he was not intimidated by it. He reflected upon the complex fate of being an American when he read Hawthorne and, still more, Henry James, who embodied one of the great possibilities consistent with that fate. In an essay on James he wrote that "it is the final perfection, the consummation of an American to become, not an Englishman, but a European — something which no born European, no person of any European nationality, can become."[3] Of the relation between Eliot and Whitman it is enough to say that Whitman is audible, for some good but more ill, in the third section of "The Dry Salvages," providing Eliot with a somewhat insecure tone. Of Mark Twain Eliot is on record as saying in praise that he was one of those writers who discover "a new way of writing, valid not only for themselves but for others,"[4] but I cannot recall any occasion on which Eliot moved in Twain's direction, despite "the river with its cargo of dead negroes" in "The Dry Salvages." The question of his relation to Poe is far more interesting, because it is strange that he should have had any interest in such a writer. In fact, he did not admire Poe's poems, he thought them adolescent things; Poe had never grown up. But there were two aspects of the matter which he could not ignore. The first concerned Poe's style of incantation which, Eliot said, "because of its very crudity, stirs the feelings at a deep and almost primitive level."[5] Eliot had his own style of incantation, and he was greatly taken by Poe as a master in the singing style. The second consideration was that Poe's work, fruitless in the English and American traditions, had entered the sensibilities of the great French poets and especially of Baudelaire,

Mallarmé, and Valéry. Eliot was interested in this event, and he
pondered it. There is almost a suggestion that Poe had somehow
achieved the final perfection of an American by becoming a
European, reincarnated in Baudelaire, Mallarmé, and Valéry.
Eliot was strongly engaged by Poe, as by Swinburne, for a similar
reason, the call of one verbalist to another.

The great interest of American literature arises, it is commonly
agreed, from the sense of American feeling as making a new start,
every day, with little or nothing regarded as capital saved from
yesterday. The world is all before the American writers. So these
writers naturally think of making everything new, they do not feel
overwhelmed by the weight of previous achievement. American
writers burn their bridges behind them, relegating the previous,
as James said of his compatriots generally in *The American Scene*,
to the category of wan misery. If *The Waste Land* is written by an
American who has set out to make himself a European, its chief
labour toward that perfection is the assumption of the burden of
history. The allusions in Eliot's poem show not the extent of his
learning but the gravity of the whole enterprise, the range of those
responsibilities he is ready to accept in such a cause. What most of
the allusions say is: "there have been other times, not utterly lost
or forgotten; we ourselves were not born this morning."

We may press the argument a little further. If English literature
is devoted to the relation between person, place, and time, it acts
by a corresponding syntax of prescribed relations. The first result
is that the chief function of one word is to lead the mind to the
next. No detail in *Middlemarch* is as important as the entire
network of relations, word by word, sentence by sentence: the
reader's mind is not encouraged to sink into the recesses of a word,
but to move forward until the prescribed affiliations are complete.
The modesty with which a word sends the reader's mind running
to the next is the verbal equivalent of dependency in a given
society, as one person accepts his enabling relation to another.
But the modern revolution in such American poems as *The Waste
Land* and *Hugh Selwyn Mauberley* depends upon a different sense

of life and therefore upon a different syntax. One's first reading of these poems leaves an impression of their poetic quality as residing in their diction: the animation of the verse arises from the incalculable force of certain individual words or phrases which stay in the mind without necessarily attracting to their orbit the words before or after. The memorable quality of those phrases seems to require a clear space on all sides, and it has little need of before and after. I take this to mean that the relations to which the words of an American poem refer are not prescribed or predictive but experimental. Around each word there is a space or a void in which nothing is anticipated, nothing enforced. Every relation must be invented, as if the world had just begun. Harold Rosenberg has argued that this is the chief characteristic of modern French poetry, though he offers a different explanation. "lifting up a word and putting a space around it has been the conscious enterprise of serious French poetry since Baudelaire and Rimbaud"; and a little later he speaks of "the space around words necessary for consciousness."[6] In Eliot's early poems an American is trying to make himself a Frenchman, perfecting himself in the creation of Jules Laforgue; an enterprise capable of producing, in the long run, the magisterial achievement of making himself a European. The space around the words is necessary for consciousness, and it puts at risk the continuity of relations, as between one person and another. In Eliot, consciousness is the most available form of virtue, to be conscious is to be holy: an equation which causes great difficulty in the later plays, and especially in *The Cocktail Party*. But the words thus surrounded by empty space receive a corresponding halo of significance, they compel the imagination not by their relation but by their isolation. Such words take unto themselves a force of radiance, an exceptional power which Eliot in the later plays ascribes to saints and martyrs. Martyrdom is Eliot's favourite version of the Sublime.

There is a passage in *Writing Degree Zero* where Roland Barthes offers virtually the same distinction between what he calls

classical language and modern language. In classical language the
meaning is continuous, linear, it is always deferred until the end.
So the mind, like the eye, runs along beside the words, and the
movement is gratifying. But in modern poetry it is the word
"which gratifies and fulfills like the sudden revelation of a truth."
The word has lost its prescribed relations, but for that very reason
it has acquired a magical power, it has become complete in itself,
a revelation in its own recesses. Giving up its old dependency, the
word acquires Sibylline presence; it stands there like Rilke's
archaic torso of Apollo. It is a mark of such words that we cannot
read them, but they read us, they affront us by presenting their
significance in relation to themselves. Barthes says of such words
that they "initiate a discourse full of gaps and full of lights, filled
with absences and over-nourishing signs, without foresight or
stability of intention, and thereby so opposed to the social
function of language that merely to have recourse to a discontinuous speech is to open the door to all that stands above
Nature." Classical language "establishes a universe in which men
are not alone, where words never have the terrible weight of
things, where speech is always a meeting with the others." Modern
language presupposes a discontinuous Nature, "a fragmented
space, made of objects solitary and terrible because the links
between them are only potential." I would say that the links
between them must be invented and are then fictive rather than
prescribed or agreed: they have the freedom of fiction and, paying
the price, the loneliness of being arbitrary. Such words, since
they cannot be continuous with nature, must be above or below
it, two conditions about equally lonely. They are exceptions
deprived of a rule. These words become names because of their
oracular power, but what they name cannot be defined; they are
like Stetson in *The Waste Land*, whose chief character is that he
does not answer, though he instigates, the questions addressed to
him. Stetson is the name for the interrogation, but he is under no
obligation to reply. *The Waste Land* is the name of another
interrogation, and its words are less answers than hints and

guesses. Barthes says of these modern words generally — "words adorned with all the violence of their irruption, the vibration of which, though wholly mechanical, strangely affects the next word, only to die out immediately" — that they "exclude men: there is no humanism of modern poetry."[7] Stetson is not related to his interrogator or to London or even to Mylae, he is an oracle who stirs a nervous quiver of interrogation, and dies out in a line from Baudelaire.

Classical language, then, is a system organized on the assumption that nature is continuous; hence the primacy of syntax. Classical poems stand in apposition to a seamless web of relations which we agree to call nature: when the web is domestic we call it society. The poems testify to those webs by enacting them in miniature. The long poem is valued as an extended ritual, offered to nature in the grandest terms, a celebration of prescribed relations. The reader may still be surprised, because he does not know at any moment which of the indefinitely large number of relations the writer will enact, but he knows that one of them will be invoked. Each word is faithful to the others. But in modern poems, according to this distinction, the words are independent and therefore lonely. In *The Waste Land* we respond most deeply to the individual words and phrases with a sense of their exposure. The words are not obscure, because we know what the dictionary says of them and, mostly, we know where they come from. But they are Sibylline because of the darkness between them: they challenge us to provide them with a continuous syntax and they mock our efforts to do so; that was not what they meant at all. The whole poem looks like the sub-plot of a lost play; what is lost is the main plot, nature as a significant action. The attempt to specify the form of *The Waste Land* is doomed because the form is not specific, it is not — to use Blackmur's word — predictive. The poem cries for its form: what it shows forth in itself is not form but the desperate analogy of form, tokens of a virtual form which would be valid if there were such a thing. What holds the several parts of the poem together is the need, which is at once the

poet's need and our own, to keep life going, including the life of
the poem in the dark spaces between the words. The problem is
not that the poem lacks form but that it has a passion for form,
largely unfulfilled, and—to make things harder—the memory of
lost forms. Those lost forms would not answer the present need,
even if they could be recovered: this is what Blackmur meant by
saying of Eliot's early poems and *The Waste Land* that "they
measure the present by living standards which most people
relegate to the past."[8] What is present and vivid to us in the poem
is the cry for form, the loud lament of that disconsolate chimera,
and the cry is so pure that it almost makes up for what is merely
lost. If the poem proliferates in little forms, it is because these are
variations on an absent theme, a theme of which only the variations are known. The variations are recited from many different
sources, and with increasing urgency toward the end of the poem,
the sources being older versions of form, present now as broken
images. In their bearing upon the reader, these images tell upon
his conscience, forcing him to live up to the exactitude of the
poem and to reject false consolations. If the poem is to be read as
prologomena to penance, it is also, in its bearing upon the reader,
an incitement to scruple.

So Blackmur on another occasion spoke of Eliot's task as a poet:
"he has in his images to remind reason of its material, to remind
order of its disorder, in order to create a sane art almost insane in
its predicament." He has "to make a confrontation of the rational
with the irrational: a deliberate reversal of roles."[9] But in fact
Eliot had to make a double confrontation, the violence going both
ways. He had to confront the rational with the irrational, with
what is below nature, and the images used for this violence are
mostly those he associated with Conrad's hollow men and *Heart of
Darkness*. In the passage which Eliot wanted to use as the
epigraph to *The Waste Land* before he came upon Petronius's
Sibyl, Conrad's Marlow says of Kurtz:

> Did he live his life again in every detail of desire, temptation, and
> surrender during that supreme moment of complete knowledge? He

cried in a whisper at some image, at some vision, — he cried out twice,
a cry that was no more than a breath — "The horror! the horror!"

The confrontation of the rational with the irrational is propelled
by the assumption that complete knowledge is possible and its
horror inescapable. So I have always believed that the reader of
The Waste Land ought to take Tiresias seriously as the name of
such a possibility, and such a horror. But the other confrontation
is equally valid: the irrational is confronted with the rational in all
those ways for which, in the poem, the rational imagination is
represented by Shakespeare, Spenser, St. Augustine, and, in the
first version, by a passage from Plato's *Republic* which Pound
deleted: "Not here, O Ademantus, but in another world."[10] The
line comes from a famous passage in Book IX where Glaucon says
that the city which has been described is merely verbal, it does not
exist anywhere on earth; and Socrates answers, "Well, perhaps
there is a pattern of it laid up in heaven for him who wishes to
contemplate it and so beholding to constitute himself its citizen."[11] The contemplation of the City of God is also complete
knowledge, above nature, its sublimity compelling to the citizen,
and its finality is asserted in the repeated Sanskrit word with
which the poem ends. A Tiresias would see the City of God as
clearly as the Unreal City, its malign counterpart. So the poem
moves between *Heart of Darkness* and "heart of light." Words
stand between reason and madness, touched by both adversaries.

We need an authoritative example; from Section III of *The
Waste Land,* "The Fire Sermon":

> But at my back in a cold blast I hear
> The rattle of the bones, and chuckle spread from ear to ear.
>
> A rat crept softly through the vegetation
> Dragging its slimy belly on the bank
> While I was fishing in the dull canal
> On a winter evening round behind the gashouse
> Musing upon the king my brother's wreck
> And on the king my father's death before him.
> White bodies naked on the low damp ground

And bones cast in a little low dry garret,
Rattled by the rat's foot only, year to year.
But at my back from time to time I hear
The sound of horns and motors, which shall bring
Sweeney to Mrs. Porter in the spring.
O the moon shone bright on Mrs. Porter
And on her daughter
They wash their feet in soda water
Et O ces voix d'enfants, chantant dans la coupole![12]

It is useless to ask of that passage such questions as the
following: who is speaking? what is the point of his narrative?
whose white bodies lay naked on the ground? Such questions
assume that there is a world-without-words to which Eliot's words
pay tribute; as, in common usage, the word "box" acknowledges
the existence of a certain object which does not depend upon a
word for its existence. A reader determined to give some kind of
answer might say, to the first question: Tiresias; but he somehow
includes the Buddha, Ferdinand Prince of Naples, Ovid, and
Verlaine. And to the second he might say: Well, the narrative is
merely ostensible, we are not meant to think of it as a story, the
words in that order make a kind of landscape in the reader's
mind, Marshall McLuhan calls it psychological landscape, which
is at once subject and object; it has to do with Eliot's theory of the
objective correlative or Santayana's theory of the correlative
object. And the answerer might say to the third question: The
king my brother and the king my father, I suppose, but again the
point is verbal and atmospheric rather than denotative. Questions
more in accord with the nature of the passage would include the
following: what is going on, when "rat's foot" is preceded by the
punning rhyme, "rattled"? What is going on when the speaker,
whoever he is, quotes several fragments from Ovid, Verlaine, the
Grail Legend, Australian popular song, Marvell, *The Tempest*,
John Day, and Middleton? Why does the passage suddenly change
its tone at that first insistent rhyme, "year" with "hear"? Why are
we given "wreck" instead of "wrack" in the quotation from *The
Tempest?* These questions are not likely to set anyone's heart
astir, but they are more in accord with Eliot's poem because they

do not call another world in judgment upon the words. The
questions keep strictly to language, and in this respect they follow
the rhetoric of the poem. Symbolist poetry yearns for a world
governed by the laws of Pure Poetry; internal laws, marking
purely internal liaisons between one word and another, without
any reference to nature as a court of appeal. In such a world, time
would take the form of prosody. In the passage from "The Fire
Sermon" no effect is allowed to escape from the words, to leave
the medium of language. The images and figures do not leave the
poem, they refuse to leave a setting which is assertively verbal. It
is permissible to say that the speaker here and throughout the
poem is Tiresias; but that is like saying that something is the
speech of God, it merely replaces one problem by another. The
words of the Sermon are not completed by our conceiving for
their speaker a personal identity. It is more useful to imagine a
possible state of feeling which is secreted in the words. The best
way to read the lines is not to ask that each phrase give up its
meaning, as if that meaning were then to replace the words; but
to ask what quality, in each sequence, the phrases share. That
quality may be found to attach itself to a state of feeling which
cannot be given in other terms. Not a seamless narrative, but a set
of lyric moments, each isolated for consciousness.

It is customary to say that the explanation for this use of
language is to be found in the works of F. H. Bradley and in Eliot's
thesis, *Knowledge and Experience in the Philosophy of F. H.
Bradley*. I quote a few sentences in which Eliot summarizes
Bradley's argument: kinship between Eliot's prose and Bradley's
has been noted. "It is only in immediate experience that knowledge and its object are one." "We have no right, except in the
most provisional way, to speak of *my* experience, since the I is a
construction out of experience, an abstraction from it; and the
thats, the browns and hards and flats, are equally ideal constructions from experience, as ideal as atoms." "The only independent
reality is immediate experience or feeling." " 'My' feeling is
certainly in a sense mine. But this is because and in so far as I am
the feeling." "Experience is non-relational."[13] These sentences

refer to Bradley's general philosophical position but more especially to certain passages in his *Essays on Truth and Reality*,
including this one:

> Now consciousness, to my mind, is not original. What comes first in
> each of us is rather feeling, a state as yet without either an object or
> subject. . . . Feeling is immediate experience without distinction or
> relation in itself. It is a unity, complex but without relations. And there
> is here no difference between the state and its content, since, in a word,
> the experienced and the experience are one.[14]

In Eliot's version, "feeling is more than either object or subject,
since in a way it includes both." Furthermore,

> In describing immediate experience we must use terms which offer a
> surreptitious suggestion of subject or object. If we say presentation, we
> think of a subject to which the presentation is present as an object. And
> if we say feeling, we think of it as the feeling of a subject about an
> object. . . . It may accordingly be said that the real situation is an
> experience which can never be wholly defined as an object nor wholly
> enjoyed as a feeling, but in which any of the observed constituents may
> take on the one or the other aspect.[15]

Perhaps this is enough to suggest what Eliot means when he speaks
of "the continuous transition by which feeling becomes object and
object becomes feeling." The language of "The Fire Sermon" is
surreptitious in the sense that its objectivity is merely ostensible.
The rat creeping through the vegetation has only as much to do
with animal life as is required to incite a certain feeling in the
speaker. The rat has crept into the words and lost itself there;
what transpires in the words is a certain feeling, in this case more
subject than object. The meaning of a phrase, a line, a word, in
"The Fire Sermon" is every impression that attaches itself to those
sounds under the pressure of consciousness; an assertion which
reminds us that the famous Chapter XIV of Bradley's *Essays on
Truth and Reality* is called "What is the real Julius Caesar?" The
real *Waste Land* is a sequence of those impressions, incited by the
sequence of words: the impressions are different for each reader.

There is nothing unorthodox in this, from the standpoint of
a philosophical idealist. It would be possible to quote Susanne

Langer just as relevantly as Bradley. It is also orthodox Symbolism, of the kind which Valéry treats in "Analecta, Tel Quel II," where he says that "the self flees all created things, it withdraws from negation to negation: one might give the name 'Universe' to everything in which the self refuses to recognize itself." The self refuses to recognize itself in any part of the objective world, so called, until the world is transformed into subjective terms, every apprehended object become subject. But the self is always willing to recognise itself in language and symbols. Thinking of Eliot's poem, one might give the name "language" to that alone in which the self recognises itself. As for Eliot himself, recognition may be willing or desperate: willing if we emphasize the luxury of the words, the gypsy phrases and cadences, the impression that a man who passes his entire life among such words is the happiest of men; desperate, if we emphasize the allusions, and Eliot's need of them, the accepted weight of responsibility, those fragments shored against his ruin. The allusions are Eliot's insignia, and they have this further point; they give his sensibility other ground than itself, ground in history, literature, religion, revelation, through the words, the ground of our beseeching.

For while the self flees every created thing and refuses to recognise itself anywhere but in words, it needs something besides itself. Perhaps language is enough, but we must leave that question open. In a chapter on solipsism Eliot writes:

> The point of view (or finite centre) has for its object one consistent world, and accordingly no finite centre can be self-sufficient, for the life of a soul does not consist in the contemplation of one consistent world but in the painful task of unifying (to a greater or less extent) jarring and incompatible ones, and passing, when possible, from two or more discordant viewpoints to a higher which shall somehow include and transmute them.[16]

In *The Waste Land* Eliot calls this higher perspective Tiresias: "we are led to the conception of an all-inclusive experience outside of which nothing shall fall," he says in the thesis on Bradley.

A year after the publication of *The Waste Land* Eliot reviewed

Joyce's *Ulysses,* and proposed there a distinction which depends
upon the idea of greater and lesser perspectives. In this distinction
between two methods of fiction, "narrative method" is based upon
the commonly accepted separation of subject and object. The
personal equivalent is the notion of a literary character, cut out
from his surroundings and endowed with certain qualities. The
medium is words, but most of them are common and they are
placed in accepted arrangements. Books based upon these arrangements are called novels, so the novel as a form of art came to an
end, according to Eliot, with Flaubert and James. (He later
repudiated this obituary, by the way.) The "mythical method" of
fiction, on the other hand, is based upon immediate experience,
the primacy of feeling, the idea of subject and object melting into
each other beyond positivist redemption, and at last transcended
in a quasi-divine perspective, Tiresias in *The Waste Land,* the
Homeric archetype in *Ulysses.* But we should not identify Tiresias
with the ultimate form of consciousness. It is necessary to think of
language (Valéry's "Saint Langage" in "La Pythie") as issuing from
a perspective grander even than Tiresias's, since Tiresias can only
see the world as one alienated from it: he does not give or
sympathize, he does not participate in the suffering and transformation of "What the Thunder Said." It is necessary for the
poem, and for poetry, to go beyond the phase of consciousness
which Eliot calls Tiresias. The "going beyond" has no name, it is
the action of the poem itself. Instead of common words in
common places there is language itself, construed now as a great
treasury of images and figures and, increasingly in Eliot, identified with the Word of God. Using language in this way, it seems
natural to have Ferdinand Prince of Naples, the Phoenician
sailor, the one-eyed seller of currants, and all the women in the
world becoming Tiresias. For Eliot, as for Bradley, there is no
question of a Wordsworthian liaison between man and nature.
The only part of Bradley's *Appearance and Reality* which Eliot
chose to quote in his notes to *The Waste Land* disengages itself
from any such hope. In Ch. XXIII Bradley says that "we behave
as if our internal worlds were the same." But we err:

Our inner worlds, I may be told, are divided from each other, but the outer world of experience is common to all; and it is by standing on this basis that we are able to communicate. Such a statement would be incorrect. My external sensations are no less private to myself than are my thoughts or my feelings. In either case my experience falls within my own circle, a circle closed on the outside; and, with all its elements alike, every sphere is opaque to the others which surround it. . . . In brief, regarded as an existence which appears in a soul, the whole world for each is peculiar and private to that soul.[17]

Perhaps our first impression here is wonder that such a view of the mind's predicament could ever have secreted, in Bradley's pupil, a major poem. But the second impression is better, that for such a poet language is the only possible home: either language or that metalanguage we call silence. But we are in danger of confounding the pupil with his master. Just as Bradley cleared himself of a charge of solipsism by arguing, in *Appearance and Reality*, that "we can go to foreign selves by a process no worse than the construction which establishes our own self,"[18] so Eliot cleared himself of a charge of philosophy by becoming a poet; that is, by attending to all the affiliations of words, including their old hankering after objects. Against the persuasion of his idealism, there are the deep persuasions of Dante, Shakespeare, Dryden, Virgil; and there is eventually the persuasion of Christian belief in which time is redeemed and the higher dream is made flesh. Perhaps these are the necessary qualifications to make while returning to the poem. Without them, we are in danger of turning the poem into a set of more or less interesting ideas; forgetting that to Eliot, as to Bradley, "a mere idea is but a ruinous abstraction"; forgetting, too, that it was Eliot who praised Henry James for possessing a mind so fine that no idea could violate it. With the passage from "The Fire Sermon" in front of us again, we see that what came first was not an idea but a feeling, "a state as yet without either an object or subject." The nearest expressive equivalent is rhythm, at this stage not yet resolved in words. In "The Music of Poetry" Eliot reported that in his own experience "a poem, or a passage from a poem, may tend to realize itself first as a particular rhythm before it reaches expression in words, and that this rhythm may bring to birth the idea and the image."[19] An account of our passage would be a blunt affair if it did not point to the changes of rhythm as among the chief moments; where the echo of Marvell's "To His Coy Mistress" imposes a new and deeper tone upon the verse; and from there until the line from Verlaine the transitions become more abrupt. Eliot remains true to the original feeling by remaining true to its rhythm. The words, when they are found, maintain a double allegiance: they are required to define the rhythm of the first feeling, and they must also allow for the melting of one experience into another.

The first consequence is that, to a reader sceptical of idealist assumptions, many of these lines appear wilfully arch and secretive: they appear to go through the motions of grammar and syntax without committing themselves to these agencies. They are neither one thing nor the other, neither wholly subject nor wholly object: without proposing themselves as paradoxes, they are paradoxical. A further result is that, in verse of this kind, incidents drawn from whatever source cannot have the status which they would have in a novel or another poem. In the *Metamorphoses* Ovid tells the story of the rape of Philomela by King Tereus of Thrace. Eliot recalls the story in "A Game of Chess." Trico's song in Lyly's *Alexander and Campaspe* has the lines:

> Oh, 'tis the ravished nightingale.
> *Jug, jug, jug, jug, tereu!* she cries.

Matthew Arnold's "Philomela" is one story, John Crowe Ransom's is another, the story is diversely told. How it appears in the mind of God, there is no knowing; what is the real Philomela is a hard question. How it appears in the inordinate mind of Tiresias is given in *The Waste Land:*

> Twit twit twit
> Jug jug jug jug jug jug
> So rudely forc'd.
> Tereu

—being the twit of the swallow, the Elizabethan nightingale-call and, by curious association, the word for "slut," a fine phrase of justice from Middleton's *A Game at Chess,* and lastly the simple vocative, "Tereu." Ovid's story is given, indeed, but only the gist of it, the story insofar as it survives transportation in the inclusive consciousness of Tiresias. In that strange place, one image melts into another; hence Eliot's idiom of melting, transition, becoming, deliquescence, and so forth.

To resume a long story: it is easy to think of Eliot as he thought of Swinburne: "only a man of genius could dwell so exclusively and consistently among words." In Swinburne, as in Poe, words alone are certain good. But it is well to qualify that report by adding another, from "The Music of Poetry," where Eliot speaks of the poet as occupied with "frontiers of consciousness beyond which words fail, though meanings still exist." In the plays this exorbitant work is done by miracle, "the way of illumination." Tiresias is the Unidentified Guest, until he too is transcended in Celia. The effort of the plays is to allow people to live by a holy language. Language, the ancient place of wisdom, is guaranteed by conscience and consciousness, as in *Four Quartets.* That is why, at last, "the poetry does not matter." The procedures of *The Waste Land,* which were sustained by the force of language itself, are transposed into the idiom of characters acting and suffering: transitions and perspectives, verbal in *The Waste Land,* take more public forms in the later poems and plays, the forms of personal action, chances, and choices. The frontier of consciousness is not the place where words fail but where self dies, in the awful surrender of faith. Bradley is not repudiated, but he is forced to accommodate himself to the Shakespeare of *A Winter's Tale* and *The Tempest:* that is one way of putting it.

I have been arguing that it is characteristic of Eliot's language in *The Waste Land* to effect an "absence in reality," and to move words into the resultant vacuum. At first, the words seem to denote things, *sensibilia* beyond the lexicon, but it soon appears that their allegiance to reality is deceptive, they are traitors in reality. So far as the relation between word and thing is deceptive, so far also is "objective" reality undermined. The only certainty is that the absence in reality has been effected by the words, and now the same words are enforcing themselves as the only presences. What we respond to is the presence of the words. In this way the words acquire the kind of aura, or the kind of reverberation, which we feel in proverbs; with this difference, that proverbs appeal to our sense of life, an inherited wisdom in our sense of things; Eliot's words appeal to primordial images and rhythms which can be felt, though they cannot well be called in evidence. I cannot explain this use of language except by suggesting that if the common arrangements of words issue from the common sense of time, Eliot's arrangements issue from the quarrel between time and value: I assume that value is a way of breaking the chain of time, the chain of one thing after another. Eliot is using words as if their first obligation were neither to things nor to time. Philip Wheelwright has called this kind of imagination "archetypal," the imagination "which sees the particular object in the light of a larger conception or of a higher concern." Nearly everything in Eliot's language arises from the pressure which he exerts, upon himself in the first instance and thereafter upon the reader, to register the force not oneself that makes for truth. We are urged beyond the divisions of subject and object to a state compounded of both; beyond the divisions of time and eternity to a point of intersection in which the double obligation is felt; beyond the divisions of speech and silence to the "word within a word," speechless and eloquent as the Christ child. I am not indeed maintaining that the word "rat" in "The Fire Sermon" has ceased to observe all relation to a rodent, but that the word is a double agent, it accepts the friction between reality and language but it does not give full allegiance to either party. The word points beyond individuality and even beyond species to an indeterminate form of verbal life in which the thing denoted is inseparable from the feelings for which the word itself is the embodiment. On one side stands the world of things; on the other, a rival world of dissociated forms, Platonic cities. Between them stands the individual word, maintaining a secret life.

Eliot's problem is easy to state. He must accept the fact that words are no longer deemed to contain a changeless truth, they are read as signs, pointers, stimuli. But he has to use words when he talks to us, so his formal and linguistic procedures are designed as desperate expedients to drive us out of ourselves and beyond our common selves. We are driven toward the recognition that truth is embodied in the Word of God, the Logos of revelation; that the world of facts and appearances is merely nature in fragments, not the abiding City of God; that beyond every specific act of knowledge there is "that supreme moment of complete knowledge," certified as form, pattern, perfection. The poem does not proceed by juxtaposing one word, one image, against another, but by setting against mere words, local and natural, the "higher viewpoint" which shall somehow include and transmute them. Against the heap of broken images, there is every token of revealed order, "the heart of light, the silence." The unreal city is made real as the city of God. Every claim we insist upon is answered by "the awful daring of a moment's surrender." Eliot ascribes to the Word of God, and to that alone, what the entire tradition of Romantic poetry has ascribed to the imagination, the inclusive power which transcends the divisions of subject and object, self and nature, by establishing itself as the unity beyond every division. Ultimately, and despite the peacemaking efforts of Wordsworth and other poets, the Romantic imagination finds in nature merely a heap of broken images, useful only because they indicate the conditions of fracture which the imagination alone can confront. Eventually, the Romantic imagination gives up the effort to make peace between self and nature, and ends the war by a decision in its own favour. Henceforth, imagination is to be the ground of our beseeching. To Eliot, this resolution is merely the latest form of heresy, the "egotistical sublime" of Pride, first of the deadly sins, the vanity of ignorance and egoism which the Eliot of *After Strange Gods* denounced in Lawrence, Hardy, and Yeats. It is the aim of Eliot's poetry to make our delusions uninhabitable. The reason why "the poetry does not matter" is that something else, the love of God and the love of people in the light of that love, is what alone matters. The weight of Eliot's poetry is therefore represented by one line in *The Waste Land:* "Shall I at least set my lands in order?" The words of that line point beyond themselves to a spiritual perspective which alone makes sense of them and redeems their human limitations. This is the work of *The Waste Land, Ash Wednesday,* and *Four Quartets,* to establish the Word which is true because it is not our invention; against the reduction of Logos to Lexis which has been affected upon the sole authority of the human will. Or, as the epigraph to *Four Quartets* quotes from Heraclitus: "We should let ourselves be guided by what is common to all; yet, although the Logos is common to all, most men live as if each of them had a private intelligence of his own."[20]

II

In everything I have said about *The Waste Land* I have assumed agreement that the poem is still fundamental to our sense of modern literature and the predicament of the imagination. It is the poem we call in evidence when we propose to show how the modern imagination enlarges its role in the play of experience: this is how the imagination makes a virtue of the necessity under which it labours. Eliot's way of dealing with experience, the tension caused by the force with which he invents and transforms his experience: our sense of these things is crucial to our reading of the poem. But if Eliot is to invent and transform his experience, as well as merely receive it in the form of chances and events, he must intervene in the process of feeling before the feelings engaged are organized by forces beyond his control: he must grasp the impulses of feeling before they have been congealed by the bureaucracy of institutions or organized into the formulae of thoughts and ideas. There is a passage in Valéry's "Propos sur l'Intelligence" in which he refers to the conscientiousness with which a man "oppose l'esprit à la vie." Eliot's way of doing this is by invoking a *vie antérieure,* a net of impulses which can be grasped long before they have reached the stage of participating in a grid of public codes. There is a sentence in *The Criterion* (XII, p. 471) where Eliot praises Hemingway, or rather the Hemingway of *The Killers* and *A Farewell to Arms,* for "telling the truth about his own feelings at the moment when they exist." It seems to me that the chief labour of Eliot's early poems is precisely to find a language for his own feelings at the earliest stage of their emergence: if he can fasten upon them then, he has a good chance of holding on to them thereafter. I assume that this is what is going on, rather than any effort to describe something separate from himself, in these lines:

> A woman drew her long black hair out tight
> And fiddled whisper music on those strings
> And bats with baby faces in the violet light
> Whistled, and beat their wings
> And crawled head downward down a blackened wall
> And upside down in air were towers
> Tolling reminiscent bells, that kept the hours
> And voices singing out of empty cisterns and exhausted wells.

If the whole passage sounds like a dream, it is because dreams consist of unofficial impulses active at a stage long before their official reception as thoughts, emotions, ideas. In normal usage language intervenes in the process of feeling too late to do anything more than apply to the aged thing called a thought its official label, so that it may be easily transported from one place to another. At that stage most of the damage to feeling has been done, and the rest is done by assimilating these thoughts to the public structure of attitude and convention which constitutes that "life" to which the poet's spirit can only oppose itself.

If this is true, the next phase of Eliot's art is to draw those early impulses toward their ideal form: this is where the notion of the highest possible perspective comes in, and it is roughly speaking a relation of existence to essence, particle to principle, the City of London seen in the light of its ideal or archetype, the City of God. Sometimes this is done by exerting upon an apparently simple sentence a degree of pressure capable of moving it toward transformation, as "What shall we do tomorrow?" (line 133) leads immediately to "What shall we ever do?" Of course the City of God cannot be visited merely by one's wishing to go there, it can only be approached or conceived as if it were a meaning beyond one's self; the energy required is a force of conscience and humility. In Eliot's early poems the approach is made by reaching through sensory events toward a principle deemed to supervise them. Valéry provides a reasonable idiom for this process when he says, of the poets who succeeded the French Symbolists, that "they opened again, upon the accidents of being, eyes we had closed in order to make ourselves more akin to its substance."[21] From accident through substance to principle or essence: a direction rather than a formula.

"These fragments I have shored against my ruins": an early version of this line, superseded but never deleted in the manuscript, reads, "These fragments I have spelt into my ruins," implying, as Hugh Kenner has argued, "that the protagonist has visited the Sibyl of Virgil, whose oracles, like those of Madame Sosostris, were fragmentary and shuffled by the winds."[22] Or in any case bits of language, unanswered questions, oracular echoes, diction without syntax. "Ruins" is strong enough to carry whatever weight we care to put upon it. A passage from Georg Simmel is helpful at this point. Simmel is considering the aesthetic of ruins in landscape and he says that a ruin gives an impression of peace because in it the tension between man and nature has resulted in a consoling image of a purely natural reality. The erection of the building was an act of the human will, while its present state results from the force of nature, whose power of decay draws things downward. But nature does not allow the work to fall into the amorphous state of its raw material: it retains the work of man to the extent of assimilating it to a purely natural order. The ruin is easily assimilated into the surrounding countryside because, unlike a house or a palace, it does not insist upon another order of reality.[23] The implication of a ruin is that everything has returned to a natural unity in which man's work, however, is not humiliated or merely set aside. But the ruin in language presents a different case. These fragments are broken from an original transparent language, the language before Babel destroyed its empire and established the thousand nationalisms of speech. The notion of an original Adamic language is the secular counterpart of an equally original Logos, the "word within a word" of Eliot's "Gerontion," the "word unheard, unspoken" of "Ash Wednesday." The corresponding unity is the essence approached through the existence of the particular poetic form, the poem we are reading. What lies beyond Tiresias is the form of the poem which contains his name and his experience. The ruin in language differs from the ruin in landscape because nature has taken no part in bringing it about, Babel is the work of human pride alone, a Fall if in some respects a fortunate Fall. So the impression of peace in a ruin in landscape is replaced, so far as the ruin in language is in question, by an impression of guilt, frustration, and pathos. The only release from this impression is the partial consolation of seeing words aspire beyond their condition to create the very form by which their fragmentary state is judged.

Notes

1. T. S. Eliot, *The Waste Land: A Facsimile and Transcript of the Original Drafts,* edited by Valerie Eliot (London: Faber and Faber, 1971).
2. Hawthorne, *The House of the Seven Gables* (Columbus: Ohio State University Press, 1955), Vol. II, p. 855.
3. T. S. Eliot: "In Memory'" in *The Little Review,* Vol. V, No. 4, August 1918, p. 44.
4. *To Criticize the Critic* (London: Faber and Faber, 1965), p. 54.
5. Ibid., p. 31.
6. Harold Rosenberg, *The Tradition of the New* (London: Paladin, reprint, 1970), pp. 86, 89.
7. Roland Barthes, *Writing Degree Zero,* translated by Annette Lavers and Colin Smith (London: Cape, 1967), pp. 54-55.
8. R. P. Blackmur, *Form and Value in Modern Poetry* (New York: Anchor, 1957), p. 143.
9. R. P. Blackmur, *Anni Mirabiles 1921-1925* (Washington: Library of Congress, 1956), p. 31.
10. *The Waste Land,* p. 31.
11. Plato, *The Republic,* Book IX, 592-A-B, quoted from the Loeb edition in the Facsimile *Waste Land,* p. 128. Frank Kermode has pointed

out that the phrase is remembered in Eliot's reference to Kipling's vision of empire: "The vision is almost that of an idea of empire laid up in Heaven" *(On Poetry and Poets,* p. 245). Plato's phrase is also quoted, in Greek, in *The Criterion,* Vol. XIV, No. 56, April 1935, p. 435, immediately after Eliot's assertion that "the City of God is at best only realizable on earth under an imperfect likeness." Cf. Kermode, *The Classic* (London: Faber and Faber, 1975), p. 38.

12. *Collected Poems 1909-1962,* pp. 70-71.

13. *Knowledge and Experience in the Philosophy of F. H. Bradley* (London: Faber and Faber, 1964), pp. 19, 30, 31, 27.

14. F. H. Bradley, *Essays on Truth and Reality* (Oxford, 1914), p. 194.

15. *Knowledge and Experience,* pp. 22, 25.

16. Ibid., pp. 147-148.

17. F. H. Bradley, *Appearance and Reality* (London, 1902), p. 346.

18. Ibid., p. 258.

19. *On Poetry and Poets,* p. 38.

20. *Heraclitus,* translated by Philip Wheelwright (New York: Atheneum, 1964), p. 19 (Fragment 2).

21. Valéry, "Avant-Propos a la connaissance de la déesse": "Ils ont rouvert aussi sur les accidents de l'être les yeux que nous avions fermés pour nous faire plus semblables à sa substance." *Oeuvres,* edited by Jean Hytier (Paris: Gallimard, 1957), Vol. I, p. 1276.

22. Hugh Kenner, "The Urban Apocalypse" in W. K. Wimsatt (editor) *Literary Criticism: Idea and Act* (Berkeley: University of California Press, 1974), p. 630.

23. Georg Simmel, *Philosophische Kultur* (1923), quoted in Jean Starobinski, *The Invention of Liberty 1700-1789,* translated by Bernard C. Swift (Geneva: Skira, 1964), p. 180.

Writing Against Time

King Lear, Act IV, Scene vii, a tent in the French camp: enter Cordelia, Kent, and a doctor. Lear is carried in, still asleep. As he wakes, Cordelia speaks to him:

> How does my royal lord? How fares your Majesty?

Lear answers:

> You do me wrong to take me out o' th' grave:
> Thou art a soul in bliss, but I am bound
> Upon a wheel of fire, that mine own tears
> Do scald like molten lead.

The actor playing Lear is free to decide at what point the King sees Cordelia, because in any case seeing is not yet believing, the soul in bliss may be Cordelia or anyone not in Hell. Even if Lear has seen Cordelia, he has not recognised her, he is merely protesting against any force that would take him out of the grave. Cordelia asks, "Sir, do you know me?", and Lear answers: "You are a spirit, I know; where did you die?" The Second Quarto has "when" rather than "where," the reading common to First Folio and First Quarto: some modern editors have chosen "when." But "where" is preferable, because the entire scene turns upon place and the dislocation of the King's mind. "When" is neither here nor there, Lear is not engaged with time, his mind runs "far wide," as Cordelia says, trying to find itself by finding other things. The next time Lear speaks he asks, "Where have I been? Where am I? Fair daylight?", and a few moments later:

> . . . for I am mainly ignorant
> What place this is, and all the skill I have
> Remembers not these garments; nor I know not
> Where I did lodge last night.

But as he gradually finds himself and recognises Cordelia, he says:

> . . . Do not laugh at me,
> For (as I am a man) I think this lady
> To be my child Cordelia.

Cordelia answers, "And so I am; I am."

In this little incident we find an exemplary figure for the reception of Shakespeare's last plays. It begins as a pure vision, a magical appearance for which there is no earthly place, "You are a spirit, I know; where did you die?" The authenticity of the vision is not questioned, though it cannot be ascribed to any source: it has no source in Lear, his character, his will. Yeats observed in an essay on Berkeley that in the eighteenth century England lived for certain great constructions "that were true only in relation to the will." We know that version of truth. But the authority of Lear's vision, seeing a spirit where we see Cordelia, does not arise from his will, at this point he has no will. The vision comes with the authority of a divine act, if spirits are deemed to reside anywhere: Lear is its unquestioning witness. At this point the vision is entirely spirit, a soul certified in its death, and lest the embodiment come too easily, thereby straining our belief, Lear is set to approach the embodiment by a little exercise. "I will not swear these are my hands," he says. "Let's see. I feel this pin prick." So much the better. "Would I were assur'd of my condition!" he prays. The evidence of touch and pain is strong, and it anticipates the full recognition of Cordelia a few moments later. Lear kneels to confess his age and folly in a rambling speech which gradually gains assurance and ends with the word "Cordelia." Cordelia's answer gives full assurance of truth in the repeated "And so I am; I am." It is reasonable to say that the incident begins with a disembodied vision and ends with the assured recognition of fact, earth, and reality. The sense of sight calls for aid from the sense of touch and then turns to its own vision, renewed and justified. This is true enough, if we allow that in the event the vision is not denied or abandoned. The reception of the fact "Cordelia" fulfils the vision "Cordelia," the two Cordelias are seen to be one. We say that the vision is embodied, incarnate, or alternatively that the mere body is transfigured. For the moment it does not matter. If we were attending to *Cymbeline* rather than to *King Lear,* it would be necessary to lean in favour of one version. At the end of *Cymbeline* we are invited to feel that a vision has been, as the Soothsayer declares, "full accomplished." If it is true, as Henri Focillon maintains in his *The Life of Forms in Art,* that there is a vocation of forms corresponding to an aspiration of feelings, it reminds us that in Shakespeare's last plays the events and characters are shaped by forces conventional and formal; that is, forces given and acknowledged rather than ordained. The forces are messengers from nature rather than from culture or character. These plays aspire to a moment in which a personal vision is "full accomplished," or a fact is transfigured. Magic is authenticated, verified upon the senses and the mind. Fact is transfigured, touched with an aura wonderfully natural and spiritual. This has often been questioned, mainly by those who maintain that in the last plays the pressure of fact is too weak to make the vision a fully earned experience, fact is too easily transcended in an asserted vision. A more severe version of this complaint is made by W. H. Auden in *The Dyer's Hand,* that *The Tempest,* for example, is a manichean play "not because it shows the relation of Nature to Spirit as one of conflict and hostility, which in fallen man it is, but because it puts the blame for this upon Nature and makes the Spirit innocent." In other words, the Shakespeare of *The Tempest* finds it easy to transcend the world of fact because he despises it or is bored with it. But there is one play in which Shakespeare's sense of fact must be kept sharp and he cannot have recourse to magical islands, divine powers, and an Ariel to command. The play is *Henry VIII,* a work which seems to disturb the symmetry of the last plays so much that scholars have tried to assign much of it to Fletcher, on evidence not at all strong.

The Famous History of the Life of King Henry the Eight cannot be set on a magical island or in Antioch or Tyre: it shows events which took place in England a mere sixty years before the performance. Shakespeare takes liberties with the facts as given in Holinshed and Foxe, he concentrates events with a certain nonchalance, but he recognises a limit beyond which he cannot presume to go in such activities. The Prologue addresses itself to those who will have the truth or nothing:

> . . . Such as give
> Their money out of hope they may believe,
> May here find truth too.

If we take the play at its word as a history play, we receive its structure as a sequence of catastrophes; the diverse falls of Buckingham, Wolsey, and the Queen show the operation, as in the earlier histories, of the wheel of Fortune. The text insists upon this cadence. When Wolsey feels the King's frown, he anticipates his own fate in terms associated with the understanding of tragedy from Boethius to Chaucer, the fall of princes:

> I have touch'd the highest point of all my greatness,
> And from that full meridian of my glory
> I haste now to my setting. I shall fall
> Like a bright exhalation in the evening,
> And no man see me more.

The figure enacts its meaning, the meteor is given in a splendid show of Latinity, "like a bright exhalation in the evening," only to die in Anglo-Saxon monosyllables, "And no man see me more." It is a characteristic tone, not only in the last plays, as John Crowe Ransom and others have observed, but more generally, because Shakespeare felt the dramatic possibilities present in keeping the Latin words aware of themselves rather than allowing them to become naturalised to the English character of the language:

> . . . No, this my hand will rather
> The multitudinous seas incarnadine,
> Making the green one red.

Or Hamlet to Horatio:

> Absent thee from felicity awhile,
> And in this harsh world draw thy breath in pain
> To tell my story.

In each case the Latin appeals to a sense of latitude and grandeur, the expansive note, and the Anglo-Saxon to a sense of abrupt conclusion and definition. Shakespeare found many occasions for such a contrast, it came naturally to him with his sense of interruption:

> Yea, all which it inherit, shall dissolve,
> And, like this insubstantial pageant faded,
> Leave not a rack behind.

But the contrasting Latin and Anglo-Saxon make a sequence especially appropriate to the history plays, where a character sees his fall in the desolate context of his former glory: normally, the glory is given in Latin, the fall in Anglo-Saxon. The cadence mimes the sense of temporal life as a concession, interrupted by death, mischance, or fate.

But in *Henry VIII* the old convention has been modified. When Shakespeare came back to the history play, a genre he had put aside for thirteen or fourteen years, his sense of life had already found its vocation of form in the romance and he was disinclined to go back to a discarded note. *Henry VIII* has for that reason been interpreted as a romance, assimilated to *A Winter's Tale* and *The Tempest*. I think we must go further. The hint is given in the moment at which history and romance are reconciled, when the vision of romance and the fact of history are simultaneously and equally acknowledged. Normally in the last plays the exemplary moment is defined as an intervention, with the implication that, in Pisanio's version in *Cymbeline*, "the heavens still must work." In *Henry VIII* there is such a moment when the King intervenes to break the sequence of falls and catastrophes. The events seem to demand now the fall of Cranmer, according to a deadly sequence already established by the falls of Buckingham, Wolsey, and Katherine. The sequence marks the ideology of time. But now Henry intervenes to save Cranmer, and the dramatic rhythm is changed. Henry stops the seemingly inevitable turn of the wheel of Fortune. Cranmer, Anne Boleyn, and Cromwell are safely at the top of the wheel, and at least for the foreseeable future, according to the new rhythm of the play, the wheel will turn no more. This is the moment at which, in Act V, Scene ii, a more expansive rhythm is established with an air of freedom, as if Fate were become Providence. When the King reconciles Cranmer and Gardiner, we are still in the world of history, but it is history touched with the wand of romance, as in *A Winter's Tale.* Henry's intervention redeems the time, changing an expected cadence of falls into a new rhythm of fulfilment and reconciliation: it is in that respect an act of imagination. But the culminating moment is still ahead, the birth of the child Elizabeth: this is the moment to which Shakespeare's entire theatre aspires.

So it must be prepared. It is generally agreed that in this play the pervading feeling is not concentrated in any one character. Henry may be the hero, but there is no suggestion that the energy of the play is concentrated in him alone or chiefly, as in other plays it is concentrated in Coriolanus, Hamlet, Macbeth, Timon, or Lear. It is more accurate to say that Henry is the point at which the work of Heaven achieves definition and force, since English history is in question. But the main direction of feeling is toward the grand rhythm of events: that is why the structure of the play is expansive rather than intensive. The play is deployed like a tableau or a triptych, where one scene opens upon another and the feeling is developed in moving from one scene or picture to the next. When we emphasize the pageantry of the play, we advert to Shakespeare's way of registering, behind these scenes, forces at work which cannot be given simply or directly in terms of character, personality, or will. Pageantry is the meaning, of which history is the experience. The meaning is national, a grand convergence of feelings not merely personal though personal indeed. If these forces are almost entirely magical in *The Tempest* and historical in *Henry VIII*, this indicates their latitude, they are the same forces, coming from the same source.

Muriel Bradbrook has argued that this kind of structure in Shakespeare is found for the first time in *Timon of Athens,* which she considers an experimental scenario for an indoor dramatic

pageant.[1] The play was composed, she maintains, late in 1609
when Shakespeare's company moved into the indoor theatre at
Blackfriars. The indoor theatre was especially suited to a dramatic structure which proceeds less by plot than by apposition
of scene. One scene is juxtaposed against another, and the main
energy arises from comparisons and contrasts. *Timon of Athens*
certainly points toward the last plays, especially in the scene of
Timon's death when the hero, reconciled with the elemental
powers, is mourned by Neptune. We are in a world of natural
sympathy and credence, for the moment. It is unnecessary to
force the argument, *Timon* is still so firmly chained to time,
place, and circumstance that it cannot admit more than a
momentary touch of romance. But there are expansive forces at
work, even in a play which seems to be chiefly an act of repudia-
tion, its chief motif the profligacy of corruption. While we think
of it as a city-play on city-themes, the last scene points beyond city
and cave to the creative elements, and the structure of the drama
moves toward the last romances. Apposition of scene also governs
the idiom of *Henry VIII*, as if to authenticate a vision by showing
that the true source is deep beneath anything that may be given
as an individual act. Henry's intervention in behalf of Cranmer
seems to be a new act, but it is not a novelty, it brings to the light
of day motives natural, creative, and impersonal, prior to individual action and speech.

To show how this moves: in the first Act the Queen protests to
the King about the exorbitance of taxes imposed upon the people.
When the King and his servants occupy the stage, they are
disguised as shepherds. Up to this point the stage has been a place
of intrigue, court disputes, Wolsey, Buckingham, Norfolk, the
normal content of history plays. When drum and trumpet sound,
Wolsey assumes the strangers are soldiers or legates from abroad:
more of the same, his familiar world. The masquers come forward
as shepherds, with music, dance, and the mime of those who
"speak no English." The English we have been hearing has struck
the ear as court-talk, urban, sinister on the whole: what we hear
now is all music and gallantry until Henry is unmasked and the

party moves off the stage. Henry has set his eye upon Anne, so the world of intrigue is not repudiated, but it has been set off against another world, where the frown of the great cannot harm. As in *A Winter's Tale,* what time has imposed as fact is answered by another sense of time, fulfilled in the movement of seasons, the "things new-born" which answer "things dying": its poet is Ovid, adept of transformation. The last plays reply to the exorbitance of time and fact by recourse to metaphor, certifying powers of natural magic in which visions are full accomplished and metamorphoses are natural. Paulina says to the statue, "Be stone no more," and Hermione comes down. Prospero conjures a banquet, the "living drollery" that sets Sebastian discoursing of unicorns and phoenixes in Arabia. Posthumus invokes "golden chance" after his vision of Jupiter. In *Henry VIII* the rejected Queen has a poetic dream of peace which releases her from the chains of time to another world:

> Cause the musicians play me that sad note
> I nam'd my knell, whilst I sit meditating
> On that celestial harmony I go to.

With the music she falls asleep and in her dream six personages in white robes dance with garlands before her.

The traditional master of natural magic is Orpheus: his voice sings to release the Queen, however briefly, to a new cycle of experience in which catastrophes are sweetened into grace. Orpheus does not merely command the stones and trees, he urges upon us a sense of that grand rhythm within which temporal discords are tuned to harmony. It is reasonable to speak of a spirit of forgiveness in these last plays, provided we do not limit its application to the human will; the spirit is natural and therefore divine in the first instance, its humanity comes later: what we advert to is the large mercy which invokes the smaller mercy, human forgiveness. Why does the condemned Buckingham forgive his enemies? Why does Katherine forgive Wolsey and the King? Why does Posthumus forgive Imogen while thinking her guilty? It is not convincing to look for answers in character or personality, the patience so often shown and declared is not given as an attribute of character but of nature; it is implicit in the natural amenity of magic, romance, and the Orphic power, the several characters are tuned to express it. The story of the night is subsumed in the great cadence, time is redeemed.

But we must go a little further, because to speak of the redemption of time implies the transformation of a given world, and there is always an ambigious hovering between transformation and transcendence. In *The King's Two Bodies* Ernst Kantorowicz has considered this question in its relation to time, distinguishing between *tempus* and *aevum*.[2] *Tempus* is mere successiveness, the dimension of unprivileged life, one thing after another, governed by chance and contingency. *Aevum* is sempiternity, the endless continuum, which is in one idiom the time of angels and fictitious personages and becomes human time when it is suffused with the radiance of meaning and value. Yeats speaks of "the cracked tune that Chronos sings," this is mere *tempus,* ideological time, a force of constraint without memory or hope. Chronos imposes a positivism of time, refuses to recognise any grand rhythm or pattern other than its own mechanical successiveness. One day is divided from another, there is no merging or unifying force which might dissolve or transcend the severances. Chronos rejects every amenity of spirit or memory. That is why Günther Grass's hero in *From the Diary of a Snail* tells his children to write against Time, because it is Time that allows Terror to become habitual. It forbids a fact to be other than its merest self. But set over against or beneath that constraining time there is another time, *aevum,* which we feel perhaps only in Wordsworthian "spots" of time, when the cracked tune is mended and the song now tells of value, significance, and continuity. One of the perennial responsibilities of literature is to devise "fictions of concord," as Frank Kermode has described them, in which the successiveness of time loses its venom and we sense in a renewed time intimations of sempiternity. Chronos is answered by Mnemosyne. In *The Faerie Queene* Mutability is answered by Nature, who says of decaying things:

> . . . being rightly wayd
> They are not changed from their first estate;
> But by their change their being doe dilate:
> And turning to themselves at length againe,
> Doe worke their owne perfection so by fate:
> Then over them Change doth not rule and raigne:
> But they raigne over change, and doe their states maintaine.

(VII. vii. 58)

So, in time, the seasons, festal days, anniversaries testify to a rhythm of events, the natural rhythm of organic and human life. The impulse to redeem time is universal, we feel it when we ask that one event be related to another in a cadence of meanings and values, acting upon motives more profound than the calendar. But in Elizabethan literature there is a special concentration upon the redemption of time by setting images of decay against images of continuity. This is Kantorowicz's theme. We refer to kingship which never dies, while kings die, a fiction of jurisprudence and canon law by which the *imperium* does not lapse, while *imperatores* die; the *imperium* is the office, a corporative fiction immune to time. In Catholic thought the Papacy does not die, only Popes die. The fiction of the King's two bodies is one of the great fictions of concord in Elizabethan literature, surviving not only the frailities and corruptions of kings but usurpations of the very office of kingship. The spirit of the office persists and renews itself. The importance of the fiction is not our theme, we merely take it for granted and recognise it as one source of metaphor, the dilation of being which transforms *tempus* into *aevum* and corresponds to hope. Hope is that part of ourselves which seizes as opportunity what despair has already written off as malice. On this virtue, the structure of *Henry VIII* is sustained. A child is born, Elizabeth. Cranmer, redeemed by Henry's protection, baptises her and, going beyond the duties of the occasion, speaks his famous prophecy, a vision of continuity and peace for which the appropriate idiom is at once magical, metaphorical, and religious. In the vision the forces which separate one person from another disappear before a sense of the unity of life itself, an epic sense of communal grandeur. Cranmer is speaking against *tempus*.

The impression of time as *aevum* may be given in many ways, but two of them are crucial. Time can be redeemed by transforming the given world, surrounding fact with a bright halo of meaning. Brute fact is raised into a higher relation, it is no longer random or successive but privileged. Time may also be redeemed by incarnating the vision, the fabulous element is domesticated. In the first way, history is transformed in the radiance of its meaning and value. In the second, romance is embodied, established on earth, a miracle play of imagination. *Henry VIII* begins with the second way and ends with the first.

In the first scene three noblemen meet. Norfolk describes for Buckingham's benefit the Field of the Cloth of Gold where Henry met the King of France, an event entirely historical but given here in terms of religious ceremony and ritual. The kings are "those suns of glory," again "those two lights of men," men but not merely men. Norfolk says that the event was so fabulous that it made legend and fable seem fact:

> . . . they did perform
> Beyond thought's compass, that former fabulous story
> Being now seen possible enough, got credit
> That Bevis was believed.

So the fabulous is established. Between the two ways there is the Orphic song sung to Katherine at the beginning of the third act:

> Orpheus with his lute made trees,
> And the mountain tops that freeze
>   Bow themselves when he did sing:
> To his music plants and flowers
> Ever sprung, as sun and showers
> There had made a lasting spring.
>
> Every thing that heard him play,
> Even the billows of the sea,
>   Hung their heads and then lay by:
> In sweet music is such art,
> Killing care and grief of heart
>   Fall asleep, or hearing die.

Mutability, care, grief of heart are the attributes of *tempus*, resolved in Katherine's vision. Immediately we are thrust back into *tempus,* Chronos's cracked tune, when Wolsey and Campeius enter to persuade Katherine to give up her queenly rights. She refuses; we are still fixed in unredeemed history, the Orphic voice is not heard again until Cranmer's prophecy in the last act when with the birth and baptism of Elizabeth history is transfigured. History and Romance become one.

They are enabled to do this because the birth of Elizabeth is felt to participate in an even greater event, the birth of the Christ child, at once a child and the Logos, incarnate. Cranmer says:

> God shall be truly known, and those about her
> From her shall read the perfect ways of honour,
> And by those claim their greatness, not by blood.
> Nor shall this peace sleep with her; but as when
> The bird of wonder dies, the maiden phoenix,
> Her ashes new create another heir
> As great in admiration as herself . . .

The symbolism of the phoenix in Elizabethan literature is well appreciated now, thanks chiefly to Kantorowicz in *The King's Two Bodies* and Frances Yates in *Astraea.* The phoenix is traditionally associated with the sun that dies and is re-born every day. The bird consumes itself and a new phoenix, identical in kind, rises from the ashes. When this figure was translated into Christian terms, it was regularly taken to mean the death and resurrection of Christ, a meaning authenticated in Lactantius's "Carmen de ave phoenice," Saint Ambrose's "Hexameron," and in the Old English poem "The Phoenix" which draws upon these sources. The secular equivalent is the *renovatio urbis.* Kantorowicz says that Bernard of Parma (d. 1263) first invoked the phoenix to represent the corporative fiction that never dies: in turn, the bird represents the sempiternity of kingship. In the phoenix, species sees itself conserved and mutability overthrown. Shakespeare's meditation on this theme is "The Phoenix and Turtle," where the lovers embody a relation in which "either was the other's mine":

> Property was thus appalled,
> That the self was not the same;

Single nature's double name
Neither two nor one was called.

Property is appalled because the situation of the lovers is a scholastic scandal. Aristotle, discussing in his *Metaphysics* the opposition of the One to the Many says that "to the one belong the same and the like and the equal, and to plurality belong the other and the unlike and the unequal" (X. ii. 1054, tr. McKeon). "The same" has several meanings, he goes on: we sometimes mean "the same numerically," again we call a thing the same if it is one both in definition and in number, as for example you are one with yourself both in form and in matter, and again if the definition of its primary essence is one, as for example equal straight lines are the same. The self, in "The Phoenix and Turtle," has transcended and affronted the scholastic limit of unity and has ceased to be merely "the same," being unity and plurality at once. In the *Politics* (II. iii. 1262) Aristotle says that the unity which Socrates commends would be like that of the lovers in the *Symposium* who desire to grow together in the excess of their affection, and from being two to become one, in which case one or both would certainly perish. But they do not perish in "The Phoenix and Turtle" even when they have grown together in this precise way: that again is what appals Property and delights Poetry.

Henry VIII gathers together nearly all the phoenix-attributes in favour of its rhetoric: most particularly the association of the magical bird with *perpetuitas* and *aevum*, royal sempiternity, the resurrection of Christ, preservation of species in the individual, *dignitas* that never dies *(imperium semper est)*, death *in individuo* but not *in genere*, and above all the fact that the phoenix is the sole example of its kind living at any one moment. Frances Yates has emphasized the association of the bird with virginity and then with the English virgin queen and the Virgin Mary.[3] There is also the vision of the Age of Gold, represented in Virgil's fourth Eclogue as introduced by the birth of a child, the *virgo:* "Iam redit et virgo, redeunt Saturnia regna." The child to be born is destined to rule a golden world of peace and reconciliation. Dante enhances the vision in the *De Monarchia*, and Spenser in Merlin's

prophecy in *The Faerie Queene*, though in that case peace
depends upon Elizabethan victory:

> Tho when the terme is full accomplished,
> There shall a sparke of fire, which hath long-while
> Bene in his ashes raked up, and hid,
> Be freshly kindled in the fruitful Ile
> Of Mona, where it lurked in exile;
> Which shall breake forth into bright burning flame,
> And reach into the house, that beares the stile
> Of royall maiesty and soveraigne name;
> So shall the Briton bloud their crowne againe reclame.
>
> Thenceforth eternall union shall be made
> Betweene the nations different afore,
> And sacred Peace shall lovingly perswade
> The warlike minds, to learne her goodly lore,
> And civile armes to exercise no more:
> Then shall a royall virgin raine, which shall
> Stretch her white rod over the Belgicke shore,
> And the great Castle smite so sore with all,
> That it shall make him shake, and shortly learne to fall.
>
> (III. iii. 48-49)

(Merlin the Enchanter is also a wit of pedagogy, with those two
forms of "learning"). Queen Elizabeth chose as the motto of her
phoenix-badge the words *semper eadem*. Lactantius rings the
changes upon a paradox that defeats *tempus: Est eadem sed non
eadem, quae est ipsa nec ipsa est.* Shakespeare's Merlin is
Cranmer, who speaks with particular authority as one of the great
martyrs of Queen Mary's reign, a hero of Foxe's *Acts and
Monuments.* It is strikingly appropriate that he should utter the
prophecy of Elizabethan peace and give it in Virgil's terms.
Everything comes together at the end of the play: the Tudor
myth, Protestant victory over Rome, a promise of perpetuity in a
legendary symbol. "Thou speakest wonders," Henry intervenes to
say, receiving "this oracle of comfort," but Cranmer has already
declared that those who doubt his words will find them true. At
this point the two ways of defeating *tempus* or redeeming time
come together: fact is enhanced, transfigured by its meaning, and

an act of pure imagination, visionary, fabulous, finds itself established. Cranmer's speech brings to an end the separation of word and deed which has been, as R. A. Foakes has pointed out,[4] a significant motif in the play. In Act III, Scene ii, when Henry has decided to dispose of Wolsey, he mocks him for the scale of his wealth, his earthly audit. Wolsey defends himself in a clever speech and Henry answers, "You have said well." Wolsey, sensing the next attack, says:

> And ever may your highness yoke together
> (As I will lend you cause) my doing well
> With my well saying.

Henry takes the point, but closes the trap upon him:

> . . . 'Tis well said again,
> And 'tis a kind of good deed to say well,
> And yet words are no deeds. My father lov'd you,
> He said he did, and with his deed did crown
> His word upon you . . .

It is the fallen world in which there is always a discrepancy between word and deed, because word is sign and not the thing itself. Only in the Orphic tradition is the discrepancy overwhelmed, word and deed are one. Cranmer speaks according to this tradition, because prophecy closes the gap between word and deed, sign and thing. Prophecy is Orphic in the virtual mode, pointing toward the conjunction of word and event in a golden future time. Elizabeth Sewell in *The Orphic Voice* studies the lore of Orpheus as testifying to the conjunction of poetry and natural history: our theme in regard to *Henry VIII* is the conjunction of romance and human history. The redemption of *tempus* in the radiance of *aevum* proposes an enhancing motive which we can see in other places, where the positivism of language is transfigured by metaphor, or the positivism of mind by imagination. But it is wrong to speak of these as if they were necessary dualisms. Imagination and mind are not two things, they are one intellectual power, separable only if we choose to call upon a limited effort of that power or upon the complete power: in the first, what we use is mind, in the second imagination. Imagination is the intellectual power which we call upon to unify the whole range of experience, however heterogeneous that range may be:

> When a poet's mind is perfectly equipped for its work, it is constantly amalgamating disparate experience; the ordinary man's experience is chaotic, irregular, fragmentary. The latter falls in love, or reads Spinoza, and these two experiences have nothing to do with each other, or with the noise of the typewriter or the smell of cooking; in the mind of the poet these experiences are always forming new wholes.[5]

Mind is the name we give to the intellectual power which we call upon when we propose to deal with the chaos of our experience merely by putting its constituents in separate compartments; when our dealing with experience is strictly administrative, the method of Ramist logic. We call upon imagination, that is, upon the whole range of our intelligence, when we are prepared to settle for nothing less than a continuous series of enhancements; *tempus* into *aevum*, fact into value, force into intellect, and the dualism of word and deed into an Orphic unity.

I have been suggesting that the structure of *Henry VIII* may be considered in terms of space or time: as a series of moral pictures, a symbolic pageant, or, if time is our element, a series of turnings in the wheel of fortune. In either version the play presents a relation between history and meaning. If we say that the events enact their well-known history, we must also find a word to describe certain moments in which the wheel is held at rest while the meaning of the events is recited. If the events are deemed to be dynamic, their meaning is given in another tone, static for want of a better word. This is in accord with our general sense that history and meaning are not synonymous: while we are in history, we are in action and process, but the meaning is not yet. For meaning to be achieved, we must stand apart from the movement of events and either find a meaning in them or impose a meaning upon them: either way, we step out of the stream. A. J. Greimas has given us a structuralist's authority for saying this. There is a passage in his *Du sens* in which he says that every apprehension of meaning has the effect of transforming stories or lives into structures removed from history, so that events are registered as states:

> Ainsi, toute saisie de signification a pour effet de transformer les histoires en permanences: qu'il s'agisse de l'interrogation sur le sens d'une vie ou sur le sens d'une histoire (ou de l'histoire), l'interrogation, c'est-à-dire le fait qu'on se place devant une manifestation linguistique dans l'attitude du destinataire des messages, a pour conséquence ceci: que les algorithmes historiques se présentent comme des états, autrement dit comme des structures statiques.[6]

In *Henry VIII,* when the wheel of fortune is held unmoving, it is to enable the meaning of the events to be expressed. The character who expresses that meaning is the one most fitted to do so, normally because he is the chief victim of the events, he understands them because he has suffered them. The play "stops" so that its meaning may be given: more accurately, the play is passing from action to meaning. Buckingham in Act II, Scene i, Wolsey in Act III, Scene ii, and the Queen in Act IV, Scene ii, move into the meaning of their history: in each case the meaning is given as a moral story, the style appropriately sententious, since the speakers are expressing a meaning which they are too late to act upon. They represent three cycles of the wheel of fortune, and their meanings cannot differ much one from another. There is a genre to contain such occasions, with a corresponding notion of decorum. The only meaning which is different in style is the King's, when he intervenes to save Cranmer. He does not merely save Cranmer; he intervenes to impose upon history his chosen meaning and to ensure that this is the only meaning history will obey. The intervention takes place in Act V, Scene ii, and it leads immediately to Cranmer's baptising the child Elizabeth and to the metaphor of the phoenix as the dominant idiom to which historical events are to subscribe. Greimas has another passage in *Du sens* where he refers to history as closure:

> . . . l'histoire, au lieu d'être une ouverture, comme on n'a cessé de le répéter, est au contraire une *clôture;* elle ferme la porte à de nouvelles significations contenues, comme virtualités, dans la structure dont elle relève: loin d'être un moteur, elle serait plutôt un frein.[7]

The meaning discovered in historical events by Buckingham, Wolsey, and Katherine is, as *King Lear* has it, "the weight of this sad time." The King's meaning is what he imposes upon events, changing their force and direction. On the stage it can be made to appear either whimsical or metaphorical: in fact it is both, because gratuitous, and for that reason capable of prescribing to history a meaning declared in metaphor and prophecy.

If it is said that the play, on this showing, prescribed to history metaphors and prophecies which in the event were humiliated rather than fulfilled: well, that is only to say that it marks one incident in the tendentious relation between history and imagination. Ideally, meaning should not have to be imposed, it should inhere in the action and end of events, value should be the structure of fact. In practice, the separation of consciousness and experience, history and imagination is a fact of temporal life. It is not the purpose of imagination to act as cheerleader for the spirit of the age but to find or make a place in aesthetic forms for values which the spirit of the age cannot even recognise. Increasingly, fundamental values must be apprehended as living beneath or beyond the structure of needs and drives which, in a consumer society, constitutes normal life. There are values so alien to those of any actual society that they can be sustained only in effigy as the virtualities of artistic form: this is the role of form, to preserve as fundamental truths the values which are otherwise homeless. So it is that the artist has been driven into the position of writing against time in the desperate hope of redeeming time. Let us suppose that history is that part of one's experience which does not have to be invented. Henry VIII acceded to the throne on April 22, 1509. Mr. Vance was a neighbour of the Joyces in Bray. Well and good; these are facts, they are not soluble in the water of fiction. If they become the locus of value, so much the better, history becomes meaning. If not, they sink into the condition of being merely one thing after another, "the cracked tune that Chronos sings." In our own time it has become nearly impossible to trust in the fruitfulness of history, or to think of public events as a dependable source of value. Mary Douglas has taken as her theme in *Natural Symbols* (1970) "the lack of commitment to common symbols." We have lost the symbolic value of the family meal; our festal days no longer remind us of human continuity or a *vie antérieure* common to all, but are monstrously corrupted and humiliated by a consumer society. The institutions we have devised to make daily life more harmonious continue to impose themselves as obstacles between feeling and value. We live with objects so secularised that we can only suppose behind them a void, an absence. The first result is that increasingly meaning becomes not a natural aura surrounding objects, events, and relationships but the work of will, spasmodic and synthetic. Meaning is invented, instigated, and produced by an imagination determined upon that labour. Proust is our exemplar. He could deal with events only when they appeared to him as chance and coincidence, wonderful because arbitrary, and even then valuable to him only because he had the instinct to make of chance events monsters of reverberation. "Le livre aux caractères figurés, non tracés par nous, est notre seul livre," he wrote, but also, "en réalité, chaque lecteur est, quand il lit, le propre lecteur de soi-même."[8] The writers who touch us most deeply today are those who make something out of nothing: James, Kafka, Proust, Beckett, Eliot. What strikes us in attending to *Henry VIII* is the degree to which meaning has leaked away from its common symbols: baptism, prophecy, the Old Testament vision of a golden age, the maiden phoenix. Nearly every word of Cranmer's speech in Act V, Scene iv (lines 14-62), has to be resuscitated by an archaeology of feeling. What we lack is not historical knowledge or even "a sense of history" but a situation in which events and the imagination which engages them are felt as equal and opposite:

> Words move, music moves
> Only in time; but that which is only living
> Can only die. Words, after speech, reach
> Into the silence. Only by the form, the pattern,

> Can words or music reach
> The stillness, as a Chinese jar still
> Moves perpetually in its stillness.[9]

"Only living": presumably events which are locked in their nature, constrained to be merely what they are, temporal in every limiting sense. "Words" are temporal, too, in that limiting sense until or unless they are redeemed in a higher form or a convincing end. "Words" and "silence" denote two different states of feeling, the second higher and purer than the first. Words issue from time *(tempus)* and are vitiated by the penury of our daily concerns. However, they know enough to aspire to a higher and purer state, given in Eliot's lines as "form" and "pattern" in which the mere contents of form are not transcended but enhanced, fulfilled, redeemed. Silence is therefore a scruple which attends upon the local satisfactions of words, the voice which says that words are often self-delusions, trivial gratifications. Silence speaks against time, to redeem time. Silence therefore corresponds to the fine excess of imagination; it cannot be described, because it has no attributes apart from the aspiration which incites it, directing feeling beyond its daily nature. The discovery of the true form or pattern of feeling is impeded by the gross forms and patterns already imposed upon it; ready-made patterns enforced by the congealed institutions which, instead of keeping true feeling alive, humiliate it. So the imagination is driven to seek out those feelings which evade the bureaucracy of institutions; in the desperate hope of founding, as if for the first time, a genuine Natural Law. Institutions can deal with feeling only by turning it into routine and formulae for the sake of a brash economy. The imagination deals with feelings preferably wayward, congenitally wild, and it wants to move them not into formulae but toward the state of value and purity for which Eliot's words are "form" and "pattern," at once moving and still. The dimension is still temporal, or rather aeval: time is not the master of events but the object of creative freedom and play. As the choric Time says in *A Winter's Tale,* moving nonchalantly through sixteen years:

> . . . it is in my power
> To o'erthrow law, and in one self-born hour
> To plant and o'erwhelm custom.   (IV. i. 7-9)

Law is Chronos, overthrown by force of Chance or the eruption of meaning and value. Custom is common usage, established mostly by force of habit and need, but set aside when this force is defeated by novelty, strangeness, the Russian Formalists' virtue of "estrangement," or by any intervention which sets against the monotone of habit a new harmony, unpredicted, a new rhythm of events. This explains why revolutionists think of themselves as poets and prophets, exploding the continuum of history (to use Walter Benjamin's phrase) as a metaphor explodes the continuum of literal prose. The power which Time here claims for himself, we regularly ascribe to the imagination when it refuses to capitulate to the spirit of the age. The imagination makes nothing happen, but it lets things happen by removing obstacles of routine and providing a context of feeling from which they appear naturally to emerge.

Is the poet, then, privileged? Yes, in the sense that he, at least to a greater extent than anyone else, is master rather than victim of the public conventions, the sinister axioms of language, and is therefore undeceived. What he cannot do, he knows he cannot do. But he can intervene in language as the King in *Henry VIII* intervened in the continuum of history and exploded it, suffusing the air with his own metaphors. The comparison, fanciful as it appears, is not invalidated by the fact that Henry's intervention is in every other sense a worldly deed, a politic answer to "this naughty world" rather than the act of a pure and disinterested will. Until meaning intervenes in historical process, either by proposing a teleology which gives events their radiance or by transfiguring the local event itself, history remains problematic if not casual or arbitrary. Meaning is implicit in a logic or a symbolism of events; or it must be imposed by each man for himself. The linguistic analogy holds, either way. But this does not authorise us to engage in an idolatry of language, making graven images of black marks on a white page or sounds in the air: we grant to the poet his privilege, but not immunity to the weather of his time. He is superior to other men only in his sensitivity to the conditions in which he works and the linguistic instrument he uses. He is the only one who has a chance to "win freedom from what is inescapably inscribed in the words we must use to speak at all."[10]

What, then, is the status of Cranmer's prophecy? Is it escapist nonsense, self-indulgence, an uplifting sermon? It emerges naturally from its context only if we feel that Henry's intervention, the birth of the child Elizabeth, the baptism, and the harmony of Church and Nation have overwhelmed the force of time; that events have been given a new meaning by being given a new end. The prophecy is the counterpart of heroic narrative. Narrative says that what has been may be again: prophecy says that what has never been will still have its time, there is meaning but the meaning is not yet, the Messiah is he who will yet come. The prophet keeps the lines of possibility open for a time when the distinction between *tempus* and *aevum* will disappear. As in Emily Dickinson's poem:

> The Possible's slow fuse is lit
> By the Imagination.[11]

Poems are fictions of possibility. The special possibility they declare is one by which we transcend ourselves or go beyond our mere selves. Roland Barthes has remarked that the petit-bourgeois is a man incapable of imagining the Other:

> Le petit-bourgeois est un homme impuissant à imaginer l'Autre. Si l'autre se présente à sa vue, le petit-bourgeois s'aveugle, l'ignore et le nie, ou bien il le transforme en lui-même.[12]

But it is not merely a question of class. We are all petit-bourgeois when we hand over the work of imagination to habit, routine, or the cancelling device by which we reduce every experience to our mere selves. We say that great poetry always surprises us, shocks us into bewilderment and attention: the surprise is a sign that we are in the presence of Barthes's "l'Autre." When Eliot gives as line 430 of *The Waste Land* Gérard de Nerval's line from "El Desdichado," "Le Prince d'Aquitaine à la Tour abolie," it is not because he wants to send us off to consult de Nerval's poem or to speculate about the Aquitanian prince or the Tarot's broken tower, but because we are to be forced into a sudden sense of "l'Autre." The more alien the line is, the better. Nothing of its meaning in de Nerval, if we happen to recognise it, is excluded from *The Waste Land;* the poet is under oath to ensure that the line will take the weight of our full attention, but the richest attention is a sense of otherness, of tragedies not our own. Tiresias is only a more dramatic name for the same movement of feeling by which we imagine forms of feeling not our own.

Notes

1. Muriel C. Bradbrook, *The Tragic Pageant of "Timon of Athens"* (Cambridge: Cambridge University Press, 1966).

2. Ernst H. Kantorowicz, *The King's Two Bodies: A Stvdy in Mediaeval Political Theology* (Princeton: Princeton University Press, 1957), pp. 81f and 171f.

3. Frances A. Yates, *Astraea: The Imperial Theme in the Sixteenth Century* (London: Routledge and Kegan Paul, 1975), p. 74.

4. R. A. Foakes (editor), *Henry VIII* (London: Methuen, 1957), p. 108n.

5. T. S. Eliot, *Selected Essays* (London: Faber and Faber, third edition, 1951), p. 287.

6. A. J. Greimas, *Du sens* (Paris: Seuil, 1970), p. 104.

7. Ibid., pp. 110-111.

8. Proust, *À la recherche du temps perdu,* edited by Pierre Clarac and André Ferre (Paris: Gallimard, 1954), Vol. III, pp. 880, 891.

9. T. S. Eliot, *Collected Poems 1909-1962* (London: Faber and Faber, 1963), p. 194.

10. J. Hillis Miller: "Narrative and History" in *ELH: English Literary History,* Vol. 4, No. 3, Fall 1974, p. 471.

11. *The Poems of Emily Dickinson,* edited by Thomas H. Johnson (Cambridge, Mass.: Harvard University Press, 1963) Vol. 3, p. 1146.

12. Roland Barthes, *Mythologies* (Paris: Seuil, 1957) p. 239.